D1316524

The Captive Public

THE
CAPTIVE
PUBLIC

How Mass Opinion
Promotes State Power

BENJAMIN GINSBERG

Basic Books, Inc., Publishers

NEW YORK

Library of Congress Cataloging-in-Publication Data

Ginsberg, Benjamin.
  The captive public.

  Bibliographic references: p. 233.
  Includes index.
  1. Power (Social sciences). 2. Public opinion.
3. Representative government and representation.
4. Voting. 5. Elections. I. Title.
JC330.G56 1986   303.3'3   86–47504
ISBN 0–465–00870–4 (cloth)
ISBN 0–465–00871–2 (paper)

For Sandy

CONTENTS

PREFACE

GEORGE ORWELL warned that organization coupled with technology gave the modern state the power to rule its citizens' opinions. The state that ruled opinion, Orwell contended, ruled absolutely. Orwell's grim vision of life in the year 1984 has been enormously influential, and properly so. The power to rule opinion *is* the power to rule absolutely. More than a century before the publication of Orwell's *1984,* however, Alexis de Tocqueville also warned of the threat posed by the state's relationship with public opinion. Ironically, while Orwell feared that the state would rule opinion, de Tocqueville warned that the chief threat to freedom in the modern era was the possibility that opinion would rule the state. In de Tocqueville's view, governmental responsiveness to opinion encouraged citizens to believe that the state was simply a servant to whom vast powers could safely be granted. As a result, he warned, it was the government ruled *by* opinion that would ultimately rule absolutely.

Orwell may have been the better dramatist, but de Tocqueville was the more perceptive prophet, at least from the perspective of western political experience. Western democratic governments do sometimes seek to manipulate their citizens' beliefs. Indeed, the character of public opinion as a political phenomenon in the West has been significantly influenced by state action over the past two centuries. Yet to an important extent the contemporary western state *is* ruled by opinion. And it is precisely its deference to public opinion that functions to expand the modern state's power. As de Tocqueville foresaw, the citizens of the western democracies have willingly granted vast powers to their governments, thinking that "what they bestow" upon their rulers "is bestowed upon themselves." Ultimately, however, the state ruled by opinion is not necessarily so different from the state that rules opinion. Indeed, the subjects of the former are often even more ready than Orwell's Winston Smith to learn to love Big Brother.

I learned a great deal from friends and colleagues while writing this book. I am especially grateful to Martin Shefter for advice and comments that made this a much better book than it could possibly have been otherwise, and to Theodore J. Lowi for the vigorous criticisms that enlivened our jointly taught course at Cornell University and stimulated my thinking on a number of important points. Several colleagues commented on portions of the manuscript that I presented at various professional meetings and seminars as the book took shape. My particular thanks to Paul Allen Beck, Walter Dean Burnham, Tom Ferguson, Kathleen Frankovic, Calvin Jillson, Michael Nelson, Benjamin Page, Joel Silbey, and Robert Weissberg. Daniel Wirls and Heidi Meyers were diligent research assistants. Cornell's Jonathan Meigs Fund provided essential financial support for my research. Dolores Robinson prepared the bulk of the manuscript. Arline Blaker, Michael Busch, and David Armstrong pitched in when I really needed them.

Earlier versions of chapters 1 and 3 were presented at meetings of the American Political Science Association. A section of chapter 2 is revised from a portion of an article I wrote with Robert Weissberg for the *American Journal of Political Science.* Chapter 5 is revised from a paper that I presented at the 1983 annual meeting of the American Political Science Association; it was subsequently published in *The Political Economy,* edited by Tom

Ferguson and Joel Rogers. Chapter 6 and a segment of chapter 2 are based on a paper that I originally presented at the 1981 meeting of the American Political Science Association. A slightly different version of this discussion appeared in my 1982 book, *The Consequences of Consent.* I am grateful to Random House, M. E. Sharpe Publishers, the American Political Science Association, and the Midwest Political Science Association for permission to reprint my material.[1] Unless I have indicated otherwise, the source of all American opinion survey data used is the Center for Political Studies of the Institute for Social Research of the University of Michigan. Data was made available through the Inter-University Consortium for Political and Social Research.

I would very much like to thank Martin Kessler, President and Publisher of Basic Books, for his confidence in the project and his sound editorial judgment. My thanks also to David Graf and Debra Manette for the care and attention they gave to the manuscript.

The Captive Public

Chapter I

Government and Opinion

AT THE DAWN of the democratic era in the West, the relationship between the citizen and the state was radically transformed. The introduction of elections, parliaments, and other institutions of popular consultation meant that, to a greater or lesser extent, western governments henceforth would be formally and routinely compelled to pay heed to their citizens' needs and wishes. The development of a measure of governmental responsiveness to public opinion is generally conceived to be one of the great achievements of western society, and perhaps it is.

Nevertheless, the state's responsiveness to opinion poses a basic dilemma. On the one hand, citizens stand to benefit from the state's solicitude for their wants and views—witness the host of economic and social services that contemporary governments provide. At the same time, however, the state's responsiveness to its citizens' desires greatly facilitates the expansion of governmental powers.

Prior to the democratic era, the power of the state had been limited by the narrowness of its constituent base. When it began to accommodate mass opinion, the state, in effect, expanded the constituency for its services. In turn, governments gained access to a larger tax base, a broader base of political support, a more sizable pool of military manpower, and so on. Thus a key factor promoting the growth of the modern state's power became its responsiveness to opinion. The great transformation in the role of public opinion at the beginning of the democratic era has helped to bring about an equally great transformation in the importance and power of the state.

This is the fundamental dilemma of democratic politics. Citizens may hold the reins of the contemporary state's power, yet this very fact encourages citizens to welcome the state's expansion. Conceiving the state to be their servant, the citizens of the western democracies are happy to permit their governments to acquire the most far-reaching powers. As the scope of governmental power increases, however, what citizens initially believed to be reins, as de Tocqueville foresaw long ago, can become the ends of their own chains.

Public Opinion and Democratic Theory

The central questions of democratic politics have always concerned the relationship between the citizen and the state. But as the state's role has expanded during the course of the twentieth century, these questions have become especially critical. When rulers acquire sufficient power to do good, can they be prevented from employing their power for evil purposes? Can citizens continue to use government to improve their lot, or is the state's power, like that of the genie, beyond control once released? In the United States, there has been a basic change in the public's view of the state over the past century. The liberal perspective that once dominated American political perceptions assumed that government was, at best, a necessary evil. The greater the state's power, it was thought, the greater the threat posed to citizens' liberties and well-being. The best government, as Thomas Jefferson put it, was the one that governed least. Many Americans continue to pay lip service to this theory by professing to abhor "big government." Nevertheless, a new democratic theory of state power has replaced liberalism as the dominant public philosophy of the latter half of the twentieth century. From this new perspective, the development of elections, parliaments, and other institutions of popular control means that the state can be made to pay heed to its citizens' needs and wishes. So long as they control the state, democratic theory holds, citizens stand to benefit from its power. Thus, according to this theory, state power is a virtue rather than a threat. Indeed, given popular control, the more powerful the state, the greater its capacity to serve. The ideal of liberal theory was a weak state. The ideal of democratic theory, by contrast, is a powerful state that is controlled by—and thus responsive to—its citizens.

Contemporary public opinion research reflects the influence of the democratic theory of state power and ultimately helps to justify the expanded rule of the state that the theory endorses. The central question addressed by students of public opinion concerns governmental responsiveness to popular preferences. Those studies that fail to address this question explicitly almost invariably take responsiveness to be among the key underlying issues.[1] Typically, responsiveness is assumed to be the chief standard against which governmental conduct should be judged. As Harold Lasswell, a founding father of modern political science, once asserted, "The open interplay of opinion and policy is the distinguishing mark of popular rule."[2] Though the evidence of actual consistency between governmental policy and popular opinion is often weak, opinion researchers presume nevertheless that a strong relationship would be highly desirable. "Somehow," one leading text avers, "the policies passed by the government must reflect the preferences of the governed."[3]

There can be little doubt that the question of responsiveness is important. However, by defining responsiveness as *the* central issue in the relationship between government and mass opinion, students of public opinion tend to convey a one-sided and potentially misleading view. It is, in essence, to view the relationship mainly in terms of the potential benefits to citizens. Indeed, the emphasis on responsiveness probably reflects and reinforces the perception that it is principally the citizen who stands to benefit from the relationship between the citizen and the state. What this focus ignores, however, are the equally important benefits that can accrue to the state.

Over the past two centuries, mass opinion has become a formal and institutional part of the western political process. Elections, parliaments, referenda, and a variety of other institutional mechanisms formally link popular sentiment with state action. To a greater or lesser extent, western governments surely do respond to mass opinion. There can be little doubt that this formal governmental responsiveness to the "will of the people" is one of the great virtues of political life in the West. However, the transformation of mass opinion into a formal and institutional part of the political process has not only furthered the interests of the citizenry; it has also promoted the interests of the state. This transformation has helped western governments to domesticate mass belief, regulate the content of popular opinion, delimit the impact of mass opinion, and harness the power of mass opinion for their own purposes. As it serves opinion, the contemporary state also serves itself.

Public Opinion and Popular Consent

Historians and social theorists have often asserted that favorable public opinion—in particular, some measure of popular support for the regime and the political order—was a necessary condition for political and social stability. "As a matter of social necessity," Sociologist Philip Selznick once remarked, every ruling group "must identify itself with a principle acceptable to the community as justification for the exercise of power."[4] The famous scholar and diplomat James Bryce declared that even the Roman Empire did not rest on force but rather on the "consent and good will of its subjects."[5] Frequently this consent and goodwill are said to depend on the capacity of rulers and ruling classes to manipulate the beliefs of subordinate strata. Plato, for example, wrote of the "noble lie" through which rulers purportedly convinced their subjects that the prevailing distribution of power was best for all. In a similar vein, Karl Marx argued that a key element in the maintenance of any class society was the ideological preeminence of the economically dominant class. Lower classes, Marx averred, were taught to see the world through the eyes of their betters and, as a result, came to acquiesce in the established economic and social order.

It is surely true that popular approbation can contribute to governmental authority and stability. Yet the notion that governments necessarily depend on the public's acceptance exaggerates the significance of mass opinion as a force in political life. Obviously in every nation the goodwill of one or another elite stratum, be it the aristocracy, the military, the haute bourgeoisie, or the party cadre, can matter a great deal. However, throughout most of human history the feelings of common citizens have been relevant to governmental affairs and stability only sporadically. Popular consent has become politically important, at least on a routine basis, only in modern times.

Indeed, to the extent that popular consent actually depends on rulers' "noble lies," it is difficult to understand precisely how even the most sublime of these fibs could have had much influence on the beliefs of subject groups. Ruling strata have always been happy to assure anyone who would listen that the extant organization of power and privilege should be venerated for its consistency with logic, morality, history, law, the public welfare, and, of course, the divine will. But whatever the merits of these affirmations—and many have been interesting more for their ingenuity than their plausibility—only during the past two centuries have the doctrines enunciated by ruling classes really begun to reach the mass public, for prior to the nineteenth-century introduction of mass education and mass communication, there were few avenues through which rulers' claims could actually be communicated to the public at large. Even religious institutions, often assumed to have served as key mechanisms of public indoctrination, really had relatively little influence on the masses until the contemporary epoch. In most areas of Europe, neither the peasantry of the Middle Ages nor the urban working class that began to emerge during the seventeenth and eighteenth centuries attended formal church institutions in substantial numbers. In medieval Europe, according to historian Gabriel LeBras, Catholicism was the religion of the ruling class.[6] In later years most Protestant denominations catered to the bourgeoisie. As a result, the religious precepts that purported to justify political authority and social hierarchy in pre-modern Europe could hardly have served as the "opium of the people." For the most part, these doctrines were understood and believed only by members of the upper class.[7]

Prior to the nineteenth century, the principal audience for the "noble lies" of the ruling class was, in fact, the ruling class itself. The legitimating ideologies served mainly to reinforce the beliefs of the upper classes in the validity of the existing order, the virtues of the regime, and the propriety of their own power and position. In effect, these myths functioned to bolster upper-class support for the state and helped ruling classes to maintain a measure of self-confidence and coherence, and, thus, a surer grasp upon the reins of power.[8] But whatever their ability to persuade themselves, before the eighteenth and nineteenth centuries ruling groups could do little to shape mass opinion. Indeed, the available evidence strongly suggests that the great mass of ordinary people had little love for the regime or the social order. Generally, the masses equated the regime with the gendarme, the bailiff, and the tax collector, and found the social order odious and repressive.[9]

Despite the opinions of consent theorists, however, this lack of popular support did not usually pose much of a threat to the existing order. First, the masses were restrained by what is often called the coercion of everyday life. Peasants and laborers, compelled to work from dawn until dark to eke out a living, hardly had sufficient free time at day's end to plot against the state. Consequently, the extent of peasant opposition to feudal authority tended to vary with the season, reaching its low point during the harvest, when there was literally no end to the working day. Of course, mass discontent often did surface in the form of riot and insurrection—phenomena that were endemic in both rural and urban Europe before the nineteenth century. But civil disturbances usually posed no real challenge to the power of the crown and aristocracy. Indeed, rulers often saw riots and uprisings as perfectly normal and acceptable mechanisms for the expression of local grievances and rarely viewed them as a cause for alarm. Given the localized and limited character of economic exchange and governmental administration, rioting usually did not even especially disrupt the affairs of trade or state. If, however, it was necessary, regimes were nearly always able to bring matters under control through the use of force. Thus food riots, religious protests, and political disturbances, as well as the extreme violence sometimes sparked by tax increases, military conscription, or compulsory labor, all generally had the same result—bloody repression.[10]

Occasionally the authorities might be compelled to placate rioters. As Theda Skocpol has observed, however, only when the
ruling class was itself divided or when the state and its dominant classes were at odds could mass discontent pose a real
threat to the state and established order.[11] Generally rulers had
little reason to heed Talleyrand's warning to Napoleon about
the limits of coercion. It was, in fact, eminently possible for a
ruling group to "sit on the bayonet" giving, at most, occasional
and fleeting thought to questions of popular support and mass
opinion.

Public Opinion and Democratic Institutions

The relationship between government and opinion began to
change during the eighteenth century. Earlier, European rulers
devoted little attention to the views of their ordinary subjects.
But after this time, no European regime could afford to ignore
the views of the masses. The most important aspect of this
change was, of course, the construction of formal mechanisms
of popular consultation—electoral institutions and parliamentary bodies—and the gradual extension of the right to vote to
the lower classes by the beginning of the twentieth century.
These changes for the first time gave ordinary citizens a formal
and routine voice in public affairs. Henceforth governments
would be formally obligated to take account of public opinion
when formulating their programs and policies.

The causes of this transformation were complex. It is conven-
tionally assumed that extension of the right to vote and to be
represented in governmental decision making resulted from ir-
resistible popular demands for participation and representation.
It is certainly true that in many instances citizens obtained the

right to vote only after a long period of struggle. However, as political scientist E. E. Schattschneider once noted, the difficulty with which voting rights were actually secured has often been overrated.[12] Quite frequently during the course of western political history, ruling strata have actually taken the initiative in expanding popular participation and representation. Indeed, in some instances western governments have granted representation and voting rights to groups that neither sought nor particularly welcomed these privileges.[13]

There are essentially four sets of circumstances that can impel rulers to give ordinary citizens a voice in public affairs. First, suffrage expansion is frequently linked to efforts on the part of groups in power to deal with internal challenges to their rule by forces that attempt to mobilize mass support against the regime. During the eighteenth, nineteenth, and twentieth centuries, cycles of mobilization and countermobilization were central features of western politics. In the United States, for example, eighteenth-century efforts by the Jeffersonians to mobilize mass support against the incumbent Federalists forced the latter to respond in kind and ultimately led to the construction of the first American party system.

Second, a regime may be confronted by social disorder that it is unwilling or unable to suppress by force. In such cases, governments often turn to expansion of suffrage as a mechanism of stabilization, in the hope of containing and channeling away disruptive forms of mass political activity. This use of suffrage has been important on at least two occasions in recent American political history. The first of these was, of course, the federal government's effort to secure voting rights for blacks during the 1960s. The second occasion was the extension of the right to vote to eighteen-, nineteen-, and twenty-year-old citizens.[14]

The third major circumstance that can impel rulers to grant their subjects a voice in the state's affairs is the existence of a serious external threat to the state's power or territorial integrity. In particular, war and preparation for war have been very closely linked to the extension of voting rights and to the evolution of representative principles over the past two centuries. This relationship among external threat, voting rights, and representation has two aspects. On the one hand, many regimes have used suffrage expansion to help rally popular support and enthusiasm for war and defense efforts. At the same time, voting rights and parliamentary representation have been important mechanisms for obtaining popular acceptance of the increased tax burdens associated with war and defense efforts—and for helping to quell the civil disorder and rioting that tax increases can often provoke. Throughout western European history, indeed, war and the financial needs that resulted were closely linked to the construction and evolution of representative bodies. The enormous funds often needed for war and preparation for war forced rulers to turn to such assemblies for assistance in obtaining revenues. These assemblies typically granted new tax powers and other forms of assistance only in exchange for concessions from the groups in power. The link between taxation and representation in western history is, as historian Rudolph Braun notes, "obvious."[15] At the same time, taxation has been a major cause of the rioting and civil disorder that have figured so prominently in the history of suffrage. Efforts to contain popular resistance to military service, expropriation of food and supplies for armies, and, above all, the tax increases associated with war and military preparation were among the factors associated with suffrage expansion in the West as recently as World War I. Interestingly enough, expansion of suffrage has often paved the way for tax increases. During the nineteenth century, in both Britain and Prussia, the introduction and increased use of the income tax followed closely upon the heels of electoral reform and suffrage expansion.[16]

Finally, popular voting and representation have been closely associated with efforts to centralize and expand national authority, often in the context of "nation building." The purpose of suffrage expansion in this context is typically to subvert popular local or regional allegiances by linking citizens directly to the central government via the ballot box. As in the case of wartime mobilization, such governments feel compelled to increase citizens' support to a level commensurate with the sacrifices and exertions that will be demanded of them.

Suffrage Expansion in the West

The cumulative force of all these factors was felt in the West during the eighteenth and nineteenth centuries. Regimes were confronted with internal challenges from the representatives of rival classes as well as with severe social disorder. At the same time, rulers' efforts to bolster national military power, unity, and development impelled them to seek the active cooperation, as opposed to merely the sullen acquiescence, of their subjects.

Class Conflict

The most important factor underying the introduction and expansion of suffrage in the West was interclass conflict. During the eighteenth and nineteenth centuries, intense conflict involving the landed gentry, the bourgeoisie, and, later, the forces of the working class produced spirals of electoral mobilization and countermobilization as each class sought to enhance its own power and position. The European bourgeoisie are sometimes credited with the invention of modern democratic institutions; indeed, the construction of electoral and parliamentary mechanisms in western Europe was largely the work of this class. Interestingly enough, though, it was often the landed gentry rather than the bourgeoisie who took the lead in extending representative and voting rights to the great mass of ordinary citizens. The bourgeoisie typically conceived electoral and parliamentary institutions to be instruments through which the weight of their numbers and collective resources could be brought to bear against the crown and aristocracy. In general, they were not especially anxious to permit the classes below their own to use these same institutions to further their own interests. Thus while nineteenth-century liberal political theorists touted the merits of representative government, these same intellectual spokesmen for the bourgeoisie often expressed grave doubts about the wisdom of enfranchising uneducated, unskilled, and "dependent" social strata. John Stuart Mill, for example, favored a system of weighted voting that would effectively give the bourgeoisie parliamentary influence far beyond their actual numbers.

After the enfranchisement of the working classes, of course, the bourgeoisie learned that their superior economic and institutional resources generally permitted them to dominate electoral and parliamentary processes despite their relatively small numbers. This discovery had the effect of enhancing the bourgeoisie's attachment to mass democracy, which they had previously resisted. The conservative parties that represented the landed gentry, on the other hand, often were willing to take the "leap into the dark" of enfranchising the lower orders. The landed gentry shared with the working classes an antipathy for many aspects of the emerging industrial order and saw in the working classes potential allies against the bourgeoisie.[17] Thus in Germany, Bismarck introduced universal suffrage over the objections of his liberal, bourgeois opponents on the assumption that the peasant and working-class elements would support conservative forces against the bourgeoisie. Similarly, in Britain, the conservatives led by Disraeli liberalized suffrage to a far greater extent than was favored by their liberal opponents. Alignments were somewhat more complex in the United States. Yet here too the Jeffersonian party, led by the southern landed gentry, was considerably more enthusiastic about mass suffrage than was the Federalist party, a political group dominated by New England commercial strata.

The conflict between bourgeoisie and landed gentry was critical to the process of popular enfranchisement. Where this conflict did not occur or was muted, enfranchisement of the masses was delayed or prevented. For example, during the late nineteenth and early twentieth centuries, in the nations of southern Europe—Spain, Portugal, and Italy—the landed gentry and bourgeoisie both feared that the mobilization of new electoral forces would sweep them aside, and colluded with one another to prevent the enfranchisement of new strata. The best-known examples of this type of collusion include Italy's governing coalition of northern industrialists and southern landowners and Spain's ruling coalition of Basque steel interests, Catalonian textile manufacturers, and Castillian wheat growers, the so-called Bilboa-Barcelona-Valladolid axis.[18] In both cases, the bourgeoisie and gentry were able to arrive at mutually acceptable terms on which to share the levers of state power. As a result, neither group was compelled to seek mass electoral backing, and so the advent of mass democracy was postponed.

The emergence of mass democracy was also delayed where the bourgeoisie became sufficiently powerful to overwhelm their landed rivals and prevent them from even attempting to mobilize mass support. Thus, for example, in the Netherlands, where the landed gentry were too weak to mount an effective opposition to the rising bourgeoisie, parliamentary and electoral institutions were constructed early in the eighteenth century but were not opened to mass participation until well into the twentieth century.[19]

In general, during the nineteenth century ruling groups, whether gentry or bourgeoisie, pursued a policy of mass mobilization against their internal enemies only if military or political factors precluded the use of force against these foes. Where rulers had the option of thwarting or suppressing electoral opposition, they generally did so. Even in those nations whose initial electoral arrangements did not formally bar opposition, incumbents usually sought to suppress whatever electoral opponents presented themselves. In the United States, for example, the Alien and Sedition Acts of 1798 were only one part of an attempt by the Federalists to outlaw the emergent Jeffersonian opposition and prevent their own displacement from office. Alexander Hamilton and other Federalist leaders even went so far as to urge that opposition be eliminated by force, if necessary. The failure of the Federalists to suppress their Jeffersonian rivals was, in large measure, due simply to the military and political weakness of the federal government of that period, which precluded any serious Federalist effort to crush an opposition that controlled several state governments and their militias.

The American case is by no means atypical. In Norway during the elections of 1879 and 1882, an alliance of rural populists and urban radicals won victories over the conservative party that controlled the regime. The conservatives considered the possibility of seeking to suppress the opposition by force. However, their plans to use the army to stage a coup against Parliament were thwarted by the organization of riflemen's associations and popular militias by the forces of the left. The result was that conservative forces limited themselves to vigorous efforts at countermobilization and the organization of political clubs and societies. The ensuing process of mobilization and countermobilization resulted in an enormous expansion of the Norwegian electorate and, ultimately, in the establishment of full parliamentary rule in Norway.[20]

Social Disorder

The second critical problem that impelled eighteenth- and nineteenth-century rulers to begin to pay heed to mass opinion was social disorder. The complex market economies that emerged from the industrial and commercial revolutions of this period were far more sensitive to mass violence and disruption than their preindustrial predecessors. As recently as the seventeenth century, mass disorder was a routine part of political life. A bit of property might be destroyed and the mob's ringleaders ultimately hanged but generally, as historian Eric Hobsbawn puts it, rioting "caused no political problems."[21]

During the ensuing centuries, the attitudes of ruling classes toward mass disorder changed substantially. The process of industrialization and especially the effort to proletarianize the working class at this time was associated with considerable mass resistance, class conflict, political disorder, and radical political agitation by movements that sought to build mass bases of support. Nineteenth-century British history, for example, is a history of popular protest and disorder—Luddism, Chartism, the 10-hour movement, and so on. Similarly, in the United States this period was marked by militant labor movements and violent strike activity. The example of the French Revolution had, of course, already suggested to ruling groups that popular agitation could, in fact, now cause "political problems." But even more important, popular unrest and disorder posed a far different and more severe threat—a "lethal threat," according to historian Karl Polanyi[22]—to the functioning of delicate market economies than had been the case before. In the nineteenth century, rioting that would hardly have caused a ripple one hundred years earlier would lead to breakdowns in the delivery of food and other goods, disruptions in trade and manufactures, and stock market collapses.

At the same time, the massive shifts of populations from rural areas to cities that accompanied industrialization during the eighteenth and nineteenth centuries produced an enormous upsurge in the incidence of crime. In the early stages of urbanization everywhere in the West, many more migrants were attracted to the cities than could be integrated into the urban workforce. This left huge populations of unemployed persons living in abject misery but, at the same time, in close proxmity to wealth and material goods they could never hope to acquire through socially sanctioned means. At the same time, immigrants to the city found that they were no longer subject to the constraints of a rural environment in which every individual and his activities were known to the community as a whole. "City air," as Weber put it, "made men free." Freedom meant, among other things, a cover of anonymity behind which individuals could pursue their affairs without fear of identification or exposure.

This mixture of impoverished masses living within sight of unattainable luxuries and a relaxation of the social constraints that traditionally held the rural poor in check had an explosive effect on crime rates everywhere in the world where it occurred. As a result, the well-to-do of nineteenth-century London, Paris, and New York alike lived in constant terror of crime and violence. Middle-class Parisians made sure to arm themselves if they ventured out at night.[23]

From the perspective of the propertied classes, crime posed an even more direct threat to life and property than political unrest. Indeed—and this is very significant—the two were often linked in their minds. Crime was an everyday reminder of the political problem. The great dread of nineteenth-century society was an alliance between the politically disaffected and the criminal element—an alliance of the dangerous classes of society.[24] This fear of disorder was a powerful stimulus to suffrage expansion. Regimes viewed the creation of formal avenues for popular political involvement as an important way of forestalling more disruptive forms of political action. The British Reform Act of 1832 is a case in point. The Grey government opened electoral opportunities to diminish the likelihood of political violence and disorder. As one supporter of electoral reform put it, the alternative to voting was "the spoilation of property and the dissolution of social order."[25]

External Threat

Another factor leading rulers to pay greater attention to public opinion was the growing severity of the external threat faced by European states during the eighteenth and nineteenth centuries. In particular, changes in the character of military force and international conflict substantially increased the costs and difficulties attendant on the maintenance of national power, independence, and territorial integrity and gave rulers a strong incentive to attempt to enlist their subjects' active cooperation in the defense of the state.

Military power and international conflict changed in four closely related ways during this period. To begin with, war and preparation for war become constant rather than intermittent facts of national life during these two centuries. While the actual number of wars and armed conflicts probably did not increase relative to the previous two hundred years, every European nation began to engage in extensive and permanent preparation for war. Each nation constructed a large standing army, which it maintained in a constant state of readiness to answer threats from other powers. In addition, every nation created a reserve force that could be mobilized in time of crisis to augment the regular forces. Normally, all adult males were required to perform regular military service followed by service in the reserves, which typically included a period of military training each year. War and preparation for war had been intermittent —albeit frequent—features of European political life. Now preparation for conflict had become a permanent and full-time aspect of each nation's existence.[26]

Second, the size of military forces increased dramatically at this time. Earlier wars were typically fought by small, professional armies. In the mid-seventeenth century, the forces that could be mustered by Prussia hardly numbered more than 40,000 men. Even at the height of the War of the Spanish Succession in 1712, the size of the British army barely reached 75,000 men. Only France, the wealthiest and most populous country in Europe, could field more than 100,000 soldiers before the eighteenth century.

Beginning with the French revolutionary and Napoleonic eras, though, the size of national military forces began to increase substantially. The Jacobin *levee en masse* in 1793 produced 300,000 conscripts for the revolutionary armies. By 1813 Napoleon was able to draft some 1.3 million of his countrymen. He drafted another 1 million for the campaigns of 1813 and 1814. Napoleon's *Grande Armee*, assembled for the Russian campaign, alone numbered 700,000 men. By the end of the nineteenth century, however, even these numbers were dwarfed by the standing armies of the major European powers. In 1874 the French standing army numbered some 1.75 million soldiers and the German army, approximately 3.5 million. By 1897 French forces including reserves numbered 3.5 million and German forces, 3.4 million men. In World War I, the French were able to place more than 3 million soldiers in the trenches of the western front alone.[27]

Third, the expense of armed conflict increased substantially during the eighteenth and nineteenth centuries. Obviously, permanence and increased size meant increased expense. The permanent maintenance of enormous standing armies and reserve forces required vast expenditures for food, pay, supplies, transport, and weapons. At the same time, technological advances in military tactics and weaponry, including artillery, communications, transport, and munitions, increased the cost of equipping an effective fighting force. Moreover, the industrial revolution made it possible for each nation—and thus necessary for all nations—to produce vast quantities of rifles, machine guns, field guns, and munitions. The extensive industrial production now required for an effective military effort not only increased the cost of armed conflict but also made the factory worker as much a soldier in the war effort as the infantryman on the front line.

Finally, the composition of armies changed at this time. Prior to the eighteenth century, armies were composed of mercenary or forcibly impressed troops whose nationality was of little or no consequence. Armies were multilingual and multinational, held together by iron discipline and material incentives. But as the need to maintain permanent reserve forces compelled rulers to rely more heavily on their own subjects to fill the military ranks, during the eighteenth and nineteenth centuries the earlier multinational armies began to give way to more or less exclusively national forces. The construction of national armies, of course, was associated with the development of the notion that military service was a duty and obligation of all male citizens.

Taken together, these factors encouraged, indeed impelled, rulers to seek popular support for the maintenance of their military power. Huge permanent armies of citizen-soldiers could be raised more easily and could be induced to fight more vigorously if imbued with enthusiasm for their cause. Popular support facilitated military conscription and ultimately made soldiers more willing to endure hardship and danger. The turning point in this regard was the French Revolution. The unprecedented size and ardor—and military success—of the citizen armies of postrevolutionary France convinced the rulers of all European nations that military power was closely linked with mass support. Throughout the nineteenth century, war and suffrage expansion went hand in hand, as the logic of the Swedish slogan, "one man, one vote, one gun" became fully apparent to western regimes. The concluding act in this drama was World War I, which directly or indirectly contributed to expansion of suffrage in Belgium, Canada, Italy, the Netherlands, the United Kingdom, and the United States.

State Building

Finally, during the eighteenth and nineteenth centuries the last acts of the European nation-building saga took place as rulers struggled to secure national boundaries, unify often disparate and hostile populations, develop national economies and infrastructures, and centralize national authority by diminishing the autonomy of territorial subunits. The emergence and expansion of modern states can, of course, be explained in a variety of different ways. Yet whatever the precise nature of the underlying causes, the fundamental requirement for the construction of nation-states was the extraction of revenues and services from their citizens. Without these resources, rulers could not defend their territorial claims against external foes, subordinate internal rivals, or unify and pacify polyglot subject populations.

To put the matter simply, there are two ways in which rulers can acquire revenues and services from their subjects—coercion and persuasion. All governments, of course, employ elements of both. Generations of American men, for example, were offered a choice between voluntary military enlistment and involuntary conscription. Behind the warm handshake of the genial recruiting sergeant lurked the cold tentacles of the remorseless Selective Service System.

In the eighteenth and nineteenth centuries, rulers began to learn that it could be advantageous to secure the support and loyalty of their subjects rather than simply to rely on force to ensure popular obedience. Again, the French Revolution was the turning point. The apparent willingness of the citizens of postrevolutionary France to work, sacrifice, and even die for their nation provided a dramatic illustration of the force that might be tapped by mobilizing popular support for national purposes. The Prussians were the first to follow the French example, but in due course all European rulers sought to enhance their own power by enlisting their subjects' sympathies. The more ambitious rulers' aims, the more interested they became in acquiring popular support for the efforts and exertions —and taxes—required for national unification and development.

The expansion of voting rights and representation was a key element in this effort to enhance national unity and power during these centuries. Indeed, even before the French Revolution, elections played an important role in the efforts of the U.S. Founding Fathers to centralize and expand national authority. At the American Constitutional Convention of 1787, James Wilson argued in favor of the popular election of members of the House of Representatives by asserting that he favored "raising the federal pyramid to considerable altitude" and for that reason wished to give it "as broad a base as possible." This sentiment was echoed by other delegates, such as Elbridge Gerry, who, although distrustful of popular influence in government, believed nonetheless that the establishment of a strong and stable central government required a regular means of obtaining popular consent through elections. Some delegates, to be sure, favored direct popular elections of national leaders in order to give citizens a voice in the new government. Virtually all the delegates, however, conceived direct popular election of national leaders to be a means of increasing the authority and influence of the new national government. Such election, it was thought, would increase the influence of the federal government in relation to the states and would give citizens the necessary "confidence" in government to enable the new regime to function effectively.[28]

The Fragility of State Power

Underlying all these moves to increase popular involvement in support of government was, of course, the weakness of the nineteenth-century western European state relative to the demands that were being made upon it. Western European states lacked adequate internal police or security forces to effectively stem the tide of domestic disorder that accompanied industrialization and urbanization. In eighteenth-century Britain, for example, the primary forces available to quiet serious disturbances were "special constables"—middle-class householders mustered for temporary duty. Sufficient numbers of special constables were not always readily available in the areas where they were most needed—few members of the middle class lived in the mining and manufacturing districts where disorder was most frequent. Moreover, even when available in sufficient numbers, these constables lacked the organization, training, and discipline required to handle serious mass disturbances.[29] Of course, behind the specials or their counterparts on the continent stood the regular army. But regular army troops could not always be spared for civil duty and besides, the army was not an especially reliable instrument of civil control. Typically, military commanders during the eighteenth and nineteenth centuries were drawn from the rural gentry, and these officers often exhibited little enthusiasm for protecting factories and commercial enterprises, sometimes preferring to leave these bourgeois properties to the mercy of the mob.[30]

Moreover, western European states lacked the capacity to collect sufficient revenues to meet their military and developmental needs. Prior to the eighteenth century, major sources of state revenue had been tithes, land taxes, customs duties, and excise taxes. These revenue sources, even when augmented by borrowing and inflation, proved woefully inadequate as governmental spending, especially for national defense, began to increase dramatically after 1800. Efforts to enhance revenue collection through increased taxation often sparked popular resentment, disorder, and resistance. Not until the introduction of the income tax in the late eighteenth and early nineteenth centuries did state revenues begin to keep pace with state expenditures. The most efficient form of income taxation, however—tax withholding at the source of earnings—requires an administrative apparatus more sophisticated than was generally available in Europe at this time.[31]

Western European states also lacked sufficient military power to subdue their foreign rivals and provide reliable protection for their own interests and territorial integrity. Small professional armies fighting for pay were no longer adequate to project national power abroad or to keep foreign foes at bay. National security now required the construction of enormous standing armies and the introduction of universal male military training. These innovations, though, required increased tax revenues as well as reliable internal security forces to convince those citizens who might exhibit some reluctance to serve the motherland of their own free will.[32]

Finally, the military, internal security, and fiscal problems of European states also limited rulers' ability to use coercion against their domestic political opponents. Indeed, the same industrial and commercial revolutions that touched off intense domestic political conflicts in the 1800s and 1900s also resulted in the creation and diffusion of wealth, organizational skills, communications techniques, and a host of other politically relevant resources that, in effect, increased the potential for opposition to state power and diminished the state's coercive capabilities.[33] All this meant that rulers could no longer be confident of their capacity to keep domestic foes in check solely through intimidation.

In essence, rulers were compelled to seek popular support because they lacked other means to curb disorder, bring their foreign and domestic foes to heel, and retain a grip on the levers of national power. Where ruling strata did have such a capacity, they made fewer concessions to the will of the people. The nations of southern Europe are a telling example. In Italy, Spain, and Portugal during the eighteenth and nineteenth centuries, as I have already noted, the bourgeoisie and gentry were able to agree to share rule and, as a result, were able to jointly use the instruments of state power to intimidate and coerce the working class and peasant opposition, collect taxes, and deal with disorder. The rulers of these nations had little incentive to court popular support. As Cornell political scientist Martin Shefter indicates, a similar phenomenon occurred in many of the regions of the world that industrialized after the West. The economies of late industrializers are often dominated by a few large corporations, banking combines, or the state itself; where this is so, incumbent elites are likely to be able to withstand political challenges by drawing on the organizational and economic resources of these institutions.[34] Ultimately western governments developed means of fulfilling their needs that did not depend on active popular cooperation. However, at this time western rulers had little choice but to attempt to acquire popular support for obtaining revenues, maintaining internal order, and dealing with foreign foes, and to turn to public opinion to bolster the state's power.

The Great Transformation

The construction of democratic electoral institutions and popular representative bodies during this era for the first time gave ordinary citizens a formal and routine voice in public affairs. Rulers were now compelled to take routine account of the opinions of ordinary citizens when making their decisions; the "will of the people" became a routine factor in civic affairs. In the West, after the nineteenth century, it becomes difficult to sustain the argument that the public's opinions do not matter. Indeed, the emergence and persistence of democratic institutions caused a great transformation in western politics, substantially altering the relationship between citizen opinion and state power. In the absence of elections, representative bodies, or other formal mechanisms for its expression, citizens' opinions still can have some impact on rulers' conduct. Routine voting is hardly the only way that citizens can reward or punish officials for their behavior. Even the most autocratic regime must beware lest its actions provoke popular disobedience, riot, or insurrection. But where formal mechanisms for its expression and enforcement are lacking, the influence of popular opinion tended to be inversely related to rulers' power. That is, rulers tended to be most concerned with their subjects' wishes when their own power to govern was weakest or most insecure and least interested in citizens' views when their own power was most secure.

The advent of democratic elections and popular representation, however, meant that even when rulers had the military and administrative capacity to compel obedience, citizens' influence was no longer necessarily reduced. The effectiveness of electoral and parliamentary sanctions, unlike the threat of riot, revolution, or insurrection, does not necessarily vary with the state's power. With the introduction of formal mechanisms for the expression of opinion, popular influence and rulers' power were no longer inversely related but could instead coexist.

It is due to this possibility for coexistence that democratic institutions potentially transform the relationship between rulers and the ruled. For, given a formal means of influencing their rulers' actions—one that is independent of rulers' military and administrative power—citizens potentially stand to benefit from rulers' power rather than from their weakness. It is the

advent of elections and the other institutions of democratic
government that makes it possible for citizens to use the power
of government for their own benefit rather than simply benefiting from their rulers' inability to muster sufficient power to
compel them to obey their rulers' commands.

Public Opinion and State Power

Unfortunately, however, the story does not end with this felici-
tous concurrence between popular influence and the state's
power. Contemporary students of public opinion assume that
the citizenry was the only beneficiary of the linkage that was
forged between government and opinion in the West. But in
some respects the ultimate beneficiary was the state. Expansion
of the role of mass opinion in political life opened the way for
expansion of the size and power of the state. The power of the
traditional state had been limited by the narrowness of its constituent base. When it began to accommodate mass opinion, the
state effectively expanded the constituency for its services and,
as a result, gained access to a larger tax base, base of political
support, military recruitment base, and so on. Responsiveness
to public opinion has been an essential element in the growth
of the modern state's power.

A tantalizing, albeit very sketchy, glimpse of the relationship
between mass opinion and the growth of the modern state's
power can be obtained by examining the relationship between
electoral mobilization and per capita governmental revenues
across nations and over time. In the democracies, at least, mass
electoral mobilization (voters as a proportion of adults in a
given nation) is a good indication of the extent to which mass
opinion has been formally incorporated into the political and

governmental process. Per capita governmental revenues are a measure of a state's capacity to extract resources from its citizens and a plausible surrogate for state power.[35]

Examination of these data suggests that electoral mobilization was closely linked to changes in the capacity of governments to extract revenues from their subjects. Obviously in the modern era, state growth is most closely linked to war. However, if we examine the period between World Wars I and II (1919–39), four of the western nations that began the period with the most fully mobilized mass electorates, namely Switzerland, France, Canada, and Belgium, also exhibited the highest rates of revenue expansion between 1919 and 1939. The rates of increase are 24 percent for Switzerland, 44 percent for France, 19 percent for Canada, and a massive 1,191 percent for Belgium. At the same time European nations that had constructed democratic institutions but nevertheless began the twentieth century with relatively low levels of electoral mobilization had much less rapid revenue growth—or even had revenue declines during the interwar period. Thus Britain, which had a constricted electorate at this time, experienced only a ten percent increase in governmental revenues, and Italy and Denmark, also nations with electorates that had not yet been fully mobilized, saw declines of 5 percent and 6 percent, respectively. Interestingly, European nations that at the beginning of the twentieth century had not yet even begun the process of constructing democratic institutions, much less mobilizing an electorate, typically exhibited substantial revenue contraction during the depression years between the two world wars. Thus per capita state revenues in Greece, Portugal, and Spain shrank by rates of 54 percent, 31 percent, and 53 percent, respectively.

In some respects the most interesting case is that of the United States. Prior to this century, the United States boasted the world's most fully mobilized mass electorate. Nevertheless, the American government's per capita revenues contracted by 13 percent after World War I. This contraction is anomalous, unless one recalls that one of the chief events in the United States at the turn of the century was a systematic demobilization of the mass electorate.[36]

These data can offer only a sketchy glimpse of a very complex set of interactions. Yet they do suggest that the extent to which governments formally incorporated mass opinion into the political process had a bearing on the evolution of their power.

The Second "Great Transformation"

As they began to respond to citizen opinion, governments, in effect, created a mass market for their services and, in so doing, opened the way for expansion of the size and power of the state. During the past fifty years, governments have learned to expand their power by actually stimulating citizen demand for their services. Indeed, Harvard political scientist Samuel Huntington and others have argued that the stimulation of "excess" citizen demand during the 1960s led to a crisis of governability in the western democracies.[37] The difficulty with this argument can be seen by considering the analogy of the business firm. Firms seldom look upon "excess" consumer demand for their products and services as a cause for alarm. Instead they will typically seek to take advantage of such excess demand by increasing their prices (and profits) and, ultimately, expanding their productive capacities.

The same is true of "excess" citizen demand for governmental goods and services. Such demand opens the way for expansion of the state's powers. During the twentieth century, political leaders have learned to use demand stimulation explicitly to increase citizen pressure for governmental services and, thereby, to open new opportunities for the expansion of state power. In the United States, this strategy was particularly evident from the time of the New Deal and through the Kennedy and Johnson administrations. It may be recalled that both these latter administrations were able to construct large bureaucracies and substantially augment federal powers in the course of responding to federally prompted citizen demand for solutions to problems that often were initially apparent only to the federal government itself. Even during the current period of retrenchment, the national government routinely continues to stimulate a variety of citizens' wants and so to harness public opinion to buttress and augment state power.

The ultimate beneficiary of the state's new responsiveness to opinion has been the state itself. Perhaps, at times, western governments are constrained by the pressure of the public's opinions. But the larger effect of accommodating mass opinion is to free and expand the state's powers.

Ultimately, however—and this is, of course, the point of de Tocqueville's warning—the second great transformation, left unchecked, can pose a threat to the first. During the nineteenth century, regimes were compelled to take an interest in mass opinion because of the state's weakness. During the twentieth century, mass opinion contributed to the strengthening of the state's power. At the threshold of the twenty-first century, the growth of state power may threaten to further undermine the significance of mass opinion. As the state's power has expanded, governments have found means of collecting taxes, dealing with disorder, and conducting warfare that depend less on the popular mood for their success (I will return to this point in chapter 7). Perhaps the institutions of mass participation and popular consultation will remain intact. But, as de Tocqueville feared, these may become merely the means through which citizens will occasionally wave the ends of their chains.

Chapter 2

The Domestication of Mass Belief

WHEN THEY BEGAN to take formal account of popular senti-ment, western governments did not simply surrender to mass opinion as they found it. Rather they began what was to be-come a protracted effort to reshape the character and political content of their subjects' views.

While contemporary western governments do listen and defer to their citizens' views, the public opinion to which these regimes bow so assiduously is not the natural and spontaneous popular force that confronted their predecessors. Instead, the opinion that contemporary rulers heed is in many respects an artificial phenomenon that national governments themselves helped to create and that their efforts continue to sustain.

This transformation in the character of opinion has four key components. First, western regimes altered the manner in which mass beliefs were formed. While earlier such beliefs were for-mulated through social processes, now state agencies were in-volved in their creation. Second, western governments changed the social basis of public opinion from class to market, thereby converting lower social classes from producers to consumers of opinion. Third, governments restructured the political foundation of mass opinion, changing the central political perspective underlying popular attitudes from an adversary to a proprietary view of the state. Fourth, governments recast the expression of mass opinion from a spontaneous, citizen-initiated act, into a formal and routine public function.

From Social Process to Political Process

Where the formation of mass beliefs had once been achieved entirely through social processes, it now became a matter involving the direct intervention of the state's agencies. This required, in particular, the introduction of systems of mass education and, later, mass communications, which permitted governments to intervene in the formation of mass beliefs and opinions. The social and political functions of the educational systems that emerged throughout the West during the nineteenth century are, by now, no secret. Two of the chief objects of schooling were pacification of the dangerous and unruly urban proletariat and the creation of firm popular attachments to the state. Educational systems were designed to teach the masses respect for order and property while inculcating love of country.

In Britain, for example, the first of these aims was paramount. Education was viewed as a key means of "gentling" the masses, building discipline, respect for private property, and the established social order.[1] According to the Newcastle Commission, "a set of good schools civilises a whole neighborhood."[2] Education was seen as a means of eradicating urban crime and disorder. Educational reformers in nineteenth-century Britain coined the slogan "Open a school and close a jail."[3] The prevailing view is well summarized by Sir James Kay Shuttleworth, who in an 1867 address reviewed the millions of pounds spent annually on theft, property protection, the punishment of crime, and so on. "Property," he concluded, "would be more secure, indigence more rare, and the whole people more provident and contented if they were better educated."[4] Education would prevent rick burning, rioting, and other forms of unpleasantness. In the eighteenth century, education was seen as a way to protect property by teaching the poor habits of industry and thrift. By the nineteenth century education came also to be seen as providing political protection for property by teaching the poor respect for the economic and social order.

Of course, the second aim of education—the inculcation of loyalty to the state—also played a role in the history of British popular education. Liberal philosopher James Mill, for example, argued that state education was important to "train the minds of the people to a virtuous attachment to their government."[5] It was on the European continent, however, that the use of education to promote popular loyalty to the regime was taken most seriously. In postrevolutionary and restoration France, education was viewed as a critical mechanism through which the new regimes could reach the masses, attract their loyalty, and break any attachments that might remain to the previous regime. At the same time, the nations defeated by the armies of the French Revolution and Napoleon saw mass education as the factor that would ultimately permit them to draw upon the same type of mass loyalty that had served the French state so well. This was, indeed, the central aim of the reforms promulgated in Prussia by Stein, Hardenberg, Scharnhorst, and Gneisenau—"to bind everyone to the state by conviction."[6]

In the United States, both aims played a role in the history of mass education. The urban school was a key mechanism for combating crime, delinquency, and so on. At the same time, the school served as a means of instilling appropriate moral and patriotic values. This was especially so during the great era of immigration. According to one authority of the period, "You cannot catch your citizen too early in order to make him a good citizen. The kindergarten age marks our earliest opportunity to catch the little Russian, the little German, Pole, Syrian and the rest and begin to make good American citizens of them."[7]

In the United States as well as Europe, educational curricula emphasized moral virtues, respect for order, and citizenship training. Patriotic, cultural, and moral matters often occupied more time than mastery of actual skills. Even ostensibly abstract academic subjects were often used for moral education. German elementary arithmetic texts in the nineteenth century, for example, taught students how to count the number of heroic German—and cowardly French—soldiers.[8] Obviously, the study of history in every nation is designed in part, perhaps primarily, to convince students of their nation's heroic past, brave leaders, and moral superiority.[9]

Some aspects of the political importance of education can be ascertained from two sets of data. First, as nineteenth-century educational reformers hoped, education seems, indeed, to "gentle" the masses. In general, the more years of education individuals receive, the less likely they are to engage in either criminal activities or political protest.[10] Obviously, in the United States and elsewhere, university and secondary school students have occasionally been the vanguard of revolution and protest. However, where the educational system is well integrated with the social and economic structure—providing students with skills that are rewarded by the established political economy—education contributes to social order. Few students in the United States actually participate in protests or demonstrations. Indeed, contrary to the popular image, few college students are even sympathetic to protest activities.[11] At the time of the Vietnam war, of course, when college graduates were subject to military conscription, support for protest was somewhat stronger in the intelligentsia.

A second effect of education can be seen by considering patterns of public support for governmental institutions and political processes in the United States. The more years of schooling to which individuals are exposed, the more likely they are to develop a positive view of those institutions and processes. For example, the higher respondents' levels of education, the more likely they are to believe that "public officials care" what people think, that the people have some "say" about what the government does, that the government is "run for the benefit of all," and that officials are basically honest.[12]

Moreover, those with the most years of school usually tend to separate any dislike they might have for particular government leaders or policies from their general orientation toward the government. That is, well-educated persons who disapprove of the incumbent president or are dissatisfied with the government's policies are generally not as likely as individuals with fewer years of schooling to become disaffected from the general system of government. This was true even during the 1970s when general levels of public trust in government fell sharply. Education promotes what is sometimes called "diffuse support" for the regime—support that is so deeply ingrained that it is not dependent on public satisfaction with particular leaders or with particular aspects of governmental performance.

From Class to Market

Prior to the nineteenth century, opinion was stratified by social class. Each social class essentially had its own opinions and beliefs, derived from its own life circumstances. Marx to the contrary notwithstanding, the views of lower classes were not especially influenced by those of the upper classes. Indeed, there was little communication between the two. For the most part the beliefs of the upper classes did not penetrate the consciousness of the lower orders.

In the nineteenth and twentieth centuries, however, all this began to change. By subsidizing the development of mass communications, promoting mass literacy, and expanding freedom of speech and of the press, western states constructed what liberal theorists came to call a "marketplace of ideas"—an arena within which the ideas of all groups could be freely communicated and would be free to compete for acceptance. A free market in ideas, like a free market in any other commodity, tends to work to the advantage of the most advanced or powerful producers. The substitution of a market for the class organization of opinion of an earlier period had the effect of promoting the ideological dominance of the economically and politically dominant classes best able to deploy the financial, institutional, and organizational resources needed to "market" ideas effectively. As a result, the lower classes became over time consumers more than producers of their own opinions, accepting many of the beliefs advanced by the upper classes.

The development of this free market in ideas had a number of components. One was the promotion of mass literacy. The ability to read and write can obviously be enormously beneficial to those individuals who possess these skills. But at the same time, literate citizens also provide an audience for the producers of ideas and beliefs. Bourgeois proponents of education for the lower classes during the nineteenth century often pointed to this fact. Teaching the masses to read would mean that ordinary people would be able to consume the ideas and beliefs of the bourgeoisie. Obviously, prior to the invention of the broadcast media, mass literacy was a necessary condition for mass consumption of ideas.

Another facet of the construction of a free market in ideas

was the subsidy and encouragement of private communications mechanisms. This process began with the lifting of previous restrictions during the early part of the nineteenth century. For example, the tax on newspapers in Britain was removed in the 1830s. The nineteenth century was, of course, the great age of governmental subsidy of mass communications mechanisms. Throughout this period, subsidy of newspapers was common, and governments also contributed to the construction of telegraph systems and rail lines. During the twentieth century, all the western regimes promoted the development of radio, telephone, television, and, now, the complex satellite-based communications networks that link the world. The development of these systems made it possible for producers of ideas to reach vast audiences. And though it is conventional to refer to "mass communications" mechanisms, it is important to point out that the masses typically receive rather than communicate ideas through these systems. The construction of mass communications mechanisms generally promoted the flow of ideas from the top to the bottom of the social hierarchy.

A third component of the construction of a free market in ideas was and is legal protection for free trade in ideas. The great principles of western jurisprudence—the absence of prior restraint on publication, the constitutional abhorrence of censorship, the protection of speakers and writers from assault by hostile audiences, the constriction of libel law, and the protection of copyrights—provide protection for producers (as opposed to consumers) of ideas. Consumers who may not wish to see an idea disseminated are nevertheless enjoined from disrupting its dissemination. Moreover, the burden of proof rests heavily on those who, for any reason whatsoever, seek to block the production and dissemination of an idea, a process that is conceived to be so important that even the most obnoxious ideas are protected. All these legal protections have a definite political constituency.

Debates over censorship and the like are sometimes seen as

arguments between right-thinking people and narrow-minded bigots. However, there is more to it than this. The opponents of censorship and proponents of freedom of communication are, in general, the most powerful producers of ideas, or, alternatively, those who believe they can expand their market share. Thus, for example, in international politics it is the western nations and their news media that promote the free flow of ideas—a flow they dominate. In domestic politics, of course, the major news media, journalists, publishers, established educators, attorneys, and others who earn a living from communicating ideas most vigorously oppose censorship. Also, censorship is usually opposed by religious groups that seek to spread their beliefs, by growing political movements, and by others who are interested in the further dissemination of their ideas. On the other hand, the chief proponents of censorship are usually the more marginal producers of ideas or established producers who cannot protect their existing market share against competition. For example, in international politics, Third World nations with weak communications industries favor curbs on the flow of information. In domestic politics, censorship is favored by declining religious sects and politicians from the hinterlands. Thus the conflict between advocates of freedom of expression and proponents of censorship is typically not so different from the more general economic debate between expanding industries that prefer free trade and declining industries that seek protection.

This pattern is also manifested in the history of free trade in ideas. Historically, the creation of a free market in ideas was very much a product of the political activities of the rising bourgeoisie who believed that the free exchange of ideas would serve their interests. Again, their presumption was that free trade would allow them, as the most efficient producers of ideas, to greatly expand their market share. This was especially evident in the battle over newspaper taxes in Britain during the 1830s. The fight to end taxes on newspapers was led by precisely the same forces that espoused free trade in other commodities. Their manifest position was that sound ideas would defeat poor ideas in the marketplace. This belief, however, was based on the presumption that the dissemination of these "sound" ideas would be far better financed than that of the "inferior" ideas of the working classes. The bourgeoisie did not depend solely on the inherent quality or merit of their ideas. And with the elimination of newspaper taxes, the bourgeois press, subsidized by advertising, was indeed able to outproduce and undersell the radical press, which was virtually destroyed as a result.[13] I shall return to discuss the marketplace of ideas more fully in chapter 4.

From an Adversary to a Proprietary View

Before the nineteenth century, subjects generally conceived themselves to be in an adversary relationship with the state. From the perspective of most ordinary subjects, the "state" simply meant the tax collector and the military recruiter. Indeed, during the great period of European state construction in the sixteenth, seventeenth, and eighteenth centuries, governmental efforts to increase levels of tax payment and military service increased subjects' conviction that the state's power was maintained mainly at their expense. As a result popular opposition became a major obstacle to state building in western Europe.[14]

In the nineteenth century, however, western governments actively sought to alter their citizens' perspectives toward the state. Western regimes began to offer their subjects a sense of entitlement—citizenship and political rights in the form of representation and suffrage, and economic rights in the form of pensions, social welfare, employment, and property ownership.

These entitlements, taken together, were designed to encourage people to believe that the state's power served their own interests and thus to change citizens' underlying political perspective from an adversarial to a proprietary view of the state. To reinforce this proprietary view, regimes sought to create or enhance patriotic sentiment and national identity among their subjects and, moreover, to equate the state with the nation in the popular mind so that citizens who identified with the latter would also support the former. Over time, these efforts began to have profound implications for mass opinion about the state. Ordinary citizens began to view the state as a source of benefits, to develop a sense of pride in and identification with their government and ultimately a willingness to support "their" state against its domestic and foreign foes.

At the present time, for example, most Americans agree on the need for a large, active and powerful state. Indeed, even self-styled "conservatives" in the 1980s differ more with their "liberal" counterparts over the proper character than the ultimate desirability of an expanded role for the state. Many of the same individuals who urge an evisceration of the social programs that mainly benefit blacks and the poor defend state subsidies for corporations, farmers, military contractors, and tobacco growers. It should be recalled that Ronald Reagan began his successful "conservative" campaign not by promising to curtail governmental activity but rather by vowing "to restore to the federal government the capacity to do the people's work."[15] In Reagan's first inaugural address, while pledging to curb the "size and influence of the federal establishment," he also declared: "Now, so there will be no misunderstanding, it is not my intention to do away with government. It is, rather, to make it work."[16]

The chief reason that few Americans would "do away" with government is precisely the political and economic benefits that citizens believe they derive from the state. Most Americans want the government to continue to provide or even to expand

its services. For example, most say they want the government
to "do more" with regard to a variety of social and economic
problems.[17] In fact, many claim to be willing to pay higher taxes
to maintain governmental services, programs, and solvency.[18]
Despite their occasional professions of fear and abhorrence of
"Big Government," two hundred years of welfare and entitlement programs have given citizens a strong sense of depen-
dence on state power and a sense that they, and not just their
rulers, have a stake in the state's preservation and protection.

The effects of economic entitlements are reinforced by the
political entitlements enjoyed by the citizens of the western
democracies. Political rights such as voting and representation
serve to convince citizens that they actually control the state
and thus stand to benefit from its power. After all, if the state
is merely a servant, why not give it the greatest possible power
to serve? Periodic citizen participation in the voting process acts
as an important reinforcement mechanism, reminding citizens
that they control the state's power.

This role of voting can be clearly seen by examining national opinion survey data drawn from two recent American
presidential elections. Both before and after the 1968 and 1972
national elections, the University of Michigan Survey Research Center asked a national sample several questions relating to trust in government and confidence in the government's
responsiveness. By comparing pre- and postelection responses
to the same questions, we can see the effects of the two elections on citizens' attitudes toward the regime. While the impact of the 1968 and 1972 elections differ somewhat, both appear to reinforce citizens' belief that they actually control
governmental power.

Table 2–1 reports the patterns of changes among respondents
asked whether people like themselves have "much say" about
what the government does, both before and after the 1968
presidential election. It is apparent, first, that a large proportion
of those respondents who first felt that people like themselves

had no influence on the government came to believe after the election that they did have quite a lot of "say." A much smaller percentage of those who thought initially that they did have considerable influence on the government changed their views after the election. Second, it is evident that positive changes are concentrated primarily among those who actually voted. Among individuals who first felt that they had little say about what the government does, 55 percent of those who actually voted came to believe after the election that they did have quite a lot of say about the government's actions. Among nonvoters, by contrast, positive changes barely outstrip negative shifts (see table 2–1).

A very similar pattern of postelection changes appears to occur in response to the question of whether or not public

TABLE 2–1

Changes in Popular Perceptions of "Say" in Government Following the 1968 Presidential Election

	Voters	Nonvoters	Total
Respondents with negative preelection perceptions who became positive following the election (%)[a]	55.0 ($N = 700$)[b]	34.6 ($N = 263$)	49.4 ($N = 963$)
Respondents with positive preelection perceptions who became negative following the election (%)	15.5 ($N = 278$)	21.2 ($N = 52$)	16.6 ($N = 330$)

[a]The question asked prior to the election was "Would you say that people like you have quite a lot of say about what the government does, or that you don't have much say at all?" The postelection form of the question asked respondents to agree or disagree with the assertion "People like me don't have any say about what the government does."
[b]The numbers in parentheses represent the base on which the proportion of changes was calculated. For example, 700 of the voters polled had negative perceptions prior to the election. Fifty-five percent of them became positive after the election; the other 45 percent remained negative.
NOTE: Reprinted, by permission of the publisher, from Benjamin Ginsberg and Robert Weissberg, "Elections and the Mobilization of Popular Support," *American Journal of Political Science* 22 (February 1978):36.

officials care what people like the respondent think (see table 2–2). Indeed, on this question the difference between voters and nonvoters is even more marked. Among voters, a sizable proportion of those who believed prior to the election that officials did not care offered a more positive appraisal after the election. Among those who did not vote, however, the proportion shifting to a negative view surpasses the percentage of respondents who later came to believe that public officials did care.

Even more interesting, however, this table indicates that individuals who voted for the losing candidate tended to be as likely as those voting for the winner to develop a more favorable view of government's responsiveness after the election. In the case of nonvoters, by contrast, the pattern of attitudinal changes is quite negative among the supporters of both candidates. It would appear that electoral participation, rather than candidate preference, is the key to understanding the attitude changes that occurred during this election.

The 1972 presidential election generated considerably more conflict and controversy than most electoral contests in recent American history. Throughout the campaign unusually sharp policy divisions were manifested between the two candidates as well as between their supporters. One might have expected that in this climate of electoral division, George McGovern's defeat could easily have repercussions for his supporters' beliefs about the political regime itself. However, to a considerable degree, attitude changes in 1972 follow the same patterns observed in 1968. Despite the bitterness of the contest, belief in the government's responsiveness increased among voters for both candidates (see table 2–3).

Like their 1968 counterparts, voters in 1972 tended in significant proportions to exhibit a stronger belief in the government's responsiveness following the election than they held prior to its occurrence. Unfortunately, these questions were not

TABLE 2-2

Changes in Popular Perceptions of Whether or Not Public Officials Care Following the 1968 Presidential Election

	Voters		Nonvoters		All		
	Humphrey	Nixon	Preferred Humphrey	Preferred Nixon	All Voters	Nonvoters	Total
Respondents with negative preelection perceptions who became positive following the election (%)[a]	45.4 (N = 130)	45.5 (N = 132)	24.6 (N = 57)	22.4 (N = 49)	41.1 (N = 33)	24.2 (N = 153)	35.7 (N = 485)
Respondents with positive preelection perceptions who became negative following the election (%)	24.5 (N = 261)	21.8 (N = 316)	62.3 (N = 53)	45.6 (N = 57)	25.1 (N = 630)	53.2 (N = 74)	30.3 (N = 770)

[a]The question asked prior to the election was "Would you say that most public officials care quite a lot about what people like you think, or that they don't care at all?" The postelection form of the question asked respondents to agree or disagree with the assertion "I don't think public officials care much what people like me think."

NOTE: Reprinted, by permission of the publisher, from Benjamin Ginsberg and Robert Weissberg, "Elections and the Mobilization of Popular Support," *American Journal of Political Science* 22 (February 1978):37.

TABLE 2–3

Changes in Popular Perceptions of "Say" in Government Following the 1972 Presidential Election

	Voted for Nixon	Voted for McGovern	Total Voters	Total Nonvoters
Respondents with negative preelection perceptions who became positive following the election (%)[a]	48.3 (N = 145)	26.5 (N = 98)	39.6 (N = 255)	27.4 (N = 175)
Respondents with positive preelection perceptions who became negative following the election (%)	10.9 (N = 329)	17.1 (N = 152)	13.1 (N = 504)	28.7 (N = 129)

[a]Both pre- and postelection respondents were asked to agree or disagree with the statement "People like me don't have any say about what the government does."
NOTE: Reprinted, by permission of the publisher, from Benjamin Ginsberg and Robert Weissberg, "Elections and the Mobilization of Popular Support," *American Journal of Political Science* 22 (February 1978):39.

asked both before and after more recent presidential elections, so we cannot examine the impact of voting in 1976, 1980, and 1984.

State and Nation

Through the educational system, as we saw, as well as through holidays, festivals, songs, ceremonies, art, and a host of other mechanisms, western regimes sought to enhance or create a sense of national identity among their often culturally, linguistically, and ethnically disparate citizens. Moreover, they sought to teach their citizens first that the government was an expression or manifestation of that national identity—that is, to be proud of their institutions and form of government—and, second, that the state served as the chief defender of the nation against foreign and domestic foes.

On the whole, western regimes have had considerable success on all three counts. In the United States, for example, a nation created quite recently through immigration, most Americans identify strongly as Americans, are proud of their form of government, and are firmly convinced of the desirability of providing the state with the enormous resources it claims to need to provide the nation with adequate security.[19]

Two hundred years ago citizens generally hated and feared the state. Today, at least in the United States, they seem quite attached to it. It is worth noting that the relative significance of political and economic entitlements on the one hand and patriotism on the other probably varies with social class. According to the data generated by a recent *New York Times*/CBS News poll, lower-income Americans manifest a more or less unconditional love of country. For example, most indicate that no political or economic considerations would ever induce them to leave the United States for another country. For upper-income Americans, by contrast, allegiance appears to be more conditional. Most say that they *would* consider moving to another country to improve their economic lot. At the same time, upper-income Americans attach more importance to their political rights than do their lower-income countrymen.[20] As the founders of the American republic very well understood, a successful regime caters more to the *interests* of its elites and more to the *emotions* of its masses.

From Spontaneous Assertion to Routine Expression

Before the nineteenth century, mass opinion was almost exclusively asserted through spontaneous and voluntary means—most typically through riot and disorder. During the 1800s, however, governments began to construct formal avenues for the assertion of mass opinion—representative bodies, elections, and the like—and to train citizens in their use. Whatever the other consequences of these institutions, they did enable regimes to reduce the threat that informal expressions of mass opinion often posed to the political order. The construction of electoral institutions was especially crucial in this regard.[21] In the twentieth century, of course, voting has come to be seen as a normal or typical vehicle for the expression of mass political opinion. But it was not always so. Indeed, if there is any natural or spontaneous form of mass political expression, it is the riot.

The fundamental difference between voting and rioting is that voting is a socialized and institutionalized form of mass political expression. The peasant uprising or urban riot is usually a spontaneous affair, sparked by some particular event or grievance. Though riots may have been commonplace, each was itself a unique event. Where and when disturbances occurred and who took part in them usually depended on a unique pattern of circumstances and spontaneous individual choices. Voting, however, is far from spontaneous. Elections provide routine institutional channels for the expression of demands and grievances. They thus transmute what might otherwise take the form of sporadic, citizen-initiated activity into a routine public function. When, where, who, and how individuals participate in elections are matters of public policy rather than questions of spontaneous individual choice. With the advent of the election, control over the agenda for the expression of polit-

ical opinion passes from the citizen to the state. The most obvious consequence of this change was a diminution of the likelihood of disruption and disorder. By establishing an institutional channel of political activity and habituating citizens to its
use, governments reduced the danger that mass political action
posed to the established political and social order. Elections
contain and channel away potentially violent and disruptive
activities and protect the regime's stability.

In principle, of course, citizens in democracies are free to
assert whatever demands, opinions, views, and grievances they
might have through a variety of means. Americans, for example, may, if they wish, lobby, petition, demonstrate, file suit in
court, and so forth. Though there are, of course, some legal
impediments to many of these forms of participation, relatively
few modes of political expression are directly barred by law.
Despite the hypothetical availability of an array of alternatives,
though, in practice the participation in American politics of
ordinary citizens as opposed to members of elite groups is generally limited to voting and a small number of other electoral
activities. It is true that voter turnout in the United States is
relatively low. However, when, for one or another reason, ordinary Americans do seek to participate, their participation generally takes the form of voting. Relatively few individuals
choose to engage in types of political action not formally a part
of the electoral process. Indeed, a large number of citizens have
never engaged in any form of political action but voting.[22] The
preeminent position of voting and other forms of electoral involvement in the American political process is not surprising,
as the American legal and political environment is overwhelmingly weighted in favor of electoral participation generally and
voting in particular. Though Americans may in principle do as
they wish, members of the mass public are strongly encouraged
to participate electorally and to ignore the potential alternatives.

Probably the most influential among the forces helping to

channel participants into the electoral arena are law and civic education. For the mere existence of suffrage does not guarantee that citizens will use it in preference to other possible forms of political action. State legislation in the United States not only gives people the vote but prescribes the creation of an elaborate and costly public machinery that makes voting a rather simple task. And civic education, to a large extent legally mandated, encourages citizens to believe that electoral participation is *the* appropriate way to express opinions and grievances. Unlike many other nations, the United States neither obligates its citizens to vote nor prohibits them from engaging in other political activities. Nevertheless, systemic influences facilitate electoral participation, particularly voting, to the near exclusion of other possible forms of political activity.

The Impact of Law

Voting is among the least demanding forms of political involvement. Despite complicating factors such as registration, the time, energy, and effort needed to vote are considerably less than are required by all but a few other political activities. It is, indeed, usually assumed that the relative ease of voting is one of the major reasons why it is more common in the United States than any other mode of participation.

Yet the relatively low degree of individual effort required to vote, however, is somewhat deceptive. The fact of the matter is that voting is simple only because it is made so by an elaborate and costly electoral system. The ease with which citizens can vote is a function of law and public policy rather than an inherent attribute of voting itself. The costs of voting are paid mainly by the state.[23] In the United States electoral contests are administered principally by states and localities, although the Constitution, federal law, and federal court decisions have an obvious bearing on the conduct of elections.

Though state voting is sometimes thought of in terms of

regulations and limitations on suffrage, in fact, the bulk of state action in this area is permissive. States must and do create the opportunity to vote before they can begin to regulate it. Indeed, states and localities legally require themselves to invest considerable effort in the facilitating of voting. At the state, county, and municipal levels, boards of elections must be established to supervise the electoral process. For every several hundred voters in each state, special political units—precincts or election districts—are created and staffed exclusively for the administration of elections. During each electoral period polling places must be set up, equipped with voting machines or ballots, and staffed by voting inspectors. Prior to an election, its date, the locations of polling places, and the names of candidates must be publicized. After each election, returns must be canvassed, tallied, reported, and often recounted.

Because virtually all of this activity is borne by municipal governments, the total annual cost of American elections is not known. Even the very spotty evidence that is available, however, suggests that election administration is quite expensive. It is not at all unreasonable to assume that the total annual cost of election administration in the United States is well over $1 billion. This, of course, does not include the enormous cost of campaigns, now partially subsidized by the federal government but which, until recently, was borne entirely by parties, candidates for office, and organized interest groups.

Obviously, in all the states there are selective legal impediments to voting. Age disqualifies some. Registration requirements have an important impact on specific sets of potential voters. Nevertheless, although the laws of every state discourage or disqualify some potential participants, overall the laws diminish the likelihood that citizens will disqualify themselves from voting. Legal facilitation reduces the effort and motivation needed to participate by voting to the point where individuals are less likely to engage in alternative forms of political action.

Civic Education

Legal facilitation, of course, cannot completely explain the prevalence of voting and the relative absence of alternative forms of mass participation in the United States. If public attitudes were completely unfavorable to elections, it is doubtful that legal facilitation alone would have much impact. The ubiquity of voting, in large part, also reflects generally favorable public beliefs about the electoral process and perhaps a low regard for alternative forms of political action.

Such favorable public attitudes to voting do not come into being spontaneously. As a matter of public policy, Americans are taught to equate participation in politics with electoral participation, and especially with voting. Civic training, designed to give students an appreciation for the American system of government, is a legally required part of the curriculum in every elementary and secondary school and, though it is not as often required by law, civic education usually manages to find its way into college curricula as well.

In the elementary and secondary schools, through formal instruction and, more subtly, through the frequent administration of class and school elections, students are taught the importance of the electoral process. By contrast, little attention is given lawsuits, direct action, organizing, parliamentary procedures, lobbying, or other possible modes of participation. Obviously the techniques involved in organizing a sit-in or protest march are seldom part of an official school course of study.[24]

The New York State first-grade social studies curriculum offers a fairly typical example of the kind of training in political participation given very young children. The State Education Department provides the following guidelines to teachers:

> To illustrate the voting process, present a situation such as: Chuck and John would both like to be the captain of the kickball team. How will we decide which boy will be the captain? Help the children to understand that the fairest way to choose a captain is by voting.

Write both candidates' names on the chalk board. Pass out slips of paper. Explain to the children that they are to write the name of the boy they would like to have as their captain. Collect and tabulate the results on the chalk board.

Parallel this election to that of the election for the Presidency.

Other situations which would illustrate the election procedure are voting for:

a game
an assignment choice
classroom helpers.[25]

Though secondary-school students periodically elect student government representatives rather than classroom helpers and are given more sophisticated illustrations than kickball team elections, the same principle continues to be taught, in compliance with legal requirements. College students are also frequently given the opportunity to elect senators, representatives, and the like to serve on the largely ornamental representative bodies that are to be found at most institutions of higher learning. Millions of college students believe this sort of experience is good preparation for life.[26]

Obviously, civic education is not always completely successful. In the late 1960s and early 1970s sizable numbers of college students and graduates staged sit-ins and demonstrations for various political causes. Segments of the educational process clearly provide skills, resources, and ideas that enable their recipients to participate more readily in a variety of political contexts than those with lower levels of educational attainment. The state's civics curriculum is hardly all that students learn in school. Nevertheless, level of education is strongly associated with interest in elections, belief in the efficacy and importance of voting, and voting itself.[27]

Civic education, of course, does not end with formal schooling. Early training is supplemented by a variety of mechanisms ranging from the official celebration of national holidays to the activities of private patriotic and political organizations. Election campaigns themselves are occasions for the reinforcement of training to vote. Campaigns include a good deal of oratory designed to remind citizens of the importance of voting and the democratic significance of elections. Parties and candidates, even if for selfish reasons, emphasize the value of participation, of "being counted," and the virtues of elections as instruments of popular government. Even though large numbers of Americans stay home on election day, this continuing civic education coupled with legal permissiveness ensures that when Americans do choose to participate they will almost always take the electoral route.

Elections as Alternatives to Political Disorder

While elections democratize citizen involvement and offer millions a routine opportunity to participate in political affairs, they also limit mass participation and cushion its likely impact on the regime. Elections facilitate participation in much the same way that floodgates can be said to facilitate the flow of water. Elections direct mass involvement into formal channels, thus removing many potential impediments to participation, but at the same time diverting it from courses that may be hazardous to the established political order.

Given the proper circumstances, of course, even those who normally value the vote and regularly participate at the polls can turn to protest and violence. Elections themselves can sometimes be sufficiently divisive that the losers withdraw from the electorate, or worse. European, Latin American, and even United States history provide any number of examples of voluntary and violent withdrawals from the electorate. However, a good bit of intriguing, though fragmentary, evidence suggests that when formal electoral channels of participation are available and citizens habituated to their use, the attractiveness of violent and disorderly mechanisms for the assertion of popular grievances is indeed diminished.

An interesting piece of evidence concerns the impact of adverse changes in economic conditions on mass political activity. Economic distress has historically been among the most important proximate causes of mass political violence and disorder. Pre–nineteenth-century urban riots and peasant risings, for example, were often responses to one or another form of economic distress. The relationship between increases in the price of bread and popular agitation during the French Revolution will always be remembered, in part because it was so carefully studied by historical sociologist George Rude, but even more because of the famous misunderstanding of the composition of cake usually attributed to Marie Antoinette.[28] Similarly, in the twentieth century adverse economic conditions have often led to popular disturbances. Even Eastern European Communist governments have, on several occasions in recent years, been shaken by mass protest over economic conditions.

Though economic distress can spark popular agitation in any nation, the form of the political activity so stimulated can vary. What is important for us here is that the form of the political activity associated with economic downturns seems to vary considerably, depending on whether or not electoral channels of political action are open and available.

Table 2–4 reports the lagged relationship between the incidence of riots and demonstrations on the one hand and percentage changes in the gross national product (GNP) on the other, for two groups of nations during the 1960s (unfortunately, more recent data are not available). The first group is composed of all those nations for which data were available that either held no regular elections or were classified as holding only "rigged" elections by the *World Handbook of Political and Social Indicators*. ("Rigged" is defined as meaning that no opposition or competition is permitted and the electoral outcome preordained.) The second group of nations consists of all those for which data were available that routinely held free and competitive elections as determined by the *World Handbook.*[29]

The differences as revealed by the table are quite striking. In those nations that do not hold regular elections or where elections are purely symbolic affairs without the possibility of opposition, changes in the GNP are negatively associated with the incidence of riots and demonstrations. That is, in those nations, economic downturns, as measured by drops in the GNP, seem positively correlated with an increased incidence of protest.

By contrast, in those nations that hold regular and competitive elections, there appears to be no relationship between adverse economic changes and the incidence of protest activity. In this group of nations, virtually no relationship whatsoever between change in GNP and riots or demonstrations is evident.

Conclusions based on gross comparisons of whole nations and also on a small number of cases during a short period of

TABLE 2–4

The Relationship Between Economic Change and Political Disorder in Dictatorships and Democracies

	Incidence of riots in 1965	Incidence of demonstrations in 1965
Change in GNP between 1963 and 1965 for nations with "rigged" elections (N = 35)	−0.28[a]	−0.16
Change in GNP between 1963 and 1965 for nations with "competitive" elections (N = 35)	−0.08	0.09

[a]Pearson correlation coefficients.
NOTE: Reprinted, by permission of the publisher, from Benjamin Ginsberg, *The Consequences of Consent* (New York: Random House, 1982), 54.

time must be considered tentative. Nevertheless, the findings are consistent with the argument that the availability of electoral channels of political agitation diminishes the likelihood that attempts by citizens to assert their grievances will take disorderly or disruptive forms. That economic downturns are associated with riots and demonstrations only where electoral channels of political activity are not available seems to suggest that elections can indeed contain and channel away the effects of stimuli that would otherwise create political disorder.

This conclusion is further supported by the fact that in the nations with open and competitive elections, the incidence of riot and protest is negatively correlated with voter turnout, which suggests that here voting and protest activity are somewhat mutually exclusive alternatives. Or, to put it another way, the greater the number of individuals who are allowed to vote, the smaller the incidence of riots and demonstrations.[30]

Economic fluctuations *do* have an impact on mass political activity in this group of nations. This impact appears more likely, however, to take the form of changes in electoral behavior than of variations in the incidence of popular riot and disorder. In the United States, for example, economic downturns appear to result in shifts of electoral support away from the incumbent party.[31] During periods of severe economic distress, moreover, electoral support for minor party candidacies tends to increase substantially.[32]

Reconstituting Mass Opinion

Thus, over two hundred years, western regimes fundamentally reconstituted mass opinion—changing its modes of formation, its social basis, its political foundations, and its form of expression. When taken together, these four changes amount to a domestication of mass public opinion. Under the pressure of market forces, the solidarity of lower-class opinion was broken; with the development of electoral institutions, the expression of mass opinion became less disruptive; when citizens began to see government as a source of benefits, opinion became fundamentally less hostile to central authority (though not always to particular authorities); with the advent of mass education, governments began to intervene directly in the formation of popular attitudes. In short, western regimes converted mass opinion from a hostile, unpredictable, and often disruptive force into a less dangerous and more tractable phenomenon. As we shall see, this change has been reflected and reinforced by polling.

Chapter 3

Polling and the Transformation of Public Opinion

THE "WILL OF THE PEOPLE" has become the ultimate standard against which the conduct of contemporary governments is measured. In the democracies, especially in the United States, both the value of governmental programs and virtue of public officials are typically judged by their popularity.[1] Twentieth-century dictatorships, for their part, are careful to give at least lip service to the idea of popular sovereignty, if only to bolster public support at home and to maintain a favorable image abroad. Some despots manage to convince even themselves that they truly speak for or, in fact, actually embody the popular will.[2]

Much of the prominence of opinion polling as a civic institution derives from the significance that present-day political ideologies ascribe to the will of the people. Polls purport to provide reliable, scientifically derived information about the public's desires, fears, and beliefs, and so to give concrete expression to the conception of a popular will. The availability of accurate information certainly is no guarantee that governments will actually pay heed to popular opinions. Yet many students and practitioners of survey research have always believed that an accurate picture of the public's views might at least increase the chance that governments' actions would be informed by and responsive to popular sentiment.[3]

Unfortunately, however, polls do more than simply measure and record the natural or spontaneous manifestation of popular belief. The data reported by opinion polls are actually the product of an interplay between opinion and the survey instrument.[4] As they measure, the polls interact with opinion, producing changes in the character and identity of the views receiving public expression. The changes induced by polling, in turn, have the most profound implications for the relationship between public opinion and government. In essence, polling has contributed to the domestication of opinion by helping to transform it from a politically potent, often disruptive force into a more docile, plebiscitary phenomenon.

Publicizing Opinion

Poll results and public opinion are terms that are used almost synonymously. As one indication of the extent to which public opinion is now identified with the polls, a sophisticated new national magazine entitled *Public Opinion* matter-of-factly devotes virtually all its attention to the presentation and discussion of survey data.

Yet, in spite of this general tendency to equate public opinion with survey results, polling is obviously not the only possible source of knowledge about the public's attitudes. Means of ascertaining public opinion certainly existed prior to the development of modern survey techniques. Statements from local notables and interest group spokespersons, letters to the press and to public officials, and sometimes demonstrations, protests, and riots provided indications of the populace's views long before the invention of the sample survey. Governments certainly took note of all these symptoms of the public's mood. As corporate executive and political commentator Chester Barnard once noted, prior to the availability of polling, legislators "read the local newspapers, toured their districts and talked with voters, received letters from the home state, and entertained delegations which claimed to speak for large and important blocks of voters."[5]

Obviously, these alternative modes of assessing public sentiment continue to be available. But it is significant that whenever poll results differ from the interpretation of public opinion offered by some other source, almost invariably the polls are presumed to be correct. The labor leader whose account of the views of the rank and file differs from the findings of a poll is automatically assumed to have misrepresented or misperceived membership opinion. Politicians who dare to quarrel with polls' negative assessments of their popularity or that of their programs are immediately derided by the press.

This presumption in favor of opinion polls stems from both their scientific and their representative character. Survey research is modeled after the methodology of the natural sciences and at least conveys an impression of technical sophistication and scientific objectivity. Occasional press accounts of deliberate bias and distortion of survey findings only partially undermine this impression.[6]

At the same time, polls can also claim to offer a more representative view of popular sentiment than any alternative source of information. Group spokesmen sometimes speak only for themselves. The distribution of opinion reflected by letters to newspapers and public officials is notoriously biased. Demonstrators and rioters, however sincere, are seldom more than a tiny and unrepresentative segment of the populace. Polls, by contrast, at least attempt to take equal account of all relevant individuals. And, indeed, by offering a representative view of public opinion, polls have often served as antidotes for false spokesmen and as guides to popular concerns that might never have been mentioned by individuals writing letters to legislators or newspaper editors.

Nevertheless, polling does more than just offer a scientifically derived and representative account of popular sentiment. The substitution of polling for other means of gauging the public's views also has the effect of changing several of the key characteristics of public opinion. Critics of survey research have often noted that polling can affect both the beliefs of individuals asked to respond to survey questions and the attitudes of those who subsequently read a survey's results.[7] However, the most important aspect of polls is not their capacity to change individuals' beliefs. Rather the major impact of polling is the way polls cumulate and translate individuals' private beliefs into collective public opinions.

Clearly the prevalence and character of beliefs in the public forum can vary greatly. Some views seldom receive public expression while others remain matters of vigorous public discussion for protracted periods. In recent years, polling has come to be one of the important factors that help to determine how, whose, which, and when private beliefs will become public matters. Indeed, the advent of polling has done much to change the aggregation, cumulation, and public expression of citizens' beliefs.

Four fundamental changes in the character of public opinion can be traced directly to the introduction of survey research. First, polling alters both what is expressed and what is perceived as the opinion of the mass public by transforming public opinion from a voluntary to an externally subsidized matter. Second, polling modifies the manner in which opinion is publicly presented by transforming public opinion from a behavioral to an attitudinal phenomenon. Third, polling changes the origin of information about public beliefs by transforming public opinion from a property of groups to an attribute of individuals. Finally, polling partially removes individuals' control over their own public expressions of opinion by transforming public opinion from a spontaneous assertion to a constrained response.

Individually and collectively, these transformations have profoundly affected the character of public opinion and, more important, the relationship of opinion to government and policy. To the extent that polling has displaced alternative modes of gauging popular sentiment, these four transformations have contributed markedly to the domestication or pacification of public opinion. Polling has rendered public opinion less dangerous, less disruptive, more permissive, and, perhaps, more amenable to governmental control.

From Voluntarism to Subsidy

In the absence of polling, the cost and effort required to organize and publicly communicate an opinion are normally borne by one or more of the individuals holding the opinion. Someone wishing to express a view about civil rights, for example, might write a letter, deliver a speech, contribute to an organization, or join a protest march. A wealthy individual might employ a public relations expert; a politically astute individual might assert that he or she represented the views of many others. But whatever the means, the organization and public communication of opinion would entail a voluntary expenditure of funds, effort, or time by the opinion holder. Polls, by contrast, organize and publicize opinion without requiring initiative or action on the part of individuals. With the exception of the small sample asked to submit to an interview, the individuals whose opinions are expressed through polls need take no action whatsoever. Polls underwrite or subsidize the costs of eliciting, organizing, and publicly expressing opinion.

This displacement of costs from the opinion holder to the polling agency has important consequences for the character of the opinions likely to receive public expression. In general, the willingness of individuals to bear the costs of publicly asserting their views is closely tied to the intensity with which they hold those views. Other things being equal, individuals with strong feelings about any given matter are more likely to invest whatever time and effort are needed to make their feelings known than are persons with less intense views. One seldom hears, for example, of a march on Washington by groups professing not to care much about abortion. As this example suggests, moreover, individuals with strongly held views are also more likely than their less zealous fellow citizens to be found at the extremes of opinion on any given question.[8] Thus as long as the costs of asserting opinions are borne by opinion holders themselves, those with relatively extreme viewpoints are also disproportionately likely to bring their views to the public forum.

Polls weaken this relationship between the public expression of opinion and the intensity or extremity of opinion. The assertion of an opinion through a poll requires little effort. As a result, the beliefs of those who care relatively little or even hardly at all are as likely to be publicized as the opinions of those who care a great deal about the matter in question. The upshot is that the distribution of public opinion reported by polls generally differs considerably from the distribution that emerges from forms of public communication initiated by citi-

zens. Political scientists Aage Clausen, Philip E. Converse, Warren E. Miller, and others have shown that the public opinion
reported by surveys is, on the aggregate, both less intense and
less extreme than the public opinion that would be defined by
voluntary modes of popular expression.[9] Similarly, poll respondents typically include a much larger proportion of individuals who "don't know," "don't care," or exhibit some
other form of relative detachment from the debate on major
public issues than the population of activists willing to express
their views through voluntary or spontaneous means.[10]

This difference between polled and voluntarily expressed
opinion can have important implications for the degree of influence or constraint that public opinion is likely to impose upon
administrators and policy makers. Polls, in effect, submerge
individuals with strongly held views in a more apathetic mass
public. The data reported by polls are likely to suggest to public
officials that they are working in a more permissive climate of
opinion than might have been thought on the basis of alternative indicators of the popular mood. A government wishing to
maintain some semblance of responsiveness to public opinion
would typically find it less difficult to comply with the preferences reported by polls than to obey the opinion that might be
inferred from letters, strikes, or protests. Indeed, relative to
these other modes of public expression, polled opinion could be
characterized as a collective statement of permission.

Certainly, even in the era of polling, voluntary expressions of
public opinion can still count heavily. In recent years, for example, members of Congress were impressed by calls, letters, and
telegrams from constituents—and threats from contributors—
regarding President Reagan's various tax reform proposals.
Groups like the National Rifle Association are masters in the
use of this type of campaign. Nevertheless, contradiction by
polls tends to reduce the weight and credibility of other sources
of public opinion, an effect that can actually help governments
to resist the pressure of constituent opinion. Constituency polls,

for example, are often used by legislators as a basis for resisting the demands of political activists and pressure groups in their districts. Polls frequently allow legislators who so desire to claim that the more vocal elements in their constituency do not truly represent the wishes of the constituency as a whole.[11]

Polling is especially useful when voluntary expressions of public opinion indicate severe opposition to a government and its programs. The relatively permissive character of polled opinion can provide a government faced with demonstrations, protests, and other manifestations of public hostility a basis for claiming that its policies are compatible with true public opinion and opposed only by an unrepresentative group of activist malcontents.

A good illustration of how polls can play this role is the case of the "silent majority" on whose behalf Richard Nixon claimed to govern. The silent majority was the Nixon administration's answer to the protestors, demonstrators, rioters, and other critics who demanded major changes in American foreign and domestic policies. Administration spokespersons frequently cited poll data, often drawing on Richard Scammon and Ben Wattenberg's influential treatise, *The Real Majority*, to question the popular standing of the activist opposition.[12] According to the administration's interpretation, its activist opponents did not represent the views of the vast majority of "silent" Americans who could be found in the polls but not on picket lines or marches, or in civil disturbances.

Undoubtedly a majority of Americans were less than sympathetic to the protestors. But from the administration's perspective, the real virtue of the silent majority was precisely its silence. Many of those Americans who remained silent did so because they lacked strong opinions on the political issues of the day. The use of polls to identify a "silent majority" was a means of diluting the political weight and undermining the credibility of those members of the public with the strongest views while constructing a permissive majority of "silent"

Americans.[13] In a sense, polls came to be used against those persons who truly had opinions.

Another illustration of the permissive character of polled opinion is Lyndon Johnson's reaction to public opinion surveys about the Vietnam war. Johnson constantly referred to the polls in his attempt to convince friends, visitors, colleagues, and most of all himself that the public supported his war policies. Indeed, Johnson's eventual realization that public opinion had turned against his administration weighed heavily in his decision not to seek another term in office.[14] The significance of this case is that polls permitted a president who was apparently actually concerned with his administration's responsiveness to public opinion to believe that he was doing what the people wanted. The polls appeared to indicate that despite the contrary assertions of protestors, demonstrators, and rioters, public opinion did not really demand an end to the war. After all, it was not until late in Johnson's term that a majority of those polled disapproved of his policies.[15] In effect, the polls permitted a public official who had some actual desire to be responsive to public opinion to more easily convince himself that he had been.

From Behavior to Attitude

Prior to the advent of polling, public opinion could often only be inferred from political behavior. Before the availability of voter survey data, for example, analysts typically sought to deduce electoral opinion from voting patterns, attributing candidates' electoral fortunes to whatever characteristics of the public mood could be derived from election returns. Often population movements served as the bases for conclusions about public preferences. Even in recent years the movement of white urbanites to the metropolitan fringe, dubbed "white flight," has been seen as a key indicator of white attitudes toward racial integration. Especially in the case of the least articulate segments of the population, governments before the advent of polls often had little or no knowledge of the public mood until opinion manifested itself in some form of behavior. Generally this meant violent or disruptive activity.

In the modern era public opinion is synonymous with polls. But certainly through the nineteenth century, public opinion was usually equated with riots, strikes, demonstrations, and boycotts. Nineteenth-century public sentiment could sometimes reveal itself through the most curious forms of behavior. In London during the 1830s, for example, a favorite mechanism for the expression of popular opinion was the "illumination." In an "illumination" those espousing a particular point of view placed lanterns or candles in their windows. Often mobs went from house to house demanding that the occupants "illuminate." Householders who declined might have their windows smashed and dwelling sacked. On April 27, 1831, a large mob formed to demand electoral reform. According to a contemporary account:

> . . . On that evening, the illumination was pretty general. . . . The mobs did a great deal of mischief. A numerous rabble proceeded along the Strand, destroying all windows that were not lighted. . . . In St. James' Square they broke the windows in the houses of the Bishop of London, the Marquis of Cleveland and Lord Grantham. The Bishop of Winchester and Mr. W.W. Wynn, seeing the mob approach, placed candles in their windows, which thus escaped. The mob then proceeded to St. James Street where they broke the windows of Crockford's, Jordon's, the Guards, and other Club houses. They next went to the Duke of Wellington's residence in Piccadilly, and discharged a shower of stones which broke several windows. The Duke's servants fired out of the windows over their heads to frighten them, but without effect. The policemen then informed the mob that the corpse of the Duchess of Wellington was on the premises, which arrested further violence against Apsley House. . . .[16]

Obviously this sort of behavior shed a good deal of light on the state of popular sentiment long before the development of survey research.

The advent of polling transformed public opinion from a behavioral to an attitudinal phenomenon. Polls elicit, organize, and publicize opinion without requiring any action on the part of the opinion holder. Of course, public presentation of an opinion via polls by no means precludes its subsequent expression through behavior. Nevertheless, polling does permit any interested party an opportunity to assess the state of the public's mood without having to wait for some behavioral manifestation. From the perspective of political elites, the obvious virtue of polls is that they make it possible to recognize and deal with popular attitudes—even the attitudes of the most inarticulate segments of the populace—before they materialize in some unpleasant, disruptive, or threatening form of political action. In democracies, of course, the most routine behavioral threat posed by public opinion is hostile action in the voting booth, and polling has become one of the chief means of democratic political elites to attempt to anticipate and avert the electorate's displeasure. But in both democratic and dictatorial contexts, governments have also employed polling extensively to help forestall the possibility of popular disobedience and unrest.

In recent years, for example, many Eastern European regimes have instituted survey programs. Polling has been used, in part, to forewarn the leadership of potential sources of popular disaffection, hostility, or antigovernment activities. As sociologist Bodgan Osolnik observed, in Eastern Europe opinion research provides "a warning that some attitudes which political actors consider to be generally accepted . . . have not yet been adopted by public opinion." Such "misunderstandings," says Osolnik, "can be extremely harmful—and dangerous."[17] Polling allows the regime an opportunity to resolve these potential "misunderstandings" before they pose a serious threat.

As early as the 1950s, to cite one concrete case, the Polish government obtained extensive survey data indicating that strong religious sentiment was widespread among the young. The regime became quite concerned with the implications of the continuing hold of "unorthodox ritualistic attitudes" on the generation that was expected to possess the strongest commitment to socialism. In response to its survey findings, the government embarked on a major program of antireligious and ideological indoctrination aimed at young people.[18] Over the past several years the government of Poland has commissioned a number of studies of public opinion on political issues designed to avert the sort of popular unrest that has frequently shaken the state.[19] Obviously, however, recent events in Poland suggest that opinion polling does not precisely guarantee political stability.

The Polish government's response to such surveys has been to seek to modify the attitudes deemed to be threatening. Attitude-change campaigns, though, are not the only possible authoritarian governmental responses. Gestapo chief Heinrich Himmler is reputed to have carefully studied polls of German attitudes toward the Nazi regime and its policies. Apparently, whenever he noted that some of those surveyed failed to respond with the appropriate opinions, he demanded to know their names.[20]

In the United States, polling has typically been used as an adjunct to policy implementation. Polling can provide administrators with some idea of what citizens are and are not likely to tolerate and, thus, help them to avoid popular disobedience and resistance. As early as the 1930s, federal agencies began to poll extensively. During that decade the United States Department of Agriculture established a Division of Program Surveys to undertake studies of attitudes toward federal farm programs.[21] At the same time, extensive use was made of surveys by the Works Progress Administration, the Social Security Administration, and the Public Health Service.[22]

In recent years polling of one sort or another has become a

routine aspect of the process of policy implementation. In their well-known study of policy implementation, political scientists Jeffrey Pressman and Aaron Wildavsky noted the matter-of-fact manner in which Floyd Hunter's Social Science Research and Development Corporation was awarded a $400,000 contract for an "economic power structure survey" as part of the Oakland (California) redevelopment project. Project officials were not certain what role this survey was to play; surveys had simply become an expected part of any major project.[23]

Nor is polling by U.S. governmental agencies confined to the domestic policy arena. Various units of the State Department and other foreign policy agencies have engaged in extensive polling abroad to assess the likely response of citizens of other nations to American foreign policy initiatives aimed at them. During the era of American involvement in Vietnam, both the Defense Department and the Agency for International Development sponsored extensive polling in that country to examine the effects of existing and proposed American programs.[24] Similarly, polling was conducted in Cuba and the Dominican Republic to assess likely popular reaction to contemplated American intervention.[25] A good deal of polling has also been sponsored in Europe by American governmental agencies concerned with European reactions to American propaganda appeals.[26] Of course, American agencies are not the only ones to make use of opinion surveys. During the 1960s, for example, Soviet administrators began to employ polls in an attempt to avoid a repetition of the sort of massive and costly popular resistance that hampered Soviet agricultural collectivization.[27]

Let me emphasize again that even the most extensive and skillful use of polling does not ensure that public opinion will manifest itself only attitudinally. Behavioral expressions of opinion in the form of protests, riots, strikes, and so on are common enough even in the era of survey research. The most accurate information about public attitudes is no guarantee that governments can or will act effectively to forestall their expression through some form of behavior. Yet polling can offer governments a measure of knowledge about public opinion while it remains purely attitudinal in form and thus poses less of an immediate threat and remains amenable to modification or accommodation.

In some instances, of course, the knowledge of popular attitudes gleaned from polls may convince those in power simply to bow to the popular will before it is too late. Such a response would certainly be consistent with the hopes expressed by polling advocates. Yet often enough the effect of polling is to lessen the threat or pressure that public opinion is likely to impose on administrators and policy makers. By converting opinion from a behavioral to an attitudinal phenomenon, polling is, in effect, also transforming public opinion into a less immediately threatening and dangerous phenomenon.

Polls can, however, also give a government a better opportunity to manipulate and modify public opinion and thus to avoid accommodation to citizens' preferences. One interesting recent example of this process is the activity of the 1965 American "Riot Commission." Charged with the task of preventing repetitions of the riots that rocked American cities during the 1960s, the National Advisory Commission on Civil Disorders sponsored and reviewed a large number of surveys of black attitudes on a variety of political, social, and economic questions. These surveys allowed the commission to identify a number of attitudes held by blacks that were said to have contributed to their disruptive behavior. As a result of its surveys, the commission was able to suggest several programs that might modify these attitudes and thus prevent further disorder. Significantly enough, the Riot Commission's report did not call for changes in the institutions and policies about which blacks had been violently expressing their views.[28] The effect of polling was, in essence, to help the government find a way to *not* accommodate the opinions blacks had expressed in the streets of the urban ghettos of the United States.

From Group to Individual

Mass behavior was not the sole source of information about popular opinion prior to the advent of polling. Reports on the public's mood could usually also be obtained from the activists, leaders, or notables of the nation's organized and communal groups. Public officials or others interested in the views of working people, for example, would typically consult trade union officers. Similarly, anyone concerned with the attitudes of, say, farmers would turn to the heads of farm organizations. Of course, interest-group leaders, party leaders, and social notables seldom waited to be asked. These worthies would—and still do—voluntarily step forward to offer their impressions of membership opinion. While such impressions might not always be fully accurate, certainly group, party, and communal leaders often do have better opportunities to meet with and listen to their adherents than would be available to outsiders. Before the invention of polling these leaders quite probably possessed the most reliable data available on their followers' views. In the absence of contradictory evidence, at least, the claims of these leaders to have special knowledge of some portion of public opinion were strong enough to help give them a good deal of influence in national affairs. In essence, public opinion was a valuable property belonging to partisan, interest, or communal groups and their heads.

The advent of polling transformed public opinion from a property of groups to an attribute of individuals. Opinion surveys can elicit the views of individual citizens directly, allowing governments to bypass putative spokespersons for public opinion. Polls have never fully supplanted communal and interest-group leaders as sources of information about popular attitudes. Yet they do lessen the need for such intermediaries by permitting whatever agencies or organizations are interested in learning the public's views to establish their own links with opinion holders. At the same time, polling often undermines the claims of group leaders and activists to speak for membership opinion. Frequently enough, polls seem to uncover discrepancies between the claims of leaders or self-appointed spokespersons on the one hand, and the opinions of the mass publics whose views these activists claim to reflect on the other. For example, during the 1960s and 1970s opponents of the American antiwar movement often took heart from poll data apparently indicating that youthful antiwar protestors who claimed to speak for "young people" really did not. Some poll data, at least, suggested that on the average individuals under thirty years of age were even more "hawkish" than respondents over the age of fifty.[29]

This conversion of public opinion from a property of groups and their leaders to a more direct presentation of popular preferences has several consequences. On the one hand, polls undoubtedly provide a somewhat more representative picture of the public's views than would usually be obtained from group leaders and notables, who sometimes carelessly or deliberately misrepresent their adherents' opinions. Even with the best of intentions, the leaders of a group may be insufficiently sensitive to the inevitable disparity of viewpoints between activists and ordinary citizens and simply assume that their followers' views are merely echoes of their own. Polling can be a useful antidote to inaccuracy as well as to mendacity.

At the same time, however, by undermining the capacity of groups, interests, parties, and the like to speak for public opinion, polling can also diminish the effectiveness of public opinion as a force in political affairs. In essence, polling intervenes between opinion and its organized or collective expression. Though they may sometimes distort member opinion, organized groups, interests, and parties remain the most effective mechanisms through which opinion can be made to have an impact on government and politics. Polls' transformation of public opinion into an attribute of individuals increases the accuracy but very likely reduces the general efficacy with which mass opinion is publicly asserted.

Consider the role of labor unions during the Nixon era. Many of the Nixon administration's policies—wage and price controls in particular—were strongly opposed by organized labor. Yet polls constantly undercut the capacity of labor leaders to oppose the programs or to threaten electoral reprisals against legislators who supported it. Poll data seemed generally to suggest that Nixon was personally popular with union members and that most of the rank and file had no strong views on the programs that troubled the unions' leadership. As a result, the administration came to feel that it was reasonably safe to ignore the importunities of organized labor on a host of public issues.[30] By enhancing the visibility of the opinions of ordinary workers, the polls surely drew a more representative picture of working-class opinion than had been offered by union officials. Yet the real cost of this more fully representative account of workers' views was, in a sense, a diminution of organized labor's influence over policy.

A similar example, also drawn from American labor history, relates to the controversy over the 1947 Taft-Hartley Act. Poll results constantly undermined the capacity of organized labor to oppose this piece of legislation, which it regarded as virulently antiunion. The polls seemed to indicate that labor union members were far less concerned than were their leaders with the act's provisions. Moreover, union members did not appear to regard legislators' positions on Taft-Hartley as a major factor that should determine their electoral choice. As a direct result of these poll data, a number of U.S. senators and representatives with large trade union constituencies were emboldened to vote for the act and, subsequently, to vote to override Truman's veto. Apparently Senator Taft himself only decided to stand for reelection after polls in Ohio indicated that union members—

a key voting bloc in the state—did not oppose him despite his sponsorship of a piece of legislation that union leaders dubbed a "slave labor act."[31]

It is not entirely a matter of coincidence that both these examples are drawn from the experience of the labor movement. Historically, the introduction of polling was, in fact, most damaging to the political fortunes of the groups that represented the interests and aspirations of the working classes. Polling erodes one of the major competitive advantages that has traditionally been available to lower-class groups and parties—a knowledge of mass public opinion superior to that of their middle- and upper-class opponents. The inability of bourgeois politicians to understand or sympathize with the needs of ordinary people is, of course, the point of one of the favorite morality tales of American political folklore, the misadventures of the "silk-stocking" candidate. To cite just one example, during the New York City mayoral race of 1894, the Committee of Seventy, a group that included the city's socially most prominent citizens, argued vehemently for improvements in the city's baths and lavatories, "to promote cleanliness and increased public comfort." The committee's members seemed undisturbed by the fact that the city and nation in 1894 were in the grip of a severe economic downturn accompanied by unusually high unemployment and considerable distress and misery among the working classes. The Committee of Seventy did not receive the thanks of many working-class New Yorkers for its firm stand on the lavatory issue.[32]

Simply as a matter of social proximity, working-class parties or associations may have better access to mass opinion than is readily available to their rivals from the upper end of the social spectrum. As one Chicago precinct captain told University of Chicago political scientist Harold Gosnell during the 1930s, "... you think you can come in here and help the poor. You can't even talk to them on their own level, because you're better, you're from the University. I never graduated from high school, and I'm one of them."[33]

Even more important than social proximity, however, is the matter of organization. In general, groups and parties that appeal mainly to working-class constituencies rely more heavily than their middle- and upper-class rivals on organizational strength and coherence. Organization has typically been the strategy of groups that must cumulate the collective energies of large numbers of individuals to counter their opponents' superior material means or institutional standing. In the course of both American and European political history, for example, disciplined and coherent party organizations were generally developed first by groups representing the working classes. French political scientist Maurice Duverger noted that "Parties are always more developed on the Left than on the Right because they are always more necessary on the Left than on the Right."[34]

What is important here is that their relatively coherent and disciplined mass organizations gave parties of the left a more accurate and extensive view of the public's mood than could normally be acquired by their less well organized opponents. In western Europe, the "branch" style of organization evolved by working-class parties in the nineteenth century gave them direct access to the views of a nationwide sample of ordinary citizens. In the United States, the urban political machines that mobilized working-class constituencies employed armies of precinct workers and canvassers who were responsible for learning the preferences, wants, and needs of each and every voter living within an assigned precinct or election district. A Chicago machine precinct captain interviewed by Gosnell, for example, "thought that the main thing was to meet and talk to the voters on a man-to-man basis. . . . It did not matter where the voters were met—in the ball park, on the rinks, at dances, or at the bar. The main thing was to meet them."[35] Through its extensive precinct organization, the urban machine developed a capacity to understand the moods and thus to anticipate and influence the actions of hundreds of thousands of voters.

The advent of polling eroded the advantage that social proximity and organization had given working-class parties in the competition for mass electoral support. Of course, any sort of political group can use an opinion survey. Polls are especially useful to carpetbaggers of all political stripes as a means of scouting what may be new and foreign territory.[36]

But historically polling has been particularly valuable to parties and candidates who lacked disciplined organizations and whose own social roots might not offer many clues to the desires of ordinary voters. Part of the historical significance of polling is that it represented a major element in the response of the right to the left's twin political advantages—greater organizational coherence and social consanguinity with ordinary citizens.

In the United States, where systematic political polling was initiated during the second half of the nineteenth century, most of the early polls were sponsored by newspapers and magazines affiliated with conservative causes and middle- and upper-class political factions. Thus the conservative *Chicago Tribune* was a major promoter of the polls during this period. Prior to the critical election of 1896, the *Tribune* polled some 14,000 factory workers and purported to show that 80 percent favored McKinley over William Jennings Bryan.[37] Many of the newspapers and periodicals that made extensive use of political polling at that time were linked with either the Mugwumps or the Prohibitionists—precisely the two political groupings whose members might be least expected to have much firsthand knowledge of the preferences of common folk. During the 1896 campaign the Mugwump *Chicago Record* spent more than $60,000 to mail postcard ballots to a random sample of one voter in eight in twelve midwestern states. An additional 328,000 ballots went to all registered voters in Chicago. The Democrats feared that the *Record* poll was a Republican trick and urged their supporters not to participate.[38] Other prominent members of the Mugwump press that frequently sponsored polls before the turn of the century included the *New York Herald,* the *Columbus Dispatch,* the *Cincinnati Enquirer,* the *Springfield* (Massachusetts) *Republican,* and the *Philadelphia Times.* [39]

This affiliation of many of the major polls with groups on the political right continued through the early years of the twentieth century. The Hearst newspapers, for example, polled extensively. *Fortune* magazine published widely read polls. The *Literary Digest,* which sponsored a famous presidential poll, was affiliated with the Prohibitionists.[40] The clientele of most of the major pre–World War II pollsters—George Gallup, Elmo Roper, and Claude Robinson, for example—was heavily Republican, reflecting both the personal predilections of the pollsters and relative capacities of Democrats and Republicans of the period to understand public opinion without the aid of complex statistical analysis.[41] In recent years the use of political polling has become virtually universal. Nevertheless, the polling efforts and uses of other forms of modern political technology by groups on the political right have been far more elaborate and extensive than those of other political factions.[42] Indeed, liberal Democrats are currently bemoaning the technological lead of their conservative Republican rivals (a point we shall return to in chapter 5).

Until the past several decades, polling was employed with much greater frequency in the United States than in Europe. It is worth noting that probably the first extensive use of political polls in Western Europe occurred after World War II under the aegis of several agencies of the U.S. government. These polls were designed, in large measure, to help centrist and right-wing political forces against their socialist and communist foes.[43]

At the present time, polling is used by parties and candidates of every political stripe in the United States and all the European democracies. Opinion surveys are hardly a monopoly of the political right. Yet the fact remains that in the absence of polling, parties and groups representing the working classes would normally reap the political advantage of a superior knowledge of public opinion. The irony of polling is that the development of scientific means of measuring public opinion had its most negative effect on precisely those groups whose political fortunes were historically most closely linked with mass public opinion.

From Assertion to Response

In the absence of polling, individuals typically choose for themselves the subjects of any public assertions they might care to make. Those persons or groups willing to expend the funds, effort, or time needed to acquire a public platform normally also select the agenda or topics on which their views will be aired. The individual writing an angry letter to a newspaper or legislator generally singles out the object of his or her scorn. The organizers of a protest march typically define the aim of their own wrath. Presumably, nineteenth-century mobs of "illuminators" determined of their own accord the matters on which the larger public would be enlightened.

The introduction of opinion surveys certainly did not foreclose opportunities for individuals to proffer opinions on topics of their own choosing. Indeed, in the United States a multitude of organizations, groups, and individuals are continually stepping forward to present the most extraordinary notions. Nevertheless, polls elicit subjects' views on questions that have been selected by an external agency—the survey's sponsors—rather than by the respondents themselves. Polling thus erodes individuals' control over the agenda of their own expressions of opinion. With the use of surveys, publicly expressed opinion becomes less clearly an assertion of individuals' own concerns and more nearly a response to the interests of others.

The most obvious consequence of this change is that polling can create a misleading picture of the agenda of public concerns, for what appears significant to the agencies sponsoring polls may be quite different from the concerns of the general public. Discrepancies between the polls' agenda and the general public's interests were especially acute during the political and social turmoil of the late 1960s and early 1970s. Though, as we saw, polling was used by the government during this period to help curb disorder, the major commercial polls took little interest in the issues that aroused so much public concern. The year 1970, for example, was marked by racial strife and antiwar protest in the United States. At least fifty-four major antiwar protests and some forty major instances of racial violence occurred.[44] Yet the 1970 national Gallup Poll devoted only 5 percent of its questions to American policy in Vietnam and only two of 162 questions to domestic race relations.[45] Similarly, in 1971, despite the occurrence of some thirty-five major cases of racial unrest and twenty-six major episodes of student violence or protest, the national Gallup Poll that year devoted only two of its 194 questions to race relations and asked no questions at all about student protest. By contrast, that year's poll asked forty-two political "horse race" questions, concerning citizens' candidate preferences and electoral expectations as well as eleven questions relating to presidential popularity.[46] An observer attempting to gauge the public's interests from poll data might have concluded that Americans cared only about election forecasts and official popularity and were blithely unconcerned with the matters that were actually rending the social fabric of the era. In fact, the commercial polls' almost total disregard for questions pertaining to civil rights, race relations, and poverty before matters reached a violent flash point in the 1960s sparked some controversy within the professional polling community. W. Phillips Davison, former president of the American Association for Public Opinion Research, called the polls' failure to anticipate the development of violent racial conflict "a blot on the escutcheon of survey research."[47]

Given the commercial character of the polling industry, differences between the polls' concerns and those of the general public are probably inevitable. Polls generally raise questions that are of interest to clients and purchasers of poll data—newspapers, political candidates, governmental agencies, business corporations, and so on. Questions of no immediate relevance to government, business, or politicians will not easily find their way into the surveys. This is particularly true of issues such as the validity of the capitalist economic system or the legitimacy of governmental authority, issues that business and government usually prefer not to see raised at all, much less at their own expense. Because they seldom pose questions about the foundations of the existing order, while constantly asking respondents to choose from among the alternatives defined by that order—candidates and consumer products, for example—polls may help to narrow the focus of public discussion and to reinforce the limits on what the public perceives to be realistic political and social possibilities.

But whatever the particular changes polling may help to produce in the focus of public discourse, the broader problem is that polling fundamentally alters the character of the public agenda of opinion. So long as groups and individuals typically present their opinions on topics of their own choosing, the agenda of opinion is likely to consist of citizens' own needs, hopes, and aspirations. Opinions elicited by polls, on the other hand, mainly concern matters of interest to government, business, or other poll sponsors. Typically, poll questions have as their ultimate purpose some form of exhortation. Businesses poll to help persuade customers to purchase their wares. Candidates poll as part of the process of convincing voters to support them. Governments poll as part of the process of inducing citizens to obey. Sometimes several of these purposes are combined. In 1971, for example, the White House Domestic Council sponsored a poll dealing with a host of social issues designed both to assist the administration with policy planning and to boost the president's reelection efforts.[48]

In essence, rather than offer governments the opinions that citizens want them to learn, polls tell governments—or other sponsors—what they would like to learn about citizens' opinions. The end result is to change the public expression of opinion from an assertion of demand to a step in the process of persuasion.

Making Opinion Safer for Government

Taken together, the changes produced by polling contribute to the transformation of public opinion from an unpredictable, extreme, and often dangerous force into a more docile expression of public sentiment. Opinion stated through polls imposes less pressure and makes fewer demands on government than would more spontaneous or natural assertions of popular sentiment. Though opinion may be expressed more democratically via polls than through alternative means, polling can give public opinion a plebiscitary character—robbing opinion of precisely those features that might maximize its impact on government and policy.

Many of those involved with survey research have long believed—or hoped—that the collection of accurate information about the public's wishes would enhance governmental responsiveness to popular opinion. No doubt there are occasions when polls help to increase the degree of correspondence between official policy and citizens' needs. But accurate information is obviously no guarantee of governmental responsiveness to popular desires. Indeed, reliable knowledge of public opinion can permit governments to manage, manipulate, and use public sentiment more effectively. At the same time that some early students of survey research purported to see only polls' implications for enhanced governmental sensitivity to opinion, others clearly recognized the value of polling as an instrument of governmental administration and policy implementation.

One academic spokesman for this latter group was David Truman. While a young World War II naval officer attached to the Joint Production Committee of the Joint Chiefs of Staff, Truman published a paper with the telling title "Public Opinion Research as a Tool of Public Administration."[49] Surveys, he indicated, can help administrators to identify and correct popular attitudes that might interfere with the successful operation of governmental programs. An example was the experience of "one of the oldest and best managed federal conservation agencies."

. . . Active operations had been started a short time before in several major conservation projects in the South. The methods employed were those which had been successfully used in the less sparsely populated sections of the West, where the population affected was comparatively close to national markets and nationwide trends. Activation of the program in the southern area was accompanied by resistance, hostility, and, in a seriously large number of cases, acts of criminal destructiveness which threatened the entire project. The findings of the government opinion researchers who were asked to study the problem revealed that the agency had, while acting in a completely legal manner, ruptured the established habits of living in the communities and to some extent had even violated certain parts of what might be called the local code of public morality. Community standards thus condoned and even encouraged individual and group acts of violence aimed at retaliation and at destroying the project.[50]

The agency's reaction to these findings was not to terminate the program that had provoked such violent popular opposition. Rather poll data allowed administrators to develop more effective means of convincing the populace of the program's value. In due course the project was able to proceed without further local resistance. Thus polling enhanced the agency's capacity to pinpoint and, ultimately, to seek to modify the public attitudes that posed a threat to its objectives.

The role of polling in this case was to transmute public opinion into a form that could be more easily managed. Rather than promote governmental responsiveness to popular sentiment, polls served to pacify or domesticate opinion, in effect helping to make public opinion safer for government. In a sense, of course, polls did contribute to the realization of a measure of consistency between public opinion and public policy: polling helped administrators change public opinion to match existing policy. In this instance as in others, opinion surveys provided officials with more or less reliable information about current popular sentiment, offered a guide to the character of the public relations efforts that might usefully be made, and served as means of measuring the effect of "information programs" on a target population. In essence, polling allowed officials a better opportunity to anticipate, regulate, and manipulate popular attitudes. Ironically, some of its early students believed that polling would open the way for "government by opinion."[51] Instead, polling has mainly helped to promote the governance of opinion. Let us now turn to the West's chief mechanism for governing opinion—the "marketplace of ideas."

Chapter 4

The Marketplace of Ideas

FREEDOM OF OPINION and expression are among the most admirable features of civic life in the western democracies. While they periodically may seek to manipulate information and shape popular perceptions, in contrast to the brutal suppression of dissident views that is so routine in much of the world, the western democracies are models of forbearance. The relative infrequency of overt repression, however, does not mean that thought and discussion in the West are free from all forms of state regulation. For the past two hundred years western governments have used market mechanisms to regulate popular perspectives and sentiments. The "marketplace of ideas," built during the nineteenth and twentieth centuries, effectively disseminates the beliefs and ideas of upper classes while subverting the ideological and cultural independence of the lower classes. Through the construction of this marketplace, western governments forged firm and enduring links between socioeconomic position and ideological power, permitting upper classes to use each to buttress the other.

Westerners often equate freedom of opinion and expression with the absence of state interference. The freedom of opinion found in the western democracies, however, is not the unbridled freedom of some state of nature. It is rather the structured freedom of a public forum constructed and maintained by the state. The maintenance of this forum has required nearly two centuries of extensive governmental effort in the areas of education, communication, and jurisprudence. The species of freedom that westerners enjoy is a product of the state's intervention, not a function of the absence of such involvement. This distinction is fundamentally important. Prior to the nineteenth century, public opinion was stratified by class, region, religion, ethnicity, and so on. Every community possessed its own opinions and beliefs based on its own experiences and circumstances. The most important aspect of this "state of nature" was that the views of lower classes were not much influenced by the beliefs of the upper classes. As I noted before, the avenues for communication among the various strata—religious channels included—were so limited that, for the most part, the attitudes and ideas of upper classes did not even penetrate the consciousness of the lower classes. Ruling classes depended on coercion, not the creation of congenial public beliefs, to maintain their power. This situation began to change in the nineteenth century. At that time and continuing into this century, most western governments launched vigorous efforts to encourage the development of mass communications, to promote popular literacy, and to expand individual freedom of speech and of the press. Through these efforts, every western state gradually dismantled internal barriers to communication and created what amounted to a national forum in which the views of all strata could be freely exchanged.

The construction of this forum, or "marketplace," was among the most important events of modern western history. First, the rise of the opinion market opened new opportunities for individual expression. The market freed individuals to hear and to voice views that differed from those of their religious, class, regional, or ethnic brethren. This is presumably why civil libertarians and other friends of diversity and dissent often played enthusiastic parts in the market's development. But while it contributed to individual freedom of opinion, the construction of the idea market also had a second important result—it opened the way for the wealthy and powerful to dominate the beliefs of the entire society.

Premarket barriers to communication among disparate social and economic groups—illiteracy, the absence of communications media, and even local restraints on expression—effectively protected weaker groups from contact with, and the influence of, the ideas and beliefs of the more powerful. These impediments to communication sheltered the beliefs and cultural identities of weaker strata in much the same way that trade barriers often protect weaker firms from their more powerful rivals. The construction of the market shattered the barriers to intergroup communication and exposed lower classes to the ideas of their social and economic superiors. This exposure undermined the ideological autonomy and cohesion of subordinate groups and gradually led them to see the world more nearly as the upper classes saw it.

In principle, of course, the market also exposed the upper classes to contact with the beliefs of their social inferiors and so gave the lower orders an opportunity to convert the entire society to their views. An idea's fate on the marketplace, after all, is usually said to depend more on its merit than its social origin. However, in the realm of opinion as in most other areas, the laws of the marketplace usually, albeit not always, favor the interests of the upper and upper-middle classes. Indeed, the fact that western regimes have historically relied so extensively on market mechanisms for the regulation of opinion, as well as most other forms of exchange, reflects and reinforces the influence of these strata. In the realm of opinion, upper- and upper-middle-class groups and the organizations and institutions they control are, first, the most powerful producers of ideas. These groups generally have far better access than their potential rivals to the social, financial, and organizational resources needed to effectively create and promote ideas. Second, these groups are usually the most influential consumers of ideas. The media, the publishing industry, and other concerns that hope to profit from the production and dissemination of opinion and information generally devote the bulk of their attention, particularly in the area of politics, to matters they deem likely to interest upper-income groups. Ideas thought unlikely to please or interest these strata are usually criticized or ignored. It is the economic importance of the "upscale" audience rather than prejudice on the part of journalists that tends to bias media news and public affairs coverage.

The ultimate significance of the construction of the idea market was to provide an institutional framework within which upper classes could use their socioeconomic and ideological powers to enhance and reinforce one another. On the marketplace, upper- and upper-middle-class forces are usually able to translate their superior economic and political resources into ideological power. Control of ideas, in turn, expands and protects their economic and political preeminence. It is the idea market more than any other western social institution that provides privileged strata with the capacity to define the universe of political and social alternatives for the entire society. In the United States in particular, the ability of the upper and upper-middle classes to dominate the marketplace of ideas has generally allowed these strata to shape the entire society's perception of political reality and the range of realistic political and social possibilities. While westerners usually equate the marketplace with freedom of opinion, the hidden hand of the market can be almost as potent an instrument of control as the iron fist of the state.

Origins of the Idea Market

Prior to the nineteenth century, opinion was a property of primary groups and classes. Disparate regional, religious, ethnic, linguistic, and economic strata generally possessed distinct ideas and beliefs based on their divergent experiences and life circumstances. The members of different primary groups generally had little contact with one another and knew remarkably little about the history, customs, or character—much less the opinions—of their nominal countrymen. In every European nation, city was separated from countryside and region from region by the lack of usable roads, the unavailability of effective communications media, and, in many cases, the absence of even a common national language. Language barriers could be formidable. For example, before the nineteenth century, Parisians traveling just a few days from the capital often reported that it was impossible to understand the patois of the local populace. Outside the larger towns, it was difficult to find anyone who spoke even a few words of French. Indeed, as late as 1860, little or no French was spoken in 25 percent of France's communes, and nearly half of France's 4 million schoolchildren possessed little more than a rudimentary grasp of the French language. Linguistic differences and the absence of effective communications mechanisms reinforced and preserved differences in customs, outlooks, and culture.[1]

Before the modern era every region—sometimes every town and village—of most European nations boasted a distinct culture and sense of identity. The same Parisian travelers who encountered language barriers in the countryside usually also found an enormous cultural gap between themselves and the local populace. Indeed, just a few miles from Paris, urban travelers often thought that they were entering a strange world, one with different customs, festivals, modes of dress, beliefs, concepts of time and distance, and even dietary habits from the world with which they were familiar. This world had its own laws of cause and effect, based on folklore and magic, and its own sense (or senses) of history in which such events as the French Revolution figured, if at all, in completely unexpected ways. In some regions, peasants identified the revolution not as a time of political change but instead as the period when trolls, ghosts, elves, and other magical creatures vanished from the world.[2] Parisians viewed country dwellers as beings more akin to natives of North America or Africa than to themselves. The inhabitants of the countryside, in their turn, usually seem to have been bewildered by the strange modes of dress, manners, and language of their Parisian visitors.[3] As to opinions and beliefs, the views and affairs of the capital had little relevance or meaning for the inhabitants of the countryside, while every region and locality had its own concerns and conception of political, economic, and social reality. Generally, the ideas that excited the cities went unnoticed in the countryside; beliefs that fueled violent passions in one region might not even produce a whisper of awareness or interest in another. Most significant was the matter of class. The members of the different social classes, even when living in geographic proximity, existed in very different worlds. Indeed, members of different classes hardly recognized each other as belonging to the same species. Watching a group of British soldiers bathe after the Battle of Waterloo, Wellington is reported to have expressed surprise that his troops were actually members of the white race. For their part, members of the working class often perceived their betters as grotesque monstrosities.[4]

The wide chasm between the worlds inhabited by the various classes had a number of consequences, among which one was of paramount importance. The gulf between the classes meant that, for the most part, rulers and ruling strata did not dominate the ideas and beliefs of the ruled. Instead, every class more or less independently developed its own ideology. It is, of course, often averred that ruling classes systematically manipulate the opinions of their subjects. Yet, as I indicated in chapter 1, only during the past two centuries have the doctrines enunciated by ruling classes really begun to reach the mass public. Before the nineteenth century there were few avenues through which rulers' claims could be communicated to a mass audience. The ideas embraced by the masses were ideas of their own creation.

The ideological autonomy of the various regions, groups, and causes began to diminish in the nineteenth century. During this period, as we saw, every European regime initiated the construction of what came to be called by liberal theorists a marketplace of ideas—a national forum in which the views of all strata would be exchanged. The construction of this marketplace had five principal components: language, literacy, perception, communications, and jurisprudence.

First, most western nations launched intense efforts to impose a single national language on the entire population. This process was costly and often entailed considerable coercion. Thus in France after 1870, the French language was the only one permitted to be used in the schools. Students or teachers found to be using any other tongue could be severely punished. Similarly, after that date the ability to read, write, and speak French became a prerequisite for even the most minor civil service appointment and the use of French became compulsory for all official business.[5] In the United States, of course, massive waves of immigration during the nineteenth century meant that millions of residents spoke no English. In response, the American national government, as well as state and local governments, made vigorous efforts to impose the English language upon these newcomers. Schools were established to provide adults with language skills. At the same time, English was the only language of instruction permitted in the public elementary and secondary schools. Generally, local governments even refused to employ bilingual teachers for foreign-born students, on the grounds that such a practice might help children to preserve

vestiges of their native tongues.[6] Knowledge of English also
became a prerequisite for American citizenship. With some no-
table exceptions, the efforts of western nations to achieve linguistic unification succeeded by the twentieth century. In
Europe, provincial dialects had lost much of their importance
by the end of World War I. By the early 1900s in France, for
example, local and regional dialects were the primary mode of
expression only of old people in the most insular areas. The
young spoke French. In the United States, second- and certainly
third-generation descendants of nineteenth-century immigrants seldom could understand even an isolated phrase of the
language their parents and grandparents once transported to
this nation's shores.

Second, and closely related to the effort to achieve linguistic
unity, was the matter of literacy. Prior to the nineteenth century, few ordinary people were able to read or write. Possession
of these skills was, for the most part, limited to the upper strata.
Widespread illiteracy in a pretechnological era meant that communication depended on word of mouth, a situation hardly
conducive to the spread of ideas across regional, class, or even
village or neighborhood boundaries. During the nineteenth and
twentieth centuries, however, all western governments actively
sought to expand popular literacy. With the advent of universal, compulsory education, of course, almost all children were
taught to read and write the mother tongue. Together with
literacy programs for adults, including extensive efforts by the
various national military services to instruct uneducated re-
cruits, this educational process led to the gradual eradication of
illiteracy in the industrial west. Like the imposition of a common language, the elimination of illiteracy opened the way for
the communication of ideas and information across primary
group lines. Indeed, even more than the imposition of a common language, the spread of literacy facilitated interclass communication, in particular, enhancing the capacity of elite strata
to communicate with the lower classes. The expansion of popu-

lar literacy, in effect, created a mass audience for those with a capacity to produce and promote their ideas—a capacity most frequently found at the upper levels of the social and economic hierarchy.[7]

The third basic ingredient for the construction of the idea market was the reconstitution of perception. Beginning in the 1800s, western regimes sought, mainly through mass education, to impose a common map or blueprint of the world upon their citizens. Mass education, of course, was a key instrument of political indoctrination or socialization, helping to disseminate such concepts as love of country and respect for property. But as important as their contribution to civic training, the schools played a central role in providing citizens with the reference points and shared understanding of the world that is essential for effective communication.[8] The central components of this shared perception included (but were not limited to): (1) a common sense of time and distance—all students were taught to "tell time" as measured by a universal and fixed clock and calendar rather than the traditional relativistic time linked to disparate local conditions such as "harvest time" and to measure distance with reference to universal and fixed standards rather than mutable, local yardsticks; (2) a common sense of geography and demography—all students were imbued (through the ubiquitous school map) with a shared sense of space and of the physical and demographic makeup of their nation and the world; (3) a common understanding of cause and effect—students were taught a scientific or rationalistic view of the world to take the place of the various traditional notions now dismissed collectively as "magic" or "superstition"; and (4) a common view of history—citizens were given a shared set of historic reference points and experiences to take the place of or at least coexist with the family, local, regional, or group histories that previously defined collective experience.

The creation of a common framework of perceptions by no means ensured agreement among the various and disparate elements of the populace, but nevertheless it was essential for the achievement of even meaningful disagreement. Even in the mid-nineteenth century French peasants often believed that the surveying equipment used in road and railroad construction was a Parisian mechanism designed to cause drought. By the twentieth century, local residents might still oppose a road or rail project, but the issue could be understood and discussed in similar terms by all parties.

The fourth facet of the construction of the marketplace of ideas was the development of communications mechanisms. This process involved a number of elements. During the early 1800s, governments built hundreds of thousands of miles of roads, opening lines of communication among the various regions and between cities and the countryside. Road building was followed later in the century by governmental promotion of the construction of rail and telegraph lines, further facilitating the exchange of goods, persons, and, not least important, ideas and information among previously disparate and often isolated areas. Such so-called internal improvements, it may be recalled, constituted the single most important activity undertaken by the American central government both before and after the Civil War. During the twentieth century, all western regimes promoted the development of radio, telephone, television, and, now, the complex satellite-based communications networks that link the world.

The final key component of the construction of a free market in ideas was, and is, legal protection for free trade in ideas. This last factor is what most clearly distinguishes the construction of the West's idea market from the efforts of authoritarian regimes with regard to belief and opinion. Obviously, the development of communication networks, linguistic unification, universal literacy, and so on were goals pursued just as avidly by autocratic nation builders in the East as by the liberal regimes of the West. The difference, as we shall see shortly, is mainly attributable to the power of the bourgeoisie in the West.

During the early part of the nineteenth century, western governments began to lift some of the traditional legal restrictions on communication. For example, Britain rescinded newspaper taxes during the 1830s. Subsequently, all western regimes, to a greater or lesser extent, developed principles of jurisprudence that protected and encouraged the production and promotion of ideas. These principles, as I observed in chapter 2, include the prohibition of prior restraint on publication; the disallowance of many, if not all, forms of censorship; protection of speakers and writers from assault by hostile audiences; restriction of the scope of libel law; and the protection of copyrights. The significance of these principles is worth reiterating. First, their chief thrust is the protection of producers and promoters of ideas rather than consumers. Consumers who may not wish to see an idea disseminated are nevertheless enjoined from disrupting its dissemination. Second, the burden of proof rests heavily upon those who, for any reason whatsoever, seek to block the production or the dissemination of an idea.

During the twentieth century, formal barriers to freedom of expression have been even further eroded, especially in the United States. Since the 1920s, at least, freedom of speech and of the press have been expanded and the opportunities for state and local governments to interfere with expression greatly diminished. While U.S. courts at one time subjected the validity of state and local governmental regulation of speech to a test of "reasonableness"—that is, a regulation had only to be "reasonable" to pass judicial muster—the criterion gave way during the 1920s to the much more stringent "clear and present danger" test, which placed more severe limits on the capacity of state and local governments to regulate speech. During the 1960s even the clear and present danger test gave way to a notion of the "preferred position" of speech under the Constitution.

This last judicial test makes it extremely difficult for state and local governments to place any limitations on speech and related forms of expression. In the United States the courts have greatly eroded the possibility for libel suits against newspapers, thus making it difficult for private agencies or individuals to seek to constrict the flow of ideas and information. At the same time, the courts have virtually eliminated the notion of obscenity. It is almost impossible for state and local governments to ban the production or distribution of materials on any moral ground.

The effect of this erosion of the remaining barriers to freedom of expression during the twentieth century has been to complete the work begun during the previous century, the work of transforming every western nation into a single unified idea market. The cumulative result of these governmental efforts was the gradual destruction of internal barriers to communication in every western nation and the construction of a forum in which the views of all groups and strata could easily be exchanged. In most western nations at this time, there are few physical or legal impediments to the transmission of ideas and information across municipal, regional, class, ethnic, or other primary group boundaries. All groups are, to a greater or lesser extent, linked by a common language, mass communications media, transportation networks, and, not least important, the shared perception of time and space and cause and effect, inculcated by the schools. In the United States, for example, the newspapers, wire services, radio, television, and news magazines present a common core of ideas and information to virtually the entire citizenry. Every region of the country can be reached by mail, phone, and broadcast media; virtually no area is inaccessible by road, rail, or air transport; and persons, ideas, and information can move freely across regions, economic strata, ethnic groups, and so on. The American government and those of the other western nations devote considerable attention and resources to promoting this flow of communication. Governments continue to regulate and, for the most part, facilitate the operations of the mass media, promote literacy and language skills, build roads, maintain postal services, block efforts by regional or local governments to censor or restrain communications, and in a variety of other ways maintain the marketplace constructed over the past two centuries. The creation and continued existence of this "free" market in ideas depends on this massive state intervention.

Viewing the World Through the Same Lenses

In several respects the construction of the idea market was among the most important events in modern western history. First, the free exchange of ideas on the marketplace has led to a remarkable confluence of views and perspectives across primary group lines. Analysts of public opinion are usually concerned with intergroup differences. However, the most striking aspect of contemporary public opinion, at least in the United States, is the substantial measure of similarity manifested by the views of disparate groups. At the present time all income groups in the United States exhibit reasonably similar orientations toward government and politics, share common perceptions of the agenda of public questions and problems, and even manifest similar attitudes on many, albeit not all, political and social issues.

One important example of a generally shared orientation toward the political process in the United States is the virtually unanimous support found within all income groups for the voting process. All income strata agree that voting is important —this despite the fact that the benefits of electoral participation might reasonably be seen very differently by members of different income strata. Thus 87 percent of those earning less than $10,000 per year, 94 percent of those earning between $10,000 and $20,000, 94 percent of those earning between $20,000 and

$30,000, and 96 percent of those earning more than $30,000 annually think that it is important to vote. Moreover, the distribution of attitudes in recent years concerning the choices to be made on such key issues as inflation, taxation, and civil rights have been substantially similar across income groups. For example, in 1980, 51 percent of the lowest income group and 55 percent of those in the highest income group agreed that progress on civil rights has been "about right" in the United States. Similarly, 63 percent of those in the lowest income group and 67 percent of those in the highest named inflation as their chief economic concern. This similarity is especially noteworthy given the differences of interest among income strata that might be expected to surface on these issues.

Regional variations in attitudes and opinions in the United States presented a very similar picture. Regional diversity certainly exists—witness regional differences in national electoral results. However, there is considerable similarity of outlook on basic political questions across all regions of the United States. For example, on the question of whether public officials are what people think—a basic question in the democratic context —the answer is "yes" for 58 percent of those living in the Northeast, 52 percent of those in the north-central United States, 56 percent of southerners, and so on. This substantial though, of course, not total similarity of outlook is also manifested across racial lines, across urban/rural lines, and, despite the prominence given the notion of a "gender gap," between the sexes. For example, in terms of race, in 1980, 70 percent of the white respondents to the University of Michigan's survey and 76 percent of the black respondents favored a 10 percent tax cut. Increased defense spending was favored by 72 percent of the whites and 58 percent of the blacks. And 50 percent of the whites and 51 percent of the blacks agreed that civil rights progress had been "about right."

Again, diversity of opinion exists on all these dimensions but, in general, the similarities outweigh the differences—at least in the contemporary United States. Of course, scientific public opinion surveys are a product of the modern era. No data exist that would allow systematic comparisons between contemporary mass opinion and the shape of popular beliefs before the twentieth century. It is nevertheless clear that the character and distribution of public opinion in the modern world differs substantially from the structure of popular beliefs in earlier eras. As mentioned, even as recently as the nineteenth century, members of different economic, regional, and ethnic groups held very different views of the world. Today, although differences of interest, principle, and belief continue to be important, most Americans, at least, see the world through similar lenses.

The development of this similarity of perspective across primary group lines is, in large measure, attributable to the operations of the idea market. In the contemporary West, individuals are continually exposed to concepts and information that originate outside their own region, class, or ethnic community. It is this steady exposure that, over time, leads members of every social group to acquire at least some of the ideas and perspectives embraced by the others. Given continual exposure to the ideas of other strata, it is virtually impossible for any group to resist some contamination and modification of its own beliefs. Thus similarities of opinion across income, race, and regional divisions are highly correlated with such factors as exposure to mass communication and education. The more exposure that members of disparate primary groups have to the mass media or to the educational system, the more likely they are to develop comparable views of the political world.

Compare, for example, the distributions of opinion on the issue of inflation within each of the different income strata, controlled for media exposure. Among those individuals reporting relatively little media use, each income group manifests quite dissimilar distributions of opinion. However, among those reporting frequent use of the media, the distribution of attitudes does not change much from one income stratum to the next (see table 4–1).

The same pattern is evident on such issues as school busing, equal rights for women, and so on. Media exposure appears to reduce the relationship between attitude and income. Among individuals who report frequent media use, the distribution of opinions varies little with income. This effect is also apparent if we compare the distribution of opinions within each region of the United States and between the two major racial groups. Again, media exposure appears to have the effect of reducing intergroup differences. For example, among respondents who seldom watch television, northeasterners and southerners disagreed on defense spending in 1980, with 81 percent of southern respondents favoring more defense spending as against 60 percent of the northeasterners. Among heavy TV viewers, by contrast, slightly more than 70 percent of each regional group favored more defense spending.

The effect of education is very similar to that of media exposure. In all but the most parochial settings, students are exposed to ideas—through books, films, lectures, and so on—that emanate from the world outside their own municipality, class, or

TABLE 4–1

Percentage of 1980 Respondents Who Believed that Inflation Was an "Extremely" Serious Problem

		View TV News "Every Day" (%)	View TV News "Almost Never" (%)
Annual Income (in thousands of dollars)	0–10	66	56
	10–20	66	59
	20–30	71	70
	30+	68	72

NOTE: These data are drawn from surveys conducted by the Center for Political Studies of the Institute for Social Research at the University of Michigan. They were made available to the author through the Inter-University Consortium for Political and Social Research.

ethnic community. As a result, education tends to erode inter-group differences in political beliefs and orientations. For example, intergroup differences on the issue of school prayer are considerably greater among the least educated than among those individuals with the most years of schooling. Thus among respondents with less than a high-school education, opinion differed sharply by income, with the lowest income group favoring prayer by an overwhelming 90 to 9 ratio while the uppermost income group divided 69 to 31 percent. Among college graduates, though, income and opinion were not related. The lowest and highest income groups split 53 to 46 percent and 47 to 43 percent, respectively. Again, education hardly leads to uniformity of opinion. Often, indeed, formal education can provide individuals on opposing sides of an issue with analytic and intellectual tools that enable them to express their differences more effectively. However, like media exposure, education tends to produce a shared world view. While it does not necessarily produce agreement, schooling generally provides disputants with at least a common language and vantage point.

In the United States, some regions and groups remained largely outside the national marketplace of ideas until World War II. The South, for example, retained its own distinct regional culture and vestiges of its "peculiar" institutions well into the postwar period. Students of public opinion may recall that until recently, southern opinion differed quite sharply on most measures from that of the nation as a whole. Since World War II, however, with the introduction and universal dissemination of television and other forms of mass communication, the expansion and quasi-nationalization of education, and the virtual elimination of local legal barriers to the communication of ideas and information, no region or group remains completely outside the national idea market. As a result, regional and intergroup differences in perspective have diminished in the United States over the past thirty years. For example, in 1956 the highest support for increased American involvement

in the world was found on the Pacific coast, where 78 percent
of poll respondents favored a more activist foreign policy. This
was some twenty points higher than support for global activism
in the least interventionist region, the South, where only 58
percent of the populace supported a more activist foreign policy. By 1980 the difference between the Pacific coast and the
South on this dimension had diminished to eight percentage
points—88 percent taking an activist position on the Pacific
coast and 80 percent in the South. At the same time, differences
among income strata on such matters as taxes, trust in government, and foreign policy have diminished over the past quarter
century. And so today, while Americans by no means agree on
all issues, regardless of race, sex, religion, income, or region,
they literally and figuratively speak the same language.

Support for Free Trade in Ideas

The construction of a national idea market and the emergence
of a measure of similarity among the views of disparate social
strata are often described as aspects of "political development"
or "modernization," terms suggesting that these phenomena
should be seen as natural and probably desirable historical processes. However, these developments were certainly not natural
or inevitable but were rather the work of particular social forces
that saw free trade in ideas—freedom of opinion and expression
—as a means of enhancing their own political and economic
power. The construction of the idea market during the nineteenth century was primarily the work of the bourgeoisie, albeit
with the occasional assistance of kings and their ministers eager
to expand and centralize national authority at the expense of
local prerogatives. The growth of the idea market during the

twentieth century was fostered by the efforts of upper-middle-class cosmopolitans assisted, in some instances, by bureaucratic centralizers.

Conflicts between advocates of unfettered expression and anyone with the temerity to propose limits on speech or the press are sometimes seen as debates that pit virtue against bigotry. However, these arguments have a political as well as a moral dimension. The chief proponents of free communication can generally be found among the most powerful producers of ideas and among those groups that believe they can increase or expand the popularity of their views. Thus, for example, in international affairs it is the western nations and their news media that advocate the free flow of ideas.[9] In domestic politics, groups, interests, and individuals who profit from communicating ideas are the most vigorous opponents of censorship. Conversely, censorship is vehemently opposed by members of proselytizing religions, growing political movements, and others who are interested in extending the dissemination of their ideas. As I noted earlier, the chief opponents of free trade are usually found among the more marginal producers of ideas, or among established producers who cannot protect their existing "market share" against competition. Thus in international affairs, Third World nations with weak communications industries favor curbs on the flow of information, while in the domestic arena, censorship is favored by declining religious sects and politicians from the hinterlands whose constituents' social and cultural views are out of step with the changes that are occurring in, and reflected by, the media broadcast from the metropole, including school textbooks. The conflict between proponents of censorship and advocates of freedom of expression is typically not so different from the more general economic debate between expanding industries that prefer free trade and declining industries that seek protection. Thus during the nineteenth century the presumption of many bourgeois politicians was that the free exchange of ideas would allow their constituents, the most efficient and effective producers of ideas, to greatly expand their market share—a view evident in the battle over newspaper taxes in Britain during the 1830s.[10]

In a similar vein, during the twentieth century the strongest support for freedom of expression has come from upper-income cosmopolitans who possess sufficient resources and access to communications media to effectively promote their ideas in the marketplace. It is for this reason that the three political movements that most vigorously championed freedom of expression in the United States during this century—the Progressive coalition, the New Deal coalition, and the New Politics coalition— were all forces in which upper-middle-class cosmopolitans figured prominently.

For example, the urban professional and managerial strata that formed the vanguard of the Progressive movement were able to exert enormous influence through the "independent" newspapers, national magazines, publishing houses, and, not least important, advertising agencies allied with, edited, or owned by the movement's members. To enhance the influence of these institutions, the Progressives championed freedom of expression, seeking, in particular, limits on the ability of state and local governments to censor or otherwise restrict the print media. The intellectual and political influence of the Progressives led to two important changes in American judicial doctrine regarding freedom of expression. First, in a series of decisions during the early twentieth century, the United States Supreme Court accepted the theretofore discredited notion that the First Amendment of the Constitution prohibited undue interference with expression by federal, state, and local authorities. Second, as I indicated earlier, the Supreme Court in the 1920s changed the judicial standard used to gauge the propriety of governmental restraints on expression from "reasonableness," to the rule of "clear and present danger," which meant that governments would henceforth be allowed to interfere with expression only in the face of an immediate threat to the

public's health or safety.[11] Taken together, these two Progres-
sive-era changes in judicial doctrine contributed substantially
to the expansion of free trade in ideas in the United States.

The New Deal coalition included among its members liberal
intellectuals and professionals with close ties to the universities,
the entertainment media, the arts, and journals of opinion. Like
the Progressives, the New Dealers relied heavily on these institutions to enhance their own influence and undermine that of
their opponents. As a result, the New Dealers, like their Progressive predecessors, were outspoken proponents of freedom
of expression. The most striking example of the importance
they attached to free trade in ideas was the successful effort of
the Roosevelt Court to elevate freedom of expression to a "preferred position" under the Constitution.[12] This, of course,
meant that protection of freedom of expression was to be given
the highest priority by the courts even when this principle came
into conflict with other constitutional precepts or governmental
interests.

The New Politics movement—to which I shall return shortly
—is a coalition of upper-middle-class intellectuals and professionals that emerged from the civil rights and antiwar struggles
of the 1960s. During the 1970s and 1980s, New Politics forces
have been at the forefront of the environmental, consumer,
feminist, and antinuclear movements. Like the Progressives and
the New Dealers, members of the New Politics movement have
enjoyed close ties to national communication media, in particular the television networks, the elite press, and liberal journals
of opinion. As a result, this movement, too, championed freedom of expression. Indeed, among the first expressions of New
Politics activism was the "free speech" movement at the University of California's Berkeley campus. The movement has, for
the most part, opposed any governmental restraints on expression—including disorderly forms of expression—and, through
such mechanisms as "sunshine" laws and "freedom of information" legislation, has sought to open governmental records and

processes to public scrutiny—that is, examination by its media allies.

Progressive, New Deal, and New Politics advocacy of freedom of expression was, in large measure, a function of their access to the national communications media. Leaders of these forces perceived free trade in ideas to be a mechanism for promoting the causes and enhancing the power of their movements. By the same token, opponents of the diminution of restraints on expression during these three eras mainly tried to prevent each group from making effective political use of the national media. Thus enemies of the Progressive movement charged that the Progressives' ideas were "godless" and, in the name of opposition to pornography and the teaching of evolution, sought to restrict the circulation of newspapers and magazines allied with the Progressive movement. Similarly, opponents of the New Deal coalition sought to silence the liberal intellectuals associated with the coalition and to gag or discredit the media that circulated their ideas by leveling charges of communism and treason against these individuals and calling for censorship of their views in the name of national security or patriotism. Finally, opponents of the New Politics movement have sought to diminish the movement's ability to use the national media and to intimidate newspapers and television networks thought to be friendly to New Politics causes by initiating boycotts, attempted buy-outs, and, most important, libel suits, such as General William Westmoreland's suit against CBS and Ariel Sharon's suit against *Time* magazine. These suits have been encouraged and often financed by conservative organizations such as the Capital Legal Foundation. When journalists charge that the threat of such suits could have a "chilling effect" on the media's willingness to question the conduct of public officials, these conservative organizations quite forthrightly respond that this is precisely their intention.[13]

The Benefits of Free Trade

It is sometimes said that the real beneficiaries of freedom of expression are the poor, minorities, and outcasts—groups whose lack of members, political power, or economic resources might otherwise leave their beliefs subject to suppression. But even though in principle everyone has an opportunity to be heard, the loudest voices on the West's idea market are seldom those of the poor and downtrodden. In general, the marketplace of ideas is dominated by the most powerful segments of the upper middle class. These strata, in turn, use the market to impose their views on the entire society.

The upper middle classes generally dominate the market both as producers and as consumers of ideas. First, at least in the United States, this stratum and the institutions it controls are the chief creators, promoters, and shapers of ideas and opinions. Few ideas spread spontaneously. Usually, whether they are matters of fashion, science, or politics, ideas must be vigorously promoted to become widely known and accepted. For example, the clothing, sports, and entertainment fads that occasionally seem to appear from nowhere and sweep the country before being replaced by some new trend are almost always the product of careful marketing campaigns by one or another commercial interest rather than spontaneous phenomena. Take, for instance, a recent sports fad, "Wallyball"—volleyball played on a racquetball court—described recently by *Newsweek* magazine as the "biggest sports/fitness craze to hit upscale America since naturalize became a verb."[14] This sports craze did not simply "hit" upscale America. It was vigorously advertised and promoted, under the auspices of Walleyball, Inc., a company formed for the purpose, by health clubs eager to generate additional revenues from their racquetball courts. Health clubs were interested in walleyball for a very simple reason. Racquetball is played by two individuals at a time. Walleyball, on the other hand, is played by as many as eight, and hence has the potential to generate considerably more revenue for the clubs. To promote this new craze, Walleyball, Inc., conducted a professional public relations campaign involving the distribution of booklets and pamphlets, promotional tours by expert players, and a national championship tournament. Indeed, quite often news articles like the *Newsweek* piece that reported the Walleyball "craze" are themselves results of promotional efforts by publicists who are skilled at attracting the interest of the news media on their clients' behalf.

Even in the sciences, ostensibly the bastions of objectivity, new theories, procedures, and findings are seldom accepted simply and immediately on their own merit. Typically the proponents of a new scientific principle or practice must campaign within the scientific community on behalf of their views. In recent years proponents of new perspectives in the fields of genetics, molecular biology, medicine, and high-energy physics —to say nothing of "softer" disciplines like economics—have conducted vigorous battles with defenders of traditional viewpoints. Occasionally such struggles become visible to the general public as one or both sides seek to generate public support for their positions. Typically, efforts to secure support within the more general public take the form of public speeches on behalf of the viewpoint in question; articles, books, and research reports written by or with the cooperation of scientists for mass consumption; and news releases purporting to present the latest scientific evidence for or against the matter at issue. These methods have been used by physicians who question (and others who defend) the value of chemotherapy for the treatment of some forms of cancer; by proponents (and opponents) of new views of the origins of the universe; by opponents (and defenders) of Keynesian economic theory; and, of course, by scientists representing various positions on the potential ecological effects of nuclear war and the possibilities for the construction of an effective defense against nuclear weapons—the so-called Star Wars program proposed by President Reagan. The manifest object of these battles, of course, is to establish the validity of a scientific position. Obviously, however, in addition to scientific principle, hinging on the outcome of these conflicts are academic appointments, access to research funds, and, in the case of Star Wars, the outcome of larger national partisan struggles. It would indeed be difficult to separate and weigh the relative importance of scientific principle and scientists' interests as causes of scientific disputes.

Indeed, at times what appear to be strictly scientific disagreements actually have political roots or are, in fact, political disputes couched in scientific language. One recent example of this phenomenon is the debate over the widely publicized theory that the extinction of the dinosaurs some 65 million years ago was caused by the catastrophic climatic effects of the impact of a large meteorite. Many proponents of this theory have drawn parallels between the fate of the dinosaurs and the potential consequences for humanity of the "nuclear winter" that some scientists assert would follow a nuclear exchange between the superpowers. The extinction of the dinosaurs, it is averred, resulted from the same sort of climatic changes that would occur after a nuclear war. It appears that at least some of the scientific proponents of the meteorite theory of dinosaur extinction are swayed less by the fossil evidence than by the theory's contemporary political implications. The majority of vertebrate paleontologists quietly reject the theory on the basis of the actual fossil evidence. According to some paleontologists, however, vocal dissenters from the meteorite theory face hostility and even obstacles to their careers within the scientific community and risk being branded as "militarists" on the ground that anyone who questions the meteorite theory of dinosaur extinction must also question the nuclear winter theory.[15]

Like their counterparts in fashion and science, successful—or at least widely held—political ideas are usually the products of carefully orchestrated campaigns by organized groups and interests rather than the results of spontaneous popular enthusiasm. Two recent examples of successful political ideas—ideas that have attracted millions of adherents—are "right to life," that is, the notion that abortions should be severely curtailed or outlawed altogether, and "nuclear freeze," the argument that the United States should halt the development and production of nuclear weapons either unilaterally or through the negotiation of a bilateral agreement with the Soviet Union. These ideas obviously differ in substance and certainly appeal to very distinct subgroups of the population. The notion of right to life is most popular among Protestant and Catholic social conservatives while the appeal of the nuclear freeze argument is strongest among liberal urban professionals. But these two political ideas are similar in one important respect. Neither was a spontaneous development; both were elaborated and successfully promoted by well-financed and well-organized groups using intelligent and sophisticated public relations techniques. Please note that I am not seeking to explain the ultimate origins of these ideas. Presumably all ideas are born in the minds of one or more individuals and are more the products of psychological factors than political calculus. What I am interested in explaining is why, of the many ideas conceived, a very small number are attractive to institutional, political, and social forces; I am not seeking to explain where ideas originate but rather why ideas are advocated.

Right to Life

Thus whatever the ultimate origins of the idea, the right-to-life issue was initiated by conservative politicians who saw it as a potential means of uniting Catholic and Protestant conservatives and linking both groups to the Republican coalition led by President Reagan.[16] These politicians convinced Catholic and evangelical Protestant leaders that they shared similar views on the question of abortion and worked with them to focus public attention on the evil of abortion. The first step in this process was, of course, to shift the media's attention and the public's sympathy away from its traditional focus on the plight of "unwed mothers" to a new concern—the agony and suffering ostensibly inflicted upon fetuses during abortions. To encourage this shift of sympathy, fetuses, which previously had not generally been seen as independent or sentient entities, were renamed "the unborn" to emphasize their humanity and were alleged to possess the attributes, feelings—and rights—of other human beings, perhaps even from the very moment of conception.

To dramatize the plight of these unborn human beings, leaders of the movement sponsored well-publicized Senate hearings where testimony, photographs, and other exhibits were presented to illustrate the violent effects of abortion procedures upon their innocent unborn subjects. At the same time publicists for the movement produced leaflets, articles, books, and films such as *The Silent Scream* to highlight the agony and pain ostensibly felt by the unborn while they were aborted. All this underscored the movement's claim that abortion was nothing more or less than the savage murder of millions of innocent human beings. Finally, Catholic and evangelical Protestant religious leaders were organized to denounce abortion from their church pulpits and, increasingly, from their electronic pulpits on the Christian Broadcasting Network (CBN) and the various other television forums available for religious programming. Religious leaders also organized demonstrations, pickets, and disruptions at abortion clinics throughout the nation.

This well-organized right-to-life campaign struck a responsive chord among millions of Americans and played a role in Reagan's victories in the 1980 and 1984 presidential elctions. Through the right-to-life issue, conservative politicians were able to unite two forces—Catholics and Protestant evangelicals —that had been bitter opponents through much of American history and were, moreover, able to stigmatize some of their liberal political opponents, most notably the Democrats' 1984 vice-presidential nominee, Geraldine Ferraro, as supporters of the murder of unborn children.

Thus the idea of right to life was hardly a result of spontaneous popular enthusiasm. The success of this notion on the marketplace of ideas depended heavily on the promotional efforts of well-organized political forces—conservative politicians, the Catholic Church hierarchy, and evangelical Protestant ministers. It is worth emphasizing that all these forces attached political as well as moral significance to the right-to-life idea. For the churchmen, it was a powerful moral stance that enhanced their image in the community and allowed them to organize and mobilize millions of sympathizers and, ultimately, to greatly strengthen their roles in national politics. For the conservative politicians, right to life was a useful way to unite conservative Catholics and Protestants, to lead both into the Reagan coalition, and, with the help of the churchmen, to stigmatize their liberal political opponents as baby killers. If the right-to-life idea had not served—and served so well—the interests of these forces, it is doubtful that they would have invested so heavily in its promotion. Political ideas are seldom developed and promoted simply because their sponsors believe them to be ethically or morally sound. Generally, ideas and interests are closely linked. This linkage is as apparent in the case of nuclear freeze as in the matter of right to life.

Nuclear Freeze

Like right to life, the idea of a nuclear freeze was developed and promoted by organized political forces seeking to further their own political interests. In particular, liberal activists conceived the idea of a nuclear freeze as a means of reviving and galvanizing the liberal antiwar coalition that had been such an important force in American politics during the Vietnam era.

Millions of Americans who might have been liberal activists or sympathizers during the 1960s and 1970s were now "Yuppies" —young urban professionals—apparently more concerned with jobs, careers, and economic issues than with the questions of peace, civil rights, and social change that had once stirred them to political action. Indeed, millions of Yuppies seemed prepared to support Ronald Reagan, the most conservative major party presidential candidate in twenty years, chiefly as a result of their newfound economic concerns.

From the perspective of liberal politicians, the nuclear freeze concept was a way of turning the agenda of political debate away from the economic concerns that generally worked to the advantage of their opponents to the issue of war and peace that had once brought them millions of sympathizers. Even the most materialistic Yuppies, after all, might be made to understand that videocassette recorders and personal computers would probably not be very useful after a nuclear war. At the same time, the issue had the potential to mobilize tens of thousands of student activists who might then also be available to work on behalf of other liberal causes and candidates. Moreover, like right to life, the demand for a nuclear freeze also served to stigmatize the opposition and attack the claims that helped buttress its political coalitions. Through the nuclear freeze campaign, conservative proponents of a strong national defense and the development and construction of new weapons systems— cornerstones of the Reagan coalition's political strategy for attracting the support of both heavy industry and large numbers of working-class people during the 1980s—could be characterized as madmen, oblivious to the threat that nuclear war posed to the survival of the human race. This claim was especially underscored by the nuclear winter scenario advanced by Cornell University astronomer Carl Sagan and other scientists. According to this thesis, even a limited nuclear exchange between the superpowers would result in such catastrophic climatological and ecological damage that food production would be disrupted or even halted throughout the world, leaving survivors of the war to freeze and starve and, perhaps, leading to the extinction of the human race. This scenario effectively answered the claim of conservative politicians that national security depended on stronger nuclear forces. If their use resulted in a nuclear winter, Americans would be killed just as surely by their own weapons as by the Soviets'. Thus, according to the liberals, the nation's survival depended on a freeze in the development of nuclear weapons, not on their continued production and deployment.[17]

To promote their cause, advocates of the nuclear freeze employed the full gamut of public relations mechanisms. Liberal senators, including Edward Kennedy, Mark Hatfield, and Alan Cranston, introduced a resolution supporting the concept of a freeze and conducted well-publicized hearings on the topic. Rallies were held throughout the nation, including a gigantic New York City rally that attracted several hundred thousand participants. Local organizations were formed, generally on college and university campuses, to foster local antinuclear activities and to enlist potential student activists. Scientists, entertainers, physicians, politicians, and educators gave speeches and held press conferences throughout the country on the dangers of nuclear war. Finally, freeze advocates helped to heavily promote films that depicted the dangers of nuclear war such as *Testament* and, most notably, "The Day After," viewed by tens of millions of Americans on the ABC television network.

The result of these efforts was a substantial increase in popular concern with issues of war and peace and, in particular, heightened public fear of nuclear war. Indeed, during the 1984 presidential campaign, Reagan strategists saw the war-and-peace issue as a potential Reagan Achilles heel and sought to offset the threat by having the President call for early negotiations with the Soviet Union to reduce each side's nuclear arsenal. In addition, Reagan called for the development of defensive systems—the so-called Strategic Defense Initiative (SDI), or

"Star Wars"—that would allegedly render offensive nuclear weapons obsolete. During his nationally televised debate with Democratic presidential candidate Walter Mondale, Reagan even went so far as to offer to share information about such defensive systems with the Soviets in order to further diminish the danger of nuclear war.

From the perspective of the Reaganites, Star Wars had two virtues. First, the proposal countered the liberals' claim that the Reagan coalition was leading the nation closer to nuclear war. After all, what would be less warlike than a proposal to render offensive nuclear weapons obsolete? Second, the proposed Star Wars program promised billions of dollars in revenues for American industry and hundreds of thousands of jobs for white-collar and, perhaps, blue-collar workers. Thus, whatever its actual military value, Star Wars potentially had enormous political value for the Reagan camp.

Because of the political benefits the Reagan coalition stood to reap from Star Wars, the SDI program was denounced as a dangerous fraud by liberal scientists and engineers, who presented technical analyses purporting to demonstrate that the defensive systems proposed by the Reagan camp would not work.[18] Liberal defense analysts and strategic planners produced articles and papers purporting to prove that the SDI system would actually have a destabilizing effect on the arms race and would inevitably increase the danger of nuclear war.[19] Liberal politicians and economists asserted that the supposed economic benefits and spinoffs of the program were actually chimerical and that, indeed, Star Wars would greatly increase the nation's budget deficits while yielding little or no economic payoff.[20] To drive home this three-pronged attack, anti–Star Wars forces began to organize on campuses throughout the nation and prepared a massive public relations offensive.

The technical merits of the anti–Star Wars case are beyond the scope of our concern, though it is difficult to resist observing that when Star Wars opponents argue on the one hand that the system could not protect the United States from a nuclear attack and on the other hand that the system would increase the probability that such an attack would occur, the logic of the case is somewhat tenuous. Nevertheless, whatever the scientific and technical facts of the matter, what is important to note is that for both the proponents and opponents of Star Wars, the issue was as much or more a matter of political power as a question of technical feasibility or even nuclear survival. For Star Wars proponents, the program was both a response to the liberals' call for a nuclear freeze and a public works program with enormous potential for political gain. For the opponents, opposition to Star Wars was a logical extension of the nuclear freeze campaign, which had been designed to change the agenda of political debate to the one area—war and peace—that liberals deemed was most favorable to themselves. If they failed to oppose Reagan's Star Wars initiative, liberals would, in effect, surrender their highest remaining ground to the Reagan coalition and, at the same time, be compelled to watch this ground used as the basis for an enormous public works program that would reward Reagan's friends and solidify their coalition.

Again, as in the case of right to life, millions of proponents of the notion of a nuclear freeze and opponents of Star Wars were perfectly sincere in their beliefs and were surely sincere when they expressed fear and dismay at the threat of nuclear war. But, nevertheless, as in the case of right to life, ideology and interest were closely linked. The idea of a nuclear freeze, whatever its merits as a solution to the problem of world peace, would never have been vigorously promoted by the coalitions of liberal political forces that were its chief advocates if the idea had not also served their political interest.

Political Ideas of the Progressive Era

Of course, these contemporary American political forces are hardly the first to advance moral principles that also tended to serve their own political interests. Perhaps the most skilled promoters of political ideas in modern American history were the turn-of-the-century Progressives, who were able to devise, promote, and implement reforms that changed the character of American politics in ways that served their own interests. Yet they were such adept promoters of ideas that most contemporary Americans simply accept the chief results of the Progressives' efforts—primary elections, nonpartisan voting, the civil service system, and voter registration—as natural, indeed desirable, elements of the political environment without having any conception of the political choice these reforms entailed—a choice that continues to shape American politics. In point of historical fact, of course, primary elections, civil service, and voter registration were all components of the Progressive attack on political parties, an attack whose principle underlying basis was the politics of social class.

The Progressives were the most adept creators, marketers, and manipulators of political symbols in all of American history. Today's political public relations firms appear amateurish by contrast. Through newspapers, magazines, civic associations, reform leagues, women's groups, university groups, and church organizations, the Progressives constantly emphasized two themes, the need to end corruption in government and politics and the necessity of expanding participation in political life. According to the Progressives, such time-honored American political practices as the patronage system, through which party leaders rewarded their allies with government jobs, were corrupt. Generations of Americans had conceived patronage to be no more than a manifestation of the profoundly democratic principle of rotation in office—after an election civil servants appointed by the defeated party were removed and replaced by a new set of officials allied with the forces that received the people's mandate to govern. The notion of a career civil service had always been regarded as "elitist" or "aristocratic."

Through their associations and publications the Progressives gradually educated the public to accept a new view of this situation. Patronage, the public was gradually taught, was not a democratic principle but rather was no more than a form of corruption. The notion of a career civil service was not "aristocratic" but instead represented the application of the principle of "merit" to political life. To this very day, Americans instinctively equate patronage with corruption and civil service with merit, oblivious to the fact that from the beginnings of the Republic to the turn of the twentieth century, their forefathers had just as instinctively equated patronage with democracy and a career service with aristocracy. It is a tribute to the political skill of the Progressives that over a relatively short period of time they were able to bring about a lasting and politically significant change in Americans' conceptions of an important political institution. Similarly, they were able to redefine the perfectly ordinary process through which party leaders selected candidates as a corrupt and dictatorial domination of politics by "bosses" in "smoke-filled" rooms and also, in the name of fighting corruption, to purge their enemies' supporters from the electorate through the adoption of voter registration requirements. Again, what is so remarkable about political reform at the turn of the century is the extent to which the Progressives were able to further the interests of their own class by devising ideas, principles, and a vision of the public good that appealed to millions of Americans and eventually came to be nearly universally accepted.

Ideas and Interests

As the Progressive example and the cases of right to life and
nuclear freeze suggest, the chief promoters and champions of
political ideas are typically those groups that stand to benefit
materially or politically from the principles in question. Obviously, the ideas presented by the Progressives and antiabortion
and nuclear freeze advocates were accepted by millions of to-
tally sincere individuals. Indeed, most of the activists, proponents, and promoters of these ideas also sincerely believed that
the positions they advocated served the public interest. Nevertheless, however sincere their proponents, political ideas are
typically vehicles for the assertion of interests. No group or
organization will invest heavily in terms of time, energy, and
resources to promote ideas that, whatever their moral value, do
not also promise to further the material interests or political
power of their proponents. It is also worth observing that for
reasons well known to students of social psychology, many
individuals do not find it terribly difficult to bring themselves
to sincerely—often fervently—believe in general principles that
just happen to be consistent with their private interests. At any
rate, the success of competing political forces is in large part a
function of their capacity to select, develop, and present ideas,
issues, and positions that enhance their own support, undercut
that of the opposition, and credibly explain why public resources should be used to finance programs that serve their
interest while being denied to programs they oppose.

Political forces may fashion and use five basic types of
ideologies to expand or bolster their support and reinforce their
programatic claims. First, they may seek to develop and promote ideas that plausibly present their own interests and those
of their allies as more general interests. These may be referred
to as public interest ideologies. Second, groups may advocate

ideas and courses of action that serve their own interests while appearing mainly to be designed to help others, typically deprived or disadvantaged strata. These might be called altruistic ideologies. Third, groups and forces frequently advance ideas that provide moral or equitable justifications for programs and policies that serve their interests—ideologies of entitlement. Fourth, groups may put forward ideas that plausibly link them and their allies with ethical and virtuous ideals while stigmatizing their opponents by identifying them with depravity and vice. These are, in effect, moralistic ideologies. Finally, political forces often espouse ideas that point out or create linkages among the interests of the members and potential members of their own political alliance while identifying and exacerbating differences of interest among the members of opposing forces —these are ideologies of coalition formation. Examples of each of these types of political ideology can be drawn from contemporary American political conflicts.

The central conflict in American politics during the past twenty years has been the struggle between what has been called the New Politics coalition and the coalition that Martin Shefter and I have elsewhere called the Reconstituted Right.[21] Each of these forces emerged from the wreckage of the New Deal regime through which Franklin Roosevelt and his successors governed the United States from the Great Depression through the postwar period. The New Politics coalition is the alliance of intellectuals and professionals that emerged from the civil rights and antiwar struggles of the 1960s and that subsequently became identified with such issues as environmentalism, consumerism, political reform, feminism, opposition to the development of nuclear energy, nuclear freeze, and, most recently, the antiapartheid campaign. National politicians closely associated with New Politics have included such individuals as former Senator George McGovern of South Dakota, who led a successful New Politics effort to capture the Democratic presidential nomination in 1972, and, more recently, Senators Alan

Cranston of California and Gary Hart of Colorado, both contenders for the 1984 Democratic presidential nomination. The New Politics coalition, in turn, can be seen as the political expression of what sociologists have called the New Class in American society. This New Class is the segment of the nation's upper class whose chief asset is human capital—high levels of education—rather than financial capital. Not coincidentially, as we shall see, the political ideas presented by the New Politics coalition often serve the interests of owners of human capital.

The second important contemporary coalition, the Reconstituted Right, consists of the bulk of the American business community, including the defense industry; the social and religious conservatives initially mobilized by George Wallace; and southern whites, northern blue-collar workers, and large segments of the suburban middle class. The formation of this coalition took place over a period of roughly twenty years and had two phases. The first of these, comprising the Nixon years, was the era of the "silent majority." The second phase, coinciding with the ascendancy of Ronald Reagan, was the era of the fully Reconstituted Right.

Ideologies of the New Politics Movement

Many of the ideas that figure most prominently in contemporary political debate are outgrowths or expressions of the conflict between the New Politics and Reconstituted Right coalitions. The former coalition has made extensive and effective use of public interest ideologies as its members campaigned vigorously on behalf of federal programs to promote more open political processes, clean air, clean water, and products free from dangerous defects. Of course, all Americans stand to benefit to some degree from these outcomes. However, in addition to the general interest served by these goals, the environmental, political, and consumer legislation supported by New Politics activists has also served the interests of the movement and of the social stratum it represents. The enactment of environmental, consumer, and occupational health and safety legislation was designed to significantly restrict the power and prerogatives of capitalists as a class by imposing limits on the goods they could produce and the ways they could produce them. In addition, environmental objections often allowed New Politics forces to block public works projects that might have channeled public resources to their enemies in the business community, in local government, and in organized labor. For example, environmental claims helped New Politics forces to virtually destroy the nuclear power industry and to prevent such projects as New York's Westway highway program. Under the rubric of constructing a more open and democratic political process, New Politics forces attacked the political institutions and procedures upon which the power of their opponents rested, then altered them in ways that would enhance their own influence.

The best-known example is the McGovern-Fraser Commission, which changed the Democratic party's presidential nomination procedures in ways that reduced the influence of the party's traditional power brokers. In addition, because they commanded considerable legal talent and enjoyed support within the judiciary, the environmental and consumer movements drafted regulatory legislation that provided manifold opportunities for public interest law firms to sue executive officials who were not enforcing environmental or consumer protection laws to their satisfaction. And organizations such as Common Cause pressed for the enactment of the Freedom of Information Act and various "sunshine laws" that would enable them to make the most of their access to the mass media. Thus in each of these cases, the public interest and the political interests of New Politics forces coincided quite nicely.

While they have relied most heavily on public interest claims, New Politics forces have also made effective use of each of the four other types of ideologies with which we are concerned. The most important moralistic ideology of the New Politics is antimilitarism, whose most recent expression, nuclear freeze, I have already discussed. Among the most prominent altruistic postures assumed by New Politics forces, especially during the 1970s, was in support of federal funds to finance programs to help minorities and the poor in inner-city neighborhoods. What was interesting about these programs was that most of them circumvented local governments and municipal bureaucracies and effectively shifted resources and power away from the working-class and middle-class ethnic groups that dominated these bureaucracies to federal agencies and private and public foundations in which New Class intellectuals and professionals had considerable influence.

The most important ideology of coalition formation recently espoused by these forces was the notion of "industrial policy" that was championed by a number of politicians including Vice President Walter Mondale during the early 1980s. Industrial policy has many variants, but the central theme is that the federal government should take a greater hand in long-range economic planning and should, in particular, supervise what was said to be the inevitable transformation of the American industrial base from obsolescent smoke-stack industries to the high-technology, energy-efficient, and nonpolluting industries that purportedly were the wave of the future. Government intervention was said to be essential to this transformation in order to minimize the human and social costs that otherwise would accompany massive changes in employment and investment. Whatever its economic merits, industrial policy can be viewed politically as an effort to forge a coalition between the New Politics movement, which would gain influence over the allocation of capital, and organized labor, whose members are promised protection against lost jobs and income during the period of transition as well as job retraining for the high-technology industries of the future. These promises were accompanied during the early 1980s by the discovery of a pressing need to repair the American "infrastructure" of roads, bridges, railways, and the like—the 1984 equivalent of New Deal public works programs for displaced workers.

The validity of industrial policy as an economic doctrine is questionable. The new jobs that may become available to members of the working class in high-technology industries are more likely to be found in Singapore than Detroit. As a political doctrine, however, industrial policy was more reasonable, at least at the outset of the 1984 presidential campaign. With the support of organized labor and the endorsement of a number of important New Politics groups, including the National Organization for Women (NOW), Mondale was able to seize the Democratic nomination despite a lackluster performance in the primaries.

Finally, the New Politics movement has developed an ingenious ideology of entitlement, namely the doctrine of "comparable worth." The central thesis of this doctrine is that individuals' incomes should be proportional to the value of their skills and training rather than a function of market mechanisms of wage allocation. Proponents of the comparable-worth doctrine assert that its principle beneficiaries would be women, who are said to suffer from discrimination in the marketplace. The implication, however, of comparable worth is that individuals—whether male or female—should be paid according to their "human capital" value—their level of education, training, and so on. What is significant about this is, of course, that the New Politics movement speaks for precisely the social class defined by its possession of high levels of this form of capital. Just as the bourgeoisie touted the moral virtues of market mechanisms because their superior capital assets generally made them their chief beneficiaries, so the New Class is happy to expound upon the virtues of comparable worth, a mechanism of wage determination that rewards its chief asset.

Ideologies of the Right

For its part, the Reconstituted Right has also made extensive use of public interest and moralistic ideologies as well as ideologies of entitlement and of coalition formation (though seldom altruistic claims) to bolster its political support and buttress its claims to public resources. Under Ronald Reagan's leadership, the Right's chief public interest assertions have concerned the need for a strong military defense and the pressing need for a more equitable tax system. Both these positions, whatever their abstract merit, have obvious political implications. At least as defined by the Right, a strong military defense has demanded enormous increases in military construction to the obvious benefit of the defense industry, an important component of the Reconstituted Right coalition.

The single most striking example of this phenomenon is President Reagan's Star Wars antimissile program, which, whatever its military value, will channel tens of billions of dollars in public funds to American industry over the coming years. Similarly, many of the components of the tax reforms supported by the Right and championed by Reagan, whatever their general effects on the American economy, work to the immediate advantage of members of Reagan's political coalition. For example, the indexing of federal income tax rates to inflation—the centerpiece of Reagan's tax cuts—worked to the clear advantage of the middle- and upper-middle-class taxpayers who had supported the Reagan coalition. Similarly, individuals with high incomes from fees and salaries are the chief beneficiaries of the Reagan administration's "tax simplification" plan, which would lower the maximum rate on earned income from 50 percent to 35 percent. Another important element of tax simplification, the proposed elimination of the federal deduction for state and local taxes, would represent a serious assault on one of the important institutional bastions of the Reconstituted Right's opponents—state and local bureaucracies in the Northeast. The enactment of this proposal would place the predominantly Democratic state and local governments in the high-tax Northeast in a bind. Either they would have to cut taxes and fire thousands of public employees (whose unions play an important role in the Democratic party), or they would encourage business firms and taxpayers to flee to regions of the country where taxes are lower, thereby suffering a decline in wealth and population—and a loss of votes in the Electoral College. The administration's tax reform proposals would also undermine Democratic party strength by eliminating the current system of public financing of presidential campaigns based on a one-dollar checkoff on federal tax returns. Because the Republican party can raise far more money from private sources, the elimination of public funding would almost certainly damage Democratic prospects in presidential elections. Thus, under the public interest rubric of tax simplification, the coalition of the Right seeks to achieve enormous political gains.

The chief moralistic claims of the Reconstituted Right involve "family issues," most notably right to life, whose political significance has already been discussed. It is worth noting that one element of the Right's family program is an entitlement claim that is potentially quite important—the notion of tuition tax credits for the parents of private and parochial school students. Proponents of this idea assert that while individuals who send their children to private or parochial schools perform a public service by relieving financially strapped local school systems of the burden of educating these children, they are penalized by being subjected to a form of double taxation—property taxes to support the public schools along with private school tuition. These circumstances, it is argued, justify some form of tax credit for these parents' tuition payments. Whatever the merits of the claim, it is clear that politically such a program could be extremely beneficial to the Reconstituted Right coalition. For it would provide millions of Catholics and fundamentalist Protestant parochial school parents and, perhaps, many upper-middle-class private school parents with a stake in continuing to support the political forces that enacted and defend the program.

Finally, ideologies of coalition formation were central to the creation and maintenance of the alliance of the Right. During the 1980 presidential campaign when this alliance was formed, Ronald Reagan and his supporters outlined a series of positions designed to attract important political and social forces to his coalition and, equally important, to reconcile the differences among these often disparate groups sufficiently to allow them to remain within the same political coalition. Thus the Reaganites promised middle-class suburbanites that they would trim social programs, cut taxes, and bring inflation under control—whatever the cost in blue-collar unemployment. Second, they told social and religious conservatives that Reagan would support antiabortion and school prayer legislation. Third, the Reaganites pledged to white southerners and other opponents of the civil rights revolution an end to federal support for affirmative action, minority quotas, and other programs designed to aid blacks. Fourth, Reagan promised American business that he would relax the environmental rules and other forms of regulation that New Politics groups had succeeded in enacting during the 1970s. Finally, the Reagan coalition offered the defense industry greatly increased rates of military spending—this under the rubric of the need to respond to a growing Soviet threat.

Each of Reagan's themes was designed to establish a link

between him and a major national political force. The main problem faced by the Reaganites was that these themes, whatever the cases for them individually, seemed contradictory. The most important of these apparent contradictions was between Reagan's promise of substantial tax relief for the middle class and his pledge to increase defense spending dramatically. This was not merely a problem of contradictory campaign promises, but reflected a potentially serious conflict within the coalition that Reagan sought to assemble. At the elite level of the nascent Reagan coalition, the defense industry wanted major spending increases. On the other hand, the millions of middle-class suburbanites whom Reagan sought to woo demanded tax relief. To construct a new conservative coalition, Reagan somehow needed to satisfy both. At this juncture, the Reaganites presented a political theory that, like the Democrats' industrial policy, masqueraded as an economic doctrine. This theory was called supply-side economics. The economic details of the theory need not concern us; indeed, most economists ridiculed it. However, like industrial policy, supply-side economics was far more important as a political theory than as an economic one. Supply-side theory purported to show that it was possible to cut taxes and increase spending simultaneously. Thus, in promising to introduce supply-side economics, Reagan was asserting that he could and would pursue policies that worked to the advantage of the two major groups in his proposed constituency whose interests had seemed most likely to clash. Just as in the case of the New Politics coalition, a number of the ideologies fashioned and promoted by the forces of the Reconstituted Right were designed, in large part, to bolster the coalition's political support and reinforce its claims on public resources.

Ideological Market Power

These examples of the political uses of ideas by the New Politics coalition and by the forces of the Reconstituted Right are noteworthy for two reasons. First, the examples suggest the extent to which the ideas expressed by political groups and forces are linked to the interests of those forces. Again, the members of political groups may be, and indeed more often than not are, perfectly sincere when they argue the merits of a particular viewpoint or the desirability of a particular course of action. However, few political leaders will devote much time or energy or many resources campaigning on behalf of abstract principles that, whatever their moral or ethical worth, do not also serve their political interests. Moreover, as I observed earlier, sincere beliefs often spring out of political and economic interest. General Motors chairman and U.S. defense secretary Charles Wilson probably had no difficulty whatsoever convincing himself that what was good for General Motors *was* good for the country.

But the New Politics and Reconstituted Right examples are also noteworthy for a second reason. Both are arguably the most powerful political groupings in the United States at this time. It is not by accident that many of the issues and ideas that have dominated the political agenda of the 1980s are the perspectives and proposals put forward by these two forces.

For example, the development and promotion of conservative themes and ideas in recent years has been greatly facilitated by the millions of dollars that individual corporations and business organizations such as the Chamber of Commerce and the Public Affairs Council spend each year on public information and what is now called in corporate circles "issues management." In addition, businessmen have contributed millions of dollars to such conservative institutions as the Heritage Foundation, the Hoover Institution, and the American Enterprise Institute. Many of the ideas that have helped the forces of the Right shape contemporary politics and policy making in the United States were first developed and articulated by scholars associated with these institutions.

Though they do not have access to financial assets that match those available to their opponents, the intellectuals and professionals associated with the New Politics movement have ample organizational skill and access to the media and, in many cases, have received years of exposure to university educations that, if nothing else, equip their recipients to create, communicate, and use ideas. During the sixties, seventies, and eighties, the chief vehicle through which liberal intellectuals and professionals advanced their ideas was the "public interest group," an institution that relied heavily on voluntary and less on paid contributions of time, effort, and interest on the part of its members.[22] Through groups like Common Cause, NOW, the Sierra Club, Friends of the Earth, Physicians for Social Responsibility, and so on, intellectuals and professionals have been able to develop and promote ideas like nuclear freeze and comparable worth.

Whatever their particular ideology, those groups and forces that can muster the most substantial financial, institutional, educational, and organizational resources—or, as we shall see later, access to state power—are the ones best able to promote their ideas in the marketplace. Obviously, these resources are most readily available to the upper and upper-middle classes. Though occasionally groups from the bottom of the class structure are able to publicize their concerns—and I shall return to the conditions under which this is most likely—it is generally the upper and upper-middle classes who possess the means needed to develop and successfully promote ideas. As a result, these classes dominate the market. It is their ideas that are generally discussed and disseminated by books, films, newspapers, magazines, and the electronic media. Conflicts on the marketplace generally reflect divisions within this social stratum.

Of course, the laws of the market—unlike those of some nations—do not preclude efforts by the members of the lower social classes to voice and publicize their concerns. In general, there are three mechanisms through which the views of the lower classes can compete on the marketplace with some hope of success.

The first of these is strong working-class organization. In European nations, such as Germany, social democratic parties built powerful organizations that published newspapers, books, and magazines; sponsored cultural activities; and organized rallies, speeches, and other public expressions of a distinctly working-class point of view. These efforts maintained a semblance of working-class culture in Europe and prevented total domination of the idea market by the bourgeoisie.[23] In the United States—where, for a variety of reasons, working-class organization was historically weak—the ideological dominion of the bourgeoisie has been much more complete.[24]

The second means through which the views of the lower classes may achieve some measure of success on the idea market is the development of some form of political alliance between upper-class and working-class forces. For example, the New Deal coalition in the United States included organized labor as well as upper-middle-class intellectuals and professionals. This latter group used its access to the print and broadcast media as well as motion pictures to publicize the concerns of the working class, though often the solutions proposed by these media to the problems of working-class people also seemed to serve the interests of their erstwhile professional and intellectual allies. Similarly, during the 1960s, upper-middle-class liberals sought to construct a political alliance with blacks and so devoted considerable energy to publicizing the concerns, needs, and aspirations of black Americans. It is significant that media attention to the entire range of civil rights issues waned sharply when the political alliance between blacks and white liberals broke during the late 1970s.[25] It was only when New Politics forces sought to revive this alliance during the mid-1980s, this time by launching a campaign against South African apartheid policies, that the issue of race relations again began to receive media attention, albeit attention focused on relations between the races five thousand miles from our shores. In any event, the concerns and grievances of American blacks have received media attention mainly in proportion to the interest that one or another segment of the white upper-middle class has had in publicizing them.

This lesson is relevant to understanding the limits of the third mechanism that can permit the lower classes to compete on the idea market—protest and disruption. Clearly, protest and violence can be important vehicles for attracting the attention and interest of the media, and this may allow groups that lack the financial or organizational resources usually needed to compete on the marketplace an opportunity to broadcast their views. During the 1960s, for example, the media coverage given civil rights demonstrators and particularly given to the violence that southern law enforcement officers in cities such as Selma and Birmingham directed against peaceful black demonstrators at least temporarily increased white sympathy for the civil rights cause. This was, of course, one of the chief aims of Dr. Martin Luther King's strategy of nonviolence.[26] In subsequent years the media has turned its attention to antiwar demonstrations and, more recently, to antiabortion demonstrations, antinuclear demonstrations, and even acts of international terrorism designed specifically to induce the western media to publicize the terrorists' causes.

However, while protest, disorder, and even terrorism can succeed in drawing media attention, these methods ultimately do not allow groups from the bottom of the social ladder to compete effectively on the idea market with their superiors.

The chief problem with protest as a communication mechanism is that, in general, the media upon which the protesters depend have considerable discretion in reporting and interpreting the events they cover. Should, for example, a particular group of protesters be identified as "freedom fighters" or "terrorists"? If a demonstration leads to violence, was this the fault of the protesters or the authorities? The answers to these questions are typically determined by the media, not by the protesters. This means that media interpretation of protest activities is more a reflection of the views of the groups and forces to which the media are responsive—usually segments of the upper-middle class—than it is a function of the wishes of the protesters themselves.

It is worth noting once again that civil rights protesters received their most favorable media coverage when a segment of the white upper-middle class saw blacks as potential political allies. After the demise of this alliance, the media focused less on the brutal treatment of peaceful black demonstrations by bigoted law enforcement officials—the typical civil rights story of the sixties—and focused more on "black militants" and "urban terrorists." Thus the effectiveness of protest as a media strategy depends, in large measure, on the character of national political alignments and coalitions. If protesters are aligned with or potentially useful to more powerful forces, then protest can be an effective mechanism for the communication of the ideas and interests of the lower classes. If, on the other hand, the social forces to which the media are most responsive are not sympathetic to the protesters or their views, then protest is likely to be defined by the print and broadcast media as mindless and purposeless violence. Obviously, demonstrations and violence are more than vehicles for the communication of ideas. Governments may be compelled to come to terms with protest movements even if the groups involved are unable to gain favorable publicity for their ideas or to promote much sympathy for their course. Yet not many protest movements can achieve their political or economic goals without some measure of success on the idea market. And, in general, success on the idea market for working-class protesters requires an alliance with at least some segment of the upper and upper-middle class.

Occasionally, of course, segments of the upper social strata engage in protest activities themselves. Typically, upper-class protesters—student demonstrators and the like—have little difficulty securing favorable publicity for themselves and their causes. Witness the universal media approval given antiapartheid protests and antinuclear protests and the benign treatment afforded the antics of even so odd a group as the "animal liberationists." This is true for a number of reasons. First, upper-class protesters are often more skilled than their lower-class counterparts in the techniques of media manipulation.[27] That is, they typically have a better sense of how to package messages for media consumption—often as a result of formal courses on the subject. For example, it is important to know what time of day a protest should occur if it is to be carried on the evening news. Similarly, the setting, definition of the issues, character of the rhetoric used, and so on all help to determine whether a protest will receive favorable media coverage, unfavorable coverage, or no coverage at all. Moreover, upper-middle-class protesters can often produce their own media coverage through "underground" newspapers, college papers, student radio and television stations, and now computer billboards. The same resources and skills that generally allow the upper-middle class to dominate the production of ideas are usually not left behind when segments of this class choose to engage in disruptive forms of political action.

The Power of Upscale Consumers

There is an additional and more important reason that upper-middle-class protesters are generally better able than their lower-class counterparts to secure favorable media attention, a factor that is related to a second general source of this group's power in the idea market. Upper-income groups dominate the marketplace not only as producers and promoters but also as consumers of ideas. As mentioned, in general, and particularly in the political realm, the print and broadcast media and the publishing industry are most responsive to the tastes and views of the more "upscale" segments of the potential audience. The preferences of these audience segments have a profound effect on the content and orientation of the press, of radio and television programming, and of books, especially in the areas of news and public affairs. The influence of the upscale audience is a function of the economics of publishing and broadcasting. Books, especially "serious" books, are purchased almost exclusively by affluent and well-educated consumers. As a result, the publishing industry caters to this market. Newspapers, magazines, and the broadcast media depend primarily on advertising revenues for their profits. These revenues, in turn, depend on the character and size of the audience that they are able to provide advertisers for their product displays and promotional efforts. The audience that a medium is able to deliver is a function first of its distribution capabilities and, second and more important for our purposes, of its content. For example, a television broadcast of a Chicago Symphony performance is likely to attract viewers different from those drawn to reruns of "The A-Team." Similarly—at least one hopes—the *National Enquirer* attracts a different sort of reader than the *New York Review*.

Obviously, advertisers are not interested in presenting their products to audiences that are unlikely to be interested or are not sufficiently well-heeled to purchase their goods. Typically advertisers seek to present their claims to audiences that are potentially interested in the products in question and sufficiently large and affluent to justify the expense of the ads. Different advertisers are interested in different consumer populations and will seek out media that cater to or seem likely to reach whatever they conceive to be the best consumer audience for their own wares.

Some advertisers, particularly those involved with the manufacture or sale of relatively inexpensive and widely used items like soap, breakfast foods, and toiletries, will attempt to reach more or less the entire population. These advertisers typically make use of mass-market magazines and newspapers as well as television and radio entertainment programs that cater to the widest possible audience. On the other hand, purveyors of more specialized products will usually make use of special-interest publications or broadcasts that they hope will reach the consumer subgroups most likely to have an interest in their merchandise. Thus manufacturers of hunting and fishing equipment may place ads in magazines or on television programs devoted to these topics; the makers of floppy disks will ordinarily conduct their ad campaigns in magazines devoted to home computing; vendors of fish-eye lenses and exposure meters will normally tout their products in publications aimed at photo hobbyists.

From the perspective of most advertisers and especially those whose products are relatively expensive, the most desirable audiences for their ads and commercials consist of younger, upscale consumers—more or less the same individuals who in their capacity as voters are nicknamed Yuppies by the press and are widely courted by politicians.[28] What makes these individuals an especially desirable consumer audience is, of course, their affluence and their spending habits. Though they represent only 10 percent of the population, individuals under the age of fifty whose family income is in the 75th percentile or better account for nearly 50 percent of the retail dollars spent on consumer goods in the United States. To reach this affluent audience, advertisers are particularly eager to promote their products in the periodicals and newspapers and on the radio and television broadcasts that are known or believed to attract upscale patronage. Thus advertisers flock to magazines like *The New Yorker, Fortune, Forbes, Architectural Digest,* and *Time.* Similarly, the pages of elite newspapers like the *New York Times* and the *Washington Post* are usually packed with advertisements for clothing, autos, computer equipment, stereo equipment, furs, jewelry, resorts and vacations, and the entire range of products and services that are such integral parts of the life-style of well-to-do business and professional strata.

Indeed, it is instructive to compare the quality and quantity of advertising on any given day in the *New York Times* with the same day's ads in the decidedly blue collar *New York Post.* First, on any given day the *Times* can be expected to carry between five and ten times as many column inches of advertising as the *Post.* Second, on many days the value of the goods advertised on the first six pages of the *Times*—jewelry, furs, designer clothing—exceeds the total value of all the goods—denture adhesives, off-brand clothing, and diet pills—advertised in the entire issue of the *Post.*

Advertisers are also quite eager to promote their products on radio and television programs favored by upscale consumers. Some entertainment programs, including in recent years such shows as "Hill Street Blues," "Cheers," "St. Elsewhere," and "Miami Vice," have drawn large numbers of affluent viewers who were eagerly followed by large numbers of avaricious advertisers.

Though affluent consumers do watch television programs and read periodicals whose contents are designed simply to amuse or entertain, the one format that most directly appeals to the upscale audience is news and public affairs. The affluent —who are also typically well educated—are the core audience of news magazines, journals of opinion like *Ramparts* and *The New Republic,* books dealing with public affairs, serious newspapers, and broadcast news and public affairs programming, including the network news and especially public affairs specials as well as dramatizations with serious contemporary political themes like ABC's now-famous "Day After" nuclear holocaust film. While other segments of the public also read newspapers and watch the television news, one's level of interest in world events, national political issues, and the like is closely related to one's level of education. As a result, the upscale audience is heavily overrepresented in the news and public affairs audience. Perhaps even more important, upscale consumers represent an even larger fraction of the buying power of the news and public affairs audience than of the general media audience. Thus in terms of numbers and, more importantly, buying power, the upper-income strata dominate the audience for news and public affairs. The concentration of these strata in the audience makes news, politics, and public affairs potentially very attractive topics to advertisers, publishers, radio broadcasters, and television executives. Indeed, from the perspectives of the television networks, news and public affairs programming is doubly attractive. First, these forms of programming can attract a desirable audience. Successful efforts to attract upscale viewers and readers mean hundreds of millions of dollars in sales and advertising revenues. And publishers of books dealing with political and social topics rely almost exclusively on the patronage of wealthy, well-educated readers. At the same time, news and public affairs are among the least expensive forms of programming to produce, usually costing only a small fraction of the per-episode price of a dramatic series or other entertainment program.[29] At any rate, the television networks and a sizable number of periodicals and newspapers vie among themselves to attract the patronage of upscale consumers by presenting features and articles with social or political themes, news reports, news analyses and commentary, and dramatizations of political or social issues designed to appeal to this audience.

To attract audiences to their news and public affairs offerings —as to any other—the media and publishing industries employ polls and other market research techniques, including the fa-

mous Nielsen and Arbitron rating services, analyses of sales, as
well as a good deal of intuition to identify the political interests,
tastes, perspectives, and biases. The results of this research—
and guesswork—affect the character, style, and content of network programming, as well as the topics of the books published
by major houses and the stories and reports presented by the
various periodicals.

Not surprisingly, given their general market power and particular presence in the public affairs audience, it is the upper-
and middle-class segment of the audience whose interests and
tastes especially influence the media's news, public affairs, and
political coverage. This is evident from the topics covered, the
style of coverage, and, in the case of network television, the
types of reporters and newscasters who appear on the screen.
First, the political and social topics given most extensive attention by the national media are mainly, albeit not exclusively,
topics that appeal to the interests of well-educated professionals, executives, and intellectuals. In recent years these topics
have included the nuclear arms race, ecological and environmental matters, budgetary and fiscal questions, regulation of
business and the economy, American policy in the Middle East,
South African apartheid policies, attacks on Americans and
American interests by terrorists, and, of course, the fluctuations
of the stock market, interest rates, the value of the dollar, the
price of precious metals, and the cost of real estate. While many
of these topics may indeed be of general importance and concern, most are of more interest to the upscale segments of the
audience than to lower-middle or working-class groups. For
example, the entire area of international affairs is mainly an
upper-middle-class concern. For upscale strata, interest in
world affairs clearly is not a result of exposure to media coverage; for lower classes, the extent of such interest is very likely
a response to the media's coverage. Thus, among relatively
well-off respondents (income of $30,000 or more), 90 percent of
the frequent TV viewers and 93 percent of the nonviewers are

interested in world affairs. Among the poorest respondents, 76 percent of the frequent viewers but only 62 percent of the nonviewers claim an interest in world affairs. Similarly, the stock market, currency fluctuations, real estate prices, and the like are matters that are obviously of most interest to the affluent.

While these matters of concern to the upscale audience receive extensive media coverage, entire categories of events, issues, and phenomena of interest to lower-middle and working-class Americans receive scant attention. For example, trade union news and events are discussed only in the context of major strikes or revelations of corruption. No network or national periodical routinely covers labor organizations. Religious and church affairs receive little coverage. The activities of fraternal, ethnic, patriotic, and veterans' organizations are generally ignored except, of course, in extraordinary situations such as the outbreak of Legionnaires' disease. Even the national sports news devotes far more time to those events enjoyed by relatively small numbers of affluent individuals, such as golf and running, than to such proletarian interests as bowling or roller derby. Of course, normally proletarian sports can become newsworthy if the upscale audience begins to take an interest in them—witness the brief spurt of national media interest in professional wrestling when that curious form of athletic theater attracted the passing attention of jaded Yuppies.

The upscale character of the national media's public affairs coverage contrasts starkly to the topics discussed in the handful of news tabloids and major daily newspapers that seek to reach the blue-collar audience. These periodicals feature some of the same events described by the major national media—the assertions of snobs notwithstanding, the *Post* is aware of the existence of a world beyond The Bronx, Queens, and Staten Island. However, from the perspective of these newspapers—and their readers—public affairs includes healthy doses of celebrity gossip; crime news; discussions of the occult and sightings of

UFOs; ethnic, fraternal, patriotic, and religious affairs; holistic medicine; and even roller derby. Executives, intellectuals, and professionals as well as the journalists and writers who serve them may sneer at this version of the news, but it is not always clear by what objective standard large portions of the contents of the *New York Times* are any more important than the materials found in the *New York Post*. Is the *Post*'s crime news inherently less significant than the *Times'* analyses of bureaucratic mismanagement? Perhaps. Is the *Post*'s celebrity gossip inherently less important to reader's lives than the *Times'* profiles of foreign and domestic politicians? As for the *Post*'s UFOs, well, the *Times* devotes at least as much attention to the UN. Perhaps the news as seen by the *Times* is more important or at least more fit to print than the news published by the *Post*, but *Times* coverage can generally be better distinguished from *Post* coverage by its class character than its ultimate importance.

The upscale perspective of the national news media also manifests itself in their political and social orientations. In general, the ideological position of the media, like its choice of topics, reflects the predispositions and views of its intended audience of upper-income managerial, technical, professional, executive, and intellectual strata. The attachment of the media to the ideology of this audience is well illustrated by the changes that have occurred over the past twenty years in the political leanings of the national print and broadcast media— in particular, the adoption of a critical posture by key sectors of the media during the 1960s and 1970s followed by a partial softening or muting of opposition during the 1980s. As conservatives like to point out, in the sixties and seventies large segments of the major national media, including the television networks—led by CBS—elite newspapers, and the news and public affairs periodicals became sharply critical of American social, economic, and international policies; of the executive branch; and of American government and society generally.[30] Thus during this period the media provided generally favorable publicity for the civil rights, antiwar, consumer, and environmental movements and for a variety of other social, economic, and political protest groups.

Clearly, this publicity had important consequences. The media played a major role in compelling the withdrawal of American forces from Indochina as well as in the formation of American domestic policy during this period. The media permitted protest movements to depict their causes as contests between the public interest and selfish interests that sought to enrich themselves by despoiling the environment, subjecting consumers to risks of cancer, or bribing public officials with cash or campaign contributions. This goes a long way toward explaining how the clear air and clean water acts of the early 1970s, which imposed billions of dollars in costs on industries and local governments, nonetheless were enacted by Congress nearly unanimously.

Another example of the adversary posture adopted by the media during the sixties and seventies was, of course, the series of investigations of public officials launched by the national press in this period. The most spectacular of these was the Watergate affair when investigations by the *Washington Post* and, later, the *New York Times,* as well as extensive publicity by the television networks, drove a sitting president from office. Investigations aimed at damaging or discrediting public officials continued through the Ford and Carter administrations. In the latter, Hamilton Jordan, a key presidential aide, was effectively neutralized by the intense publicity given a charge of cocaine use; the absence of any evidence seemed not to dampen the media's enthusiasm for the case. This pattern of adversary journalism continued into the early 1980s with the successful attacks on President Reagan's original national security advisor Richard Allen (for the crime of accepting a wristwatch from a Japanese corporation) and on Environmental Protection Agency officials, Anne Burford Gorsuch and Rita Lavelle.

Conservatives, of course, have often charged that these media

investigations and the favorable publicity given critics and protesters resulted from journalists' and broadcasters' liberal bias.
Many writers and reporters may indeed be liberals. However,
their particular biases do not really explain the media's behavior
during the 1960s and 1970s. There were, after all, no significant
changes in the ownership or operational control of the major
newspapers or networks between the late 1950s and 1960s, and
during the former period these news media were markedly
uncritical in their treatment of the government, national officials, policies, and agencies. Indeed, much of the Pentagon
"propaganda" described and subjected to scathing criticism by
CBS television in its famous 1964 blast at the military, "The
Selling of the Pentagon," had been broadcast by CBS itself
during the previous decade.

The media's motives for attacking national officials and publicizing the causes of the consumer, environmental, and antiwar
movements in the sixties and seventies were more economic
than political. CBS, for example, under the leadership of its
president, Frank Stanton, a sociologist by training, pioneered in
the use of sophisticated market research techniques to assess
the demographic character of audiences for various types of
programming. Market research, of course, revealed that the
audience for news and public affairs programs had a higher
level of education and income—and therefore a greater attrac-
tion to advertisers—than the audience for any other type of
programming and that during prime time the members of this
upscale audience tended to remain with the network whose
evening news program they had watched. Market research also
revealed that this audience had particular tastes in the news: it
liked news analysis and critical programming. It wanted to
know what really went on in Washington and in Vietnam, not
simply what the White House press secretary and the generals
said in news briefings. CBS responded to these findings with
alacrity—it invented the genre of televised investigative journalism—and the other networks followed its lead. At any rate,

the tastes and character of the audience rather than the biases of journalists were the factors underlying the media's critical posture during the sixties and seventies. Indeed, if the media did employ a disproportionate number of reporters and writers with liberal biases, it was because these individuals appealed to the audience the media sought to court. After all, writers and reporters can present their biased views only so long as these promote sales, ratings, and desirable "demographics."

The essentially economic roots of the media's ideological perspectives came into particularly sharp focus in the mid-1980s. As mentioned, during this period large segments of the upscale audience became somewhat more conservative in their political orientations and more interested in economic matters than in the civil rights and antiwar issues of the sixties. In 1980 Ronald Reagan made a concerted effort to woo "Yuppie" votes by promising and later providing tax reform measures whose principal beneficiaries were upper-income professionals. Millions of these Yuppies supported Reagan in 1984, and large numbers even began to identify themselves as Republicans in national polls, essentially surrendering their signs and placards for bond portfolios and American Express cards. This change in the orientation of its core audience, coupled with a concerted attack by conservative forces, soon led to a media retreat from the critical posture of the previous decade. Watergate-style investigations of official misconduct began to diminish in number and intensity after 1981.

During the 1984 election, national press coverage of Ronald Reagan generally was, if not laudatory, at least not hostile in tone—this despite the fact that most national journalists had personal disdain for Reagan. At the same time, of course, the national media zealously pursued investigations of the personal and family finances of liberal Democratic vice-presidential candidate Geraldine Ferraro and in the process inflicted serious damage on the Democratic campaign. Moreover, just as the media permitted New Politics forces in the 1960s and 1970s to define their goals as the public interest without subjecting their claims to serious scrutiny, the Reaganites have been allowed to declare tax reform to be in the public interest with only scattered media opposition. If the upscale audience for the news becomes more conservative during the coming decades, then we can expect the national media to drop its critical posture altogether and return to the more docile and, indeed, patriotic style of the immediate postwar period. Who knows what will follow —perhaps a CBS special on the heroic deeds of Attila the Hun? Though the precise subject matter of future media coverage remains uncertain, it is certain that in their capacities as consumers, as in their capacities as producers, the upper and upper-middle classes will continue to dominate the idea market.

It is, of course, reasonable to ask whether the views of upscale consumers might not be consequences rather than antecedents of the media's presentations. After all, the media can influence opinion. But while there is undoubtedly some interaction between elite opinion and media content, the evidence suggests that in the case of the upper classes, the relationship between media content and consumer opinion is *not* a function of media influence upon opinion. On the other hand, the evidence does indicate that the content of the media exerts a strong influence upon the attitudes and orientations of individuals from the lower social classes who are heavily exposed to print and broadcast news and public affairs coverage. We saw a bit earlier that for upscale classes interest in world affairs was not related to levels of media exposure, while for lower classes this level of interest *was* related to media exposure. This same sort of pattern manifests itself in terms of attitudes on most political issues. Among upscale strata, political attitudes are unrelated to extent of media use. Nonusers and heavy users of the media manifest similar views. Among lower-class viewers and readers, by contrast, political attitudes and extent of media use are highly correlated. For example, on the question of the importance of inflation, upscale TV viewers and nonviewers in roughly equal percentages (69 versus 71 percent) rated inflation an "extremely" serious issue. Among low-income respondents there was a twelve-point difference (67 versus 55 percent) between TV users and nonusers. Though this should by no means be construed as conclusive evidence, these data at least suggest that whatever influence the media have on political attitudes is concentrated at the lower rungs of the social ladder and, furthermore, that whatever relationship may exist between the content of the media and the views of the upscale audience are indeed results of the impact of the latter upon the former. This pattern of relationships, in turn, has important implications for understanding the social role of the media and the idea market generally.

The Impact of the Marketplace

At the beginning of this chapter, I argued that the idea market functioned to impose the views of upper classes on the entire society. This is precisely the implication of the media findings and discussion. What we have seen is that the media generally reflect the views of the upper-class audience and influence the views of the lower-class audience, in essence, communicating and imposing the views of upper classes on the entire society. This conclusion is buttressed by an important piece of evidence. If we examine the distribution of opinion within the lower-income sector of the populace, not only do the political views of heavy media users differ from those who do not report much media exposure but, significantly, the distribution of opinions among lower-income heavy users tends to be more similar to the distribution of opinion within the upscale public.

For example, in 1980, among wealthy respondents, opposition to the proposed equal rights amendment was virtually identical among frequent and infrequent television news viewers (32 versus 34 percent). Among poor respondents, by contrast, those who seldom watched TV news manifested a 50 percent opposition rate while among frequent viewers the rate was nearly identical to that of wealthy respondents—34 percent. Similarly, among wealthy respondents approval of environmental regulation did not vary with media use. Fifty-two percent of the frequent TV news viewers and 45 percent of the infrequent viewers favored keeping strong regulations. While 70 percent of the poor nonviewers favored keeping strong environmental regulations, however, 51 percent of the frequent TV news viewers favored keeping the regulations—a percentage similar to that of wealthier respondents. In essence, lower-income individuals whose opinions are least similar to those manifested by upper classes are those who are most isolated from the idea market by low levels of media use.

Thus the marketplace of ideas is dominated by the views of elite strata. The more exposed they are to the market, the more likely ordinary people are to see the world through the eyes of the upper classes. How ironic that in the name of freedom of opinion and expression, westerners have sought to remove all impediments—legal, technological, social—to the communication of ideas. This is seen by all as essential to freedom. Indeed, those who attempt to impose barriers or to insulate views from the marketplace of ideas are generally said to be enemies of all that is right and proper. As they remove impediments to expression, however, westerners are not simply making opinion more free. Instead they are making it more fully subject to market mechanisms of control. As they removed ideological barriers, western regimes reduced rather than increased the potential for a broad range of opinions and viewpoints. While ostensibly promoting freedom of opinion, the West reduced the potential for a diversity of opinions.

Chapter 5

Money, Opinion, and Power

THE RELATIONSHIP between economic power and control of mass opinion has become even stronger in recent years because of the development of new, capital-intensive information and communications technologies. This is especially evident in the realm of electoral politics. Over the past three decades, sophisticated communications technology has supplanted mass organization as the ultimate weaponry of American electoral conflict. Until the mid-twentieth century, electoral contests were dominated by party coalitions capable of deploying huge armies of workers to mobilize voters. Organization has not become politically irrelevant. But declines in party strength coupled with increases in the potency and availability of the new technology have led competing groups in the 1980s to shift their reliance from large-scale organizations to computers, opinion survey analyses, and electronic media campaigns directed by small staffs of public relations experts. This change in the character of competitive political practices is, in some respects, analogous to the transformation of military technology over the past century. The enormous infantry armies that dominated World War I battlefields have given way in importance to powerful modern weapons systems operated from electronic command posts by small groups of technicians.

The displacement of organizational methods by the new political technology is sometimes seen merely as a matter of changing "campaign styles." But this change is, in essence, a shift from labor- to capital-intensive competitive electoral practices and has far-reaching implications for the balance of power among contending political groups. Labor-intensive organizational tactics allowed parties whose chief support came from groups nearer the bottom of the social scale to use the numerical superiority of their forces as a partial counterweight to the institutional and economic resources more readily available to the opposition. The capital-intensive technological format, by contrast, has given a major boost to the political fortunes of those forces—usually found on the political right—whose sympathizers are better able to furnish the large sums now needed to compete effectively. Indeed, the new technology permits financial resources to be more effectively harnessed and exploited than was ever before possible. As a result, the significance of the right's customary financial advantage has been substantially increased. Money and the new political technology, not some spontaneous "shift to the right" by mass public opinion, were the keys to the stunning successes scored by conservative Republicans in 1978 and 1980 and the Republicans' surprisingly strong showing during what amounted to an economic depression in 1982.

Clearly, their greater capacity to employ the new campaign techniques no more guarantees victory in every race to parties and factions speaking for the relatively well-to-do than superior numbers and organization ever meant that the political formations representing the relatively worse-off would always succeed. Obviously, a variety of factors, especially including the performance of the domestic economy and the state of the nation's foreign involvements, will inevitably have an impact on electoral outcomes. Nevertheless, the new technology loads the electoral dice in favor of the right. The expanding role of the new electoral techniques means that over the coming decades, groups closer to the political left will increasingly find themselves engaged in a type of political warfare that they are poorly equipped to win. The supersession of organization by the new technology may prove to be the functional equivalent of a critical electoral realignment, substantially redistributing power and profoundly transforming political possibilities in the United States.

Popularity and Political Power

Americans have always believed that in the democratic context, popular support was the key source of political power. The framers of the American Constitution, for example, anticipated that the most popular governmental institutions would inevitably become the most powerful—a view echoed by contemporary scholars.[1] Similarly, present-day analysts often attribute the power of presidents or other public officials to their popular standing. And in the same vein, the extent of their popular support is virtually always seen as the prime ingredient of the political influence of groups, social movements, and political parties. This notion that power derives from popularity has held an extraordinarily powerful grip on political perceptions in the United States. Indeed, James Bryce once elevated the idea to a universal principle, asserting that the support of the people "has been the chief and ultimate power in nearly all nations at all times."[2]

There can be little doubt that power and popularity are

closely intertwined. Certainly, expressions of popular sentiment in the form of elections, opinion polls, and referenda are
a routine part of American political and policy-making processes. Nevertheless, the precise character of the association
between power and popularity in American politics is not entirely clear. It is at least as plausible to view popularity as an
effect as to conceive it to be a cause of political power. Surely
groups possessing substantial economic resources, institutional
leverage, or social position can use these to enhance their public
support. Presumably, the power of the Kennedys, Rockefellers,
and other "first families" of recent American politics was more
a cause than an effect of their political popularity—though
popularity, in turn, may have enhanced their power.

Questionable presumptions about the character of the relationship between power and popularity have played an extremely important role in the study of American electoral politics. Typically, students of American politics, like members of
the public at large, presume that the support of public opinion
determines electoral outcomes. It is because of this presumption
that the academic voting literature focuses so intently upon
voters' beliefs and their social, psychological, and demographic
correlates. Obviously, citizens' votes do formally determine
election results. But this formal power does not mean that voters are the decisive actors on the electoral stage. First and most
obvious, the mass electorate's power to decide is constrained by
the alternatives it is offered. Its options are defined by the
interests, parties, and candidates vying for power, not by voters
themselves. Opposing groups are certainly free to take voters'
preferences into account, but, often enough, other factors play
a more significant role in determining what possibilities will be
proposed to the electorate.[3]

More important, however, voters' choices are often results
rather than causes of successful electoral efforts. The voter-
centered perspective of the electoral literature is based on the
implicit assumption that voters' opinions are formed and elec-

toral choices made more or less independently of the efforts of contending forces to mobilize mass support. This assumption is a political counterpart of the concept of the autonomy of consumer preferences in neoclassical economic theory and is vulnerable to the same criticism.[4] Consumers' preferences and choices often are consequences of successful merchandising efforts and reflect the market power of competing firms more than the exogenous or autonomous judgments of individuals. By the same token, voters' opinions and choices are often—albeit not always—products of the efforts of contending groups to build mass followings, and mainly reflect these groups' relative capacity to achieve a measure of visibility, to communicate cogent appeals, and to offer voters solidary and material incentives sufficiently compelling to secure their allegiance.

As economist Joseph Schumpeter once put it, "The will of the people" is ultimately "the product not the motive power of the political process."[5] Perhaps all voters cannot always be convinced of all things. But it is significant that in a variety of national and historical settings, individuals with very similar social origins and life conditions have been recruited by political forces that differed substantially from one another in aims and methods. Conversely, individuals whose social origins and personal circumstances have been very different frequently have been persuaded to join the political camps of the same or very similar parties.[6] Of course, once they are established, consumer preferences can sometimes be "sticky" with respect to short-term market incentives. Brand loyalty is the classic example. Established electoral preferences may be similarly resistant to change. The durability of partisan attachments in the United States, for example, is well known. But over time, citizens' preferences are frequently protean and malleable—witness the instances in which parties and candidates have gradually been able to convince large groups to shift their political allegiances across enormous ideological chasms.[7]

The ability of competing forces to contact, rally, and maintain mass followings—the political "market power"—is heavily dependent on the social and economic resources they are able to deploy in the electoral arena. Effective electoral competition requires substantial financial, institutional, educational, and organizational assets. When groups that lack economic means or access to major social institutions compete for electoral support with groups in possession of such resources, the outcome, as critics of pluralist theories like to point out, is seldom in doubt.

In general, changes in the relative economic power and social resources of competing interests are, sooner or later, followed by political readjustments. Historically, major economic and social transformations in the United States have triggered political aftershocks in the form of critical electoral realignments. These realignments have functioned to redistribute political authority in a manner that reflected the new economic and social balance. In the contemporary American political setting, the supersession of mass electoral organization by new political technologies does not precisely represent a change in the underlying distribution of resources among opposing political interests. This transformation of electoral formats does, however, substantially alter the relative importance of two key political resources—money and personnel—and, as a result, the relative power of the groups possessing each. The likely product of this change, too, is the eventuality that Schumpeter envisaged, a change in the manifest expression of the popular will.

From Organization to Technology

For more than a century and a half, organization was the most potent weapon available to contending electoral forces. Political parties in nineteenth-century Europe, most notably the

German Sozialdemokratisch Partei Deutschlands (SPD), built elaborate partisan machinery, enrolled hundreds of thousands of dues-paying members, and molded these adherents into disciplined political battalions. Even during their heyday, political parties in the United States were never able to construct centralized structures on a national basis. However, at the state and local levels, powerful party machines organized in every precinct, election district, or other electoral subdivision dominated the electoral arena and, through it, the governmental apparatus itself. Turn-of-the-century political analyst Moisei Ostrogorski describes the typical nineteenth-century party machine:

The stronghold of this "ring" is the local committee of the party. Each political subdivision, the rural town or the city ward, or even the ward precinct, has its committee, appointed annually at the primary of the party. Above this committee of first instance there are, in the local organization, one or two more committees: the ward committee in the cities, which is generally composed of members of the precinct committees; and the county committee, which is the central committee for the county with its towns and villages, or the city committee in the large cities which have a central independent organization. The members of the county committee are appointed by the committees of the wards and of the towns or by the respective delegates of these territorial units to the county convention; the city committee is formed in a similar way. . . . The local committee . . . manipulates the whole organization, and in particular during the stage which precedes the election, that of the nomination of candidates. The [local committee] makes up the slate . . . convenes the primary . . . appoints the "inspectors of election" . . . decides who is entitled to take part. . . . The influence of the county committee, to which the ward committees and village committees of the district lead up, is still more excessive. It rules over the local organization with powers which are sometimes despotic. . . . The county committee decides, without appeals, on all the contests which arise in the organization. It wields disciplinary powers in it: it can suspend, or even turn out, the officers of the associations or of the local committees . . . it can dissolve a whole local organization when it encounters opposition in it. . . .[8]

The leading party machines of the nineteenth and early twentieth centuries could mobilize tens of thousands of patronage employees for political work. On a day-to-day basis, party functionaries maintained close contact with voters and their families, if necessary assisting constituents with personal, financial, and legal problems while at the same time learning their views and securing their trust. During election campaigns the party machines deployed their forces to trumpet the candidates' virtues, rally popular support, and bring the faithful to the polls. In terms of their organization, size, and behavior, the competing parties resembled nothing so much as armies of foot soldiers on the march—regiments of party workers engaging the enemy in a street-by-street, house-by-house struggle to maximize electoral support. Victory generally went to the party with the most energetic and best-drilled legions. Before the turn of the century, politicians even thought in military terms, conceiving elections as battles between huge opposing armies and their generals.[9]

Quite obviously mass organization is a political technique that can be used by groups espousing any viewpoint or representing any social or economic interest. In the United States, both Democrats and Republicans constructed political machines; in Europe socialists, liberals, conservatives, and others organized for political action. But although it can be used by any sort of group, organization is not a neutral political tactic. The construction of strong, permanent mass organizations has most often been a strategy pursued by groups that must aggregate the energies and resources of large numbers of individuals to counter their opponents' superior material means or institutional standing. During the course of European political history, disciplined and coherent party organizations were generally developed first by groups representing the political aspirations of the working classes. Parties, Duverger notes, "are always more developed on the left than on the right because they are always more necessary on the left than on the right."[10] In the United

States, the first mass party was built by the Jeffersonians as a counterweight to the incumbent Federalists' superior social, institutional, and economic resources. In a subsequent period of American history, the efforts of the Jacksonians to construct a coherent mass-party organization were impelled by a similar set of circumstances. Only by organizing the power of numbers could the Jacksonian coalition hope to compete successfully against the superior resources that could be mobilized by its adversaries. Precisely these efforts at party building, it may be recalled, led to the Jacksonian era's famous controversies over the use of a "spoils system" for staffing federal administrative posts and Jackson's practice of depositing federal funds in "pet" state banks. The spoils system obviously meant the appointment of loyal party workers to the national bureaucracy. The pet banks were controlled by individuals with close ties to the party.

In both the United States and Europe, the political success of party organizations forced their opponents to copy them in order to meet the challenge. It was, as Durverger points out, "contagion from the left" that led politicians of the center and right to attempt to build strong party organizations. These efforts were sometimes successful. In the United States, for example, the Whigs carefully copied the organizational techniques devised by the Jacksonians and were able to win control of the national government in the famous "hard cider" campaign of 1840. But even when groups nearer the top of the social scale responded in kind to organizational efforts by the lower classes, the net effect nonetheless was to give lower-class groups an opportunity to compete on a more equal footing. In the absence of coherent mass organization, middle- and upper-class factions almost inevitably had a substantial competitive edge over their lower-class rivals. Even if both sides organized, the net effect was to erode the relative advantage of the well-off. Parties of the right, moreover, were seldom actually able to equal the organizational coherence of the working-class opposition. As Durverger and others have observed, middle- and upper-class parties generally failed to construct organizations as effective as those built by their working-class foes who typically commanded larger and more easily disciplined forces.[11] Of course, even the superior organization of the left did not fully offset the variety of social and economic resources available to groups on the right. But its organizational advantages nevertheless gave the left an opportunity to compete on a much more equal footing than would otherwise have been possible.

Erosion of Organizational Strength

The advantages derived by the left from organizational tactics often led centrist and right-wing politicians to conclude that organized, partisan politics posed a serious threat to the established social order and to their own political power. George Washington's warning against the "baneful effects of the spirit of party" was echoed by the representatives of social, economic, and political elites in many nations who saw their right to rule challenged by groups able to organize the collective energies and resources of mass publics.

Opposition to party was the basis for a number of the institutional reforms of the American political process promulgated at the turn of the century during the so-called Progressive era. Many Progressive reformers were undoubtedly motivated by a sincere desire to rid politics of corruption and to improve the quality and efficiency of government in the United States. But, simultaneously, from the perspective of middle- and upper-class Progressives and the financial, commercial, and industrial elites with which they were often associated, the weakening or elimination of party organization promised to have a number of other important political functions. The enervation of party would mean that power could more readily be acquired and retained by the "best men"—that is, those with wealth, position, and education. The weakening of party organization, moreover, would have the effect of denying access to power to reformers' political opponents who, indeed, relied heavily on party organization. Not coincidentally, Progressive reforms were aimed especially at the destruction of the powerful urban machines built by the representatives of lower-class, ethnic voters.

The list of antiparty reforms of the Progressive era is a familiar one. The Australian ballot reform took away the parties' privilege of printing and distributing ballots and introduced the possibility of split-ticket voting. The introduction of nonpartisan local elections eroded grass-roots party organization. The extension of "merit systems" for administrative appointments stripped party organizations of their vitally important access to patronage and thus reduced their ability to recruit workers. The development of the direct primary reduced party leaders' capacity to control candidate nominations. There reforms obviously did not destroy political parties as entities but, taken together, they did substantially weaken party organizations in the United States.

After the turn of the century, the organizational strength of American political parties gradually diminished. Between the two world wars, organization remained the major tool available to contending electoral forces, but in most areas of the country the "reformed" state and local parties that survived the Progressive era gradually lost their organizational vitality and coherence and became less effective campaign tools. Again, Progressive reform did not mean the elimination of the political party as an entity. Most areas of the nation continued to boast Democratic and Republican party groupings. But reform did mean the evisceration of the permanent mass organizations that had been the parties' principal campaign weapons. In the new, reformed, legal and institutional environment of American politics, an environment that included merit systems, direct primaries, and nonpartisan elections, the chance that any group could construct and maintain an effective, large-scale mass organization was reduced.

As a result of Progressive reform, American party organizations entered the twentieth century with rickety substructures. And as the use of civil service, primary elections, and the other Progressive innovations spread during the period between the two world wars, the strength of party organizations continued to be eroded. By the end of World War II, political scientists were already beginning to bemoan the absence of party discipline and "party responsibility" in the United States.[12] This erosion of the parties' organizational strength set the stage for the introduction of new political techniques that represented radical departures from the campaign practices perfected during the nineteenth century. In place of manpower and organization, contending forces began to employ intricate electronic communications techniques to woo electoral support. This new political technology includes five basic elements.

1. *Polling.*   Surveys of voter opinion provide the information that candidates and their staffs use to craft campaign strategies. Candidates employ polls to select issues, assess their own strengths and weaknesses as well as those of the opposition, check voter response to the campaign, and determine the degree to which various constituent groups are susceptible to campaign appeals. In recent years pollsters have become central figures in most national campaigns. Indeed, Patrick Caddell, who polled for the 1976 Carter campaign, became part of Carter's inner circle of advisors and ultimately played a role in major policy decisions.[13] Virtually all contemporary campaigns for national and statewide office as well as many local campaigns make extensive use of opinion surveys.

2.   *The Broadcast Media.*   Extensive use of the electronic media—television in particular—has become the hallmark of

the modern political campaign. By far the most commonly used broadcast technique is the thirty- or sixty-second television spot advertisement—such as Lyndon Johnson's famous "daisy girl" ad*—which permits the candidate's message to be delivered to a target audience before uninterested or hostile viewers can cognitively, or physically, tune it out. Television spot ads and other media techniques are designed to establish candidate name identification, create a favorable image of the candidate and a negative image of the opponent, link the candidate with desirable groups in the community, and communicate the candidate's stands on selected issues. These spot ads can have an important electoral impact. Generally, media campaigns attempt to follow the guidelines indicated by candidates' polls. Thus media ads are particularly aimed at constituency groups that are, according to poll data, especially amenable to the candidate's blandishments or whose loyalties are especially in need of reinforcement. At the same time, advertisements seek to tap salient electoral sentiments, again, as identified by poll data.

One observer notes that the broadcast media are so central to modern campaigns that most other candidate activities are tied to their media strategies.[14] For example, a sizable percentage of most candidates' newspaper ads are now used mainly to advertise radio and television appearances. Other candidate activities are designed expressly to stimulate television news coverage. For instance, incumbent senators running for reelection or for higher office almost always sponsor committee or subcommittee hearings to generate publicity. In recent years, Senate hearings on hunger, crime, health, and defense have been used mainly to attract television cameras. Similarly, a number of

---

*This spot, which aired during the 1964 presidential race, opened with a little girl pulling the petals off a daisy. Gradually the image of nuclear warheads and the sound of a technician's countdown were superimposed, finally obliterating the original picture of the innocent child. The clear implication of this chilling scenario was that Barry Goldwater, Johnson's principal opponent, might lead the United States into nuclear war if given the power of the presidency.

candidates have found that walking the streets of the South Bronx could lead to useful news coverage.

3. *Phone Banks.* Through the broadcast media, candidates communicate with voters *en masse* and impersonally. Phone banks allow campaign workers to make personal contact with hundreds of thousands of voters. "Personal" contacts of this sort are thought to be extremely effective. Again, poll data serves to identify the groups that will be targeted for phone calls. Computers select phone numbers from areas in which members of these groups are concentrated. Staffs of paid or volunteer callers, using computer-assisted dialing systems and prepared scripts, then place calls to deliver the candidate's message. The targeted groups are generally those identified by polls as either uncommitted or weakly committed, as well as strong supporters of the candidate who are contacted simply to encourage them to vote. Phone banks are used extensively in pivotal contests. Before the 1980 Iowa caucuses, for example, Democratic and Republican presidential hopefuls placed a total of more than 3 million phone calls to Iowa's 1.7 million registered voters. During the same year, former President Carter was reported to have personally placed between twenty and forty calls every night to homes in key primary and caucus states. On some New Hampshire blocks, a dozen or more residents eventually received telephone calls from the President.[15]

4. *Direct Mail.* Direct mail serves both as a vehicle for communicating with voters and as a mechanism for raising funds. The first step in a direct-mail campaign is the purchase or rental of a computerized mailing list of voters deemed to have some particular perspective or social characteristic. Often sets of magazine subscription lists or lists of donors to various causes are employed. A candidate, for example, interested in reaching conservative voters might rent subscription lists from *National Review, Human Events,* and *Conservative Digest.* Or one interested in appealing to liberals might rent subscription lists from the *New York Review* or the *New Republic.* Considerable fine-tuning is pos-

sible. After obtaining the appropriate mailing lists, candidates usually send pamphlets, letters, and brochures describing themselves and their views to voters believed to be sympathetic. Different types of mail appeals are made to different electoral subgroups. Often the letters sent to voters are personalized. The recipient is addressed by name in the text and the letter appears actually to have been signed by the candidate. Of course, these "personal" letters are written and even signed by a computer. Probably the first campaign to make extensive use of direct-mail advertising was Winthrop Rockefeller's successful bid to become Governor of Arkansas in 1966. Rockefeller's IBM 1401 and 360 computers—primitive and slow by contemporary standards—produced more than one million pieces of mail for the state's 500,000 voters.[16]

In addition to use as a political advertising medium, direct mail has also become an important source of campaign funds. Computerized mailing lists permit campaign strategists to pinpoint individuals whose interests, background, and activities suggest that they may be potential donors. Letters of solicitation are sent, and some of the money raised is then used to purchase additional mailing lists. Direct-mail solicitation can be enormously effective. During the 1980 presidential races, for example, Representative Phillip Crane raised more than $3 million; the Republican National Committee released some 18 million pieces of mail and raised more than $12 million.[17]

5. *Professional Public Relations.* Modern campaigns and the complex technology upon which they rely are typically directed by professional public relations consultants. Virtually all serious contenders for national and statewide office retain their services. Increasingly, candidates for local office, too, have come to rely on professional campaign managers. Consultants offer candidates the expertise necessary to conduct accurate opinion polls, produce television commercials, organize direct-mail campaigns, and make use of sophisticated computer analyses. Some consulting firms specialize in particular aspects of cam-

paigning. Tarrance Associates, for example, specializes in polling; Richard Viguerie specializes in direct mail; Rothstein-Buckley and Roger Ailes concentrate on the broadcast media. A growing number of firms, though, like Spencer-Roberts, Napolitan Associates, and DeVries and Associates, will direct every aspect of an electoral effort.[18] A "full-service" firm will arrange

advertising campaigns for radio, television and newspapers, including layout, timing and the actual placing of advertisements; public relations and press services, including the organization of public meetings, preparation and distribution of press releases and statements and detailed travel arrangements for the candidate; research and presentation of issues, including preparation of position papers, speechwriting and arranging for consultations between candidates and outside experts in appropriate areas of public policy; fund-raising solicitations, both by mail and through testimonial dinners and other public events; public opinion sampling to test voter response to the campaign and voter attitudes on major issues; technical assistance on radio and television production, including the hiring of cameramen and recording studios for political films and broadcasts; campaign budgeting assistance designed to put campaign funds to the best possible use; use of data processing techniques to plan campaign strategy based on computer evaluations of thousands of bits of information; and mobilization of support through traditional door-to-door campaigns and telephone solicitation of voters.[19]

Most professional consultants prefer to work for one party or for candidates with a particular ideology. Matt Reese, for example, generally works for Democratic candidates; Stuart Spencer consults for Republicans; Richard Viguerie serves as a fund raiser for candidates of the New Right. Many firms, however, do not limit themselves to candidates of any one persuasion. While David Garth, for example, is best known for his work for liberal Democrats, his firm will conduct campaigns for Republicans—under the supervision of his partner, Ronald Maiorana, a former press secretary for Nelson Rockefeller. A major New

York City firm, Dressner, Morris, and Tortorello, will gladly assist any candidate willing to pay the appropriate fees. Richard Morris, one of the firm's partners, declares, "We're not a political club, we're a business."[20]

Several of the components of this "new" political technology were, of course, developed long before World War II. Professional public relations firms first became involved in electoral politics in 1934 when the firm of Whittaker and Baxter helped to defeat Upton Sinclair's Socialist candidacy for the California gubernatorial race of that year. Primitive opinion polls were used in American elections as early as 1824, and relatively sophisticated surveys were employed extensively during the 1880s and 1890s.[21] But after World War II, the introduction of television and the computer provided the mechanisms that became the electronic heart of the modern campaign. These innovations coincided with a growing realization on the part of politicians and activists that the capacity of traditional party organizations to mobilize voters had greatly diminished. As this realization spread, a small number of candidates began to experiment with new campaign methods. The initial trickle of political innovators became a flood when politicians observed that the new techniques were generally more effective than the more traditional efforts that could be mounted by the now-debilitated party organizations.

In a number of well-publicized congressional, senatorial, and gubernatorial campaigns during the postwar years, candidates using the new campaign methods decisively defeated rivals who continued to rely on the older organizational techniques. The successful campaigns mounted by Richard Nixon in the 1948 California Senate race, Jacob Javits in his 1948 New York congressional race, and Winthrop Rockefeller in the 1966 Arkansas gubernatorial contest were very visible examples of the power of technology. The flood of technologically oriented campaigns became a deluge after 1971. The Federal Elections Campaign Act of that year prompted the creation of large numbers of political action committees (PACs) by a host of corporate and ideological groups. This development increased the availability of funds to political candidates—conservative candidates in particular—which meant in turn that the new technology could be used more extensively. Initially, the new techniques were employed mainly by individual candidates, who often made little or no effort to coordinate their campaigns with those of other political aspirants sharing the same party label. For this reason, campaigns employing the new technology sometimes came to be called candidate-centered efforts, as distinguished from the traditional party-coordinated campaign. However, nothing about the new technology precluded its use by political party leaders seeking to coordinate a number of campaigns. In recent years party leaders, Republicans in particular, have learned to make good use of modern campaign technology. The difference between the old and new political methods is not that the latter is inherently candidate-centered while the former is strictly a party tool. The difference is, rather, a matter of the types of political resources upon which each method depends.

Money and Electoral Politics

The displacement of organizational methods by the new political technology is, in essence, a shift from labor- to capital-intensive competitive electoral practices. Campaign tasks that were once performed by masses of party workers and a modicum of cash now require fewer personnel but a great deal more money. Of course, even when manpower and organization were the key electoral tools, money had considerable political significance. Indeed, nineteenth-century American patronage machines could have neither built nor maintained their huge campaign establishments without the boodle they arrogated from a variety of sources, including the public treasury. In effect, machine politics functioned as a primitive form of public funding of election campaigns.

Nevertheless, the chief resource of nineteenth-century politics was manpower—the sympathizers, loyalists, functionaries, and activists who staffed the party organization and operated its electoral machinery. National political campaigns in the United States employed millions of workers. Ostrogorski, for example, estimates that as many as 2.5 million individuals were employed in political work during the 1880s.[22] The direct cost of campaigns, however, was relatively low. Thus estimates indicate that in 1860 Abraham Lincoln spent only $100,000— approximately twice the amount spent by his chief opponent, Stephen Douglas. Even as recently as 1948, Thomas Dewey spent only $2.1 million in his loss to Harry Truman, who spent only $2.7 million—a far cry from the $61 million spent by Richard Nixon and $30 million spent by George McGovern in 1972.[23]

Modern campaigns depend heavily on money, for each element of the new political technology is enormously expensive. A sixty-second spot announcement on prime-time network television costs as much as $100,000 each time it is aired. In 1980, for example, Carter and Reagan each spent about $16 million on television messages. Similar amounts were spent by Reagan and Mondale in 1984. Opinion surveys can also be quite expensive. Polling costs in a statewide race can easily reach or exceed the six-figure mark.[24] And campaign consultants can charge substantial fees. David Garth, for example, is reported to charge $25,000 per month plus expenses and a 15 percent commission for television time. For his services during the 1981 New York City mayoral race, Garth charged Edward Koch a total of $380,000.[25] And direct-mail campaigns, which can eventually become important sources of funds, are very expensive to initiate. According to one Democratic National Committee chairman, John White, the inauguration of a serious national direct-mail effort requires at least $1 million in "front end cash" to pay for mailing lists, brochures, letters, envelopes, and postage.[26]

The expense of the new technology is reflected in the enormous costs of the 1980, 1982, and 1984 American national elections. Senate candidates in 1980 spent some $476 million, while candidates for the House of Representatives spent another $120 million. The two major presidential candidates received and spent $60 million in public funds; in addition, at least another $13.7 million was spent by various independent groups supporting Reagan. Most estimates place the total cost of the 1980 and 1984 campaigns at over $1 billion each.[27] The 1982 off-year races were also extremely expensive. According to the Federal Election Commission (FEC), Senate candidates spent approximately $114 million, while candidates for the House of Representatives spent a total of $176 million. Another $103 million was spent by independent groups supporting various candidates.

Certainly, manpower is not irrelevant to modern political campaigns. Candidates continue to utilize the services of tens of thousands of volunteer campaign workers. Nevertheless, the new technology has made money the key political resource. Now even the recruitment of volunteer campaign workers has become a matter of electronic technology. Employing a technique called instant organization, paid telephone callers use phone banks to contact individuals in areas targeted by a computer. Volunteer workers are recruited from among these individuals. A number of recent campaigns—Richard Nixon's 1968 effort was the first—have successfully utilized this technique.

Traditional, labor-intensive campaign techniques worked to the advantage of the political left. The new, capital-intensive campaign format, however, clearly serves the interests of the political right. Almost invariably, groups and forces on the right have superior access to the massive financial resources needed to make effective use of the new technology. During the 1980 elections, for example, according to the FEC, the Republican party was able to raise and spend approximately five times the sum available to their Democratic opponents—$170 million for the Republicans in federal, state, and local races, compared with some $35 million for the Democrats. In the same year, the Democratic congressional campaign committee was able to raise only $750,000, while its Republican counterpart spent some $3 million. The Democratic senatorial campaign committee spent $800,000 while the Republicans raised and spent $5.5 million. The Democratic National Committee spent $15 million, while the Republican National Committee spent some $73 million. At the same time, independent conservative groups such as the National Conservative Political Action Committee (NCPAC) and the Fund for a Conservative Majority spent some $14 million on behalf of the Reagan candidacy. These same "New Right" groups also spent several million dollars on behalf of a number of Republican senatorial candidates. Neither the Carter campaign nor the campaigns of Democratic legislative candidates was able to secure comparable support. In 1982 the Democratic and Republican senatorial campaign committees each raised and spent approximately $600,000. However, while the Democratic congressional campaign committee was able to spend only $1 million, its Republican counterpart raised and spent some $4.6 million. At the same time, the Republican National Committee outspent the Democratic National Committee by a factor of five—$14.7 million for the Republicans versus only $2.9 million for the Democrats. Independent conservative groups raised enormous quantities of money in 1982 —NCPAC accumulated $10 million; Jesse Helms's National Conservative Club raised $9.7 million; the Fund for a Conservative Majority amassed approximately $3 million. All told, however, these groups spent less than $1 million on 1982 electoral contests. The remainder was earmarked for the 1984 presidential primaries and general election.[28]

Before 1980, Democratic candidates had been able to rely on two key sources of financial support to counter the Republicans' fund-raising abilities. First, many corporate donors who preferred the Republicans nevertheless contributed heavily to Democratic campaigns on the presumption that the great majority of incumbents—who were, of course, mainly Democrats —would win reelection no matter what efforts might be made to defeat them. Second, organized labor traditionally contributed heavily enough to the Democrats to partially offset business and conservative support for the Republicans. The value to the Democrats of incumbency was reduced somewhat in 1980 and 1984 when a large number of corporate donors came to realize that with sufficient funds and the new technology, formerly unassailable Democratic incumbents might be defeated. Midway through the 1980 race, for example, many corporate political action committees halted virtually all their contributions to Democratic incumbents and redoubled their efforts on behalf of the Republicans.[29]

In 1982, a landmark off-year election, Democratic incumbents—especially those generally deemed to be holding safe seats—had little difficulty raising money. Indeed, on the average, Democratic incumbents raised and spent only $35,000 less than incumbent Republicans. Nevertheless, the funds raised by incumbent Democrats for their own races could never fully offset the electoral impact of the Republican national party's 5 to 1 spending edge compared to the Democrats. In essence, Democratic funds were raised and spent mainly in the districts already most likely to be carried by a Democrat. The funds available to the Republicans at the national level, by contrast, could be used in contests where infusions of cash could have the most telling effects. Thus Democratic incumbents, who were most likely to win anyway, generally had a comfortable funding edge over their Republican challengers. In contests involving an incumbent Democrat and a Republican challenger, the average amount spent by the Democratic candidate was

$240,000, while the average Republican expenditure was some $90,000 less—$150,000.

The Republican party invested its funds, first, to protect its incumbents. As a result, Republican incumbents were able to outspend their Democratic challengers by an average margin of nearly $140,000—$275,000 for the Republicans to $137,000 for the Democrats. Second, the Republicans directed their funding to contests involving open seats. In 60 percent of all such contests, Republican candidates outspent their Democratic rivals. The average margin was $78,000—$297,000 for the Republicans to $219,000 for the Democrats. Finally, the Republicans focused on races that were likely to be close—those races in which spending can matter most. Seventy percent of the eighty-eight 1982 congressional races in which the final margin of victory was 5 percent or less were won by the candidate who spent the most. In 75 percent of these races, the Republican candidate outspent the Democratic candidate. On average, the Republican spending advantage was $110,000—$375,000 for the Republicans to $265,000 for the Democrats. This difference helps to explain why 50 percent of the close races in 1982 were won by Republicans (as against 38 percent of all congressional races in 1982).

The significance of labor support for the Democrats also decreased substantially after 1980. In 1980, 318 labor unions formed PACs. But for the first time their number was overshadowed by the 1,226 corporate PACs that took part in the race. In 1982 the number of labor PACs declined to 228, but the total amount contributed by labor groups increased 47 percent, to more than $20 million. This expansion of labor's efforts, however, was more than offset by the opposition. In 1982 the number of PACs affiliated with corporations increased to 1,310 and their total contribution level rose 36 percent, to $29.3 million. These corporate PACs were joined by 520 "trade, membership and health" committees—groups such as the American Medical Association and the National Realtors Association. These committees contributed $22.8 million in 1982. Realtors alone gave $2 million to congressional and senatorial candidates. At the present time, labor unions, corporations, and trade associations are feverishly organizing PACs. However, since there are some 50,000 corporations in the United States and thousands of trade associations compared with only a few hundred labor unions, the opportunity for expanded corporate and trade involvement would appear to be much greater than the possibility of increased financial efforts by organized labor.

Innovation from the Right

This portrayal of the new political technology as a weapon of the right is reinforced by an examination of the history of American campaign practices. Just as the organizational format that dominated nineteenth-century electoral politics was generally pioneered by the left, the trail for the newer technological format was largely blazed by conservative forces. Indeed, groups on the right often saw the new technology as a means of employing their superior financial resources to compensate for their historic organizational deficiencies. In some respects, the most interesting example of technological innovation by the right is the very oldest component of the "new" technology—polling. As we saw in chapter 3, because it eroded one of the major competitive advantages that has traditionally been available to lower-class groups and parties—a knowledge of mass public opinion superior to that of their middle- and upper-class opponents—the introduction of polling was detrimental to the political fortunes of the social formations that represented the interests and aspirations of the working classes.

What is true of polling is also true of most of the other

elements of the new political technology. Groups on the political right have pioneered and perfected the use of these methods. Even when right-wing forces were not the first actually to use a particular technique, they were usually the ones to fully exploit and develop its potential. For example, direct-mail fund raising was first used extensively in a presidential race by George McGovern. However, Richard Viguerie has assembled a mailing list of more than 30 million individuals interested in conservative causes. Liberal Democrats are generally far behind Viguerie and other right-wing fund raisers in terms of the quality and sophistication of their techniques.[30]

The development of the new technology in Europe and other parts of the world has followed the American pattern. That is, technological innovations pioneered on the right have been copied, with more or less success, by parties closer to the left.[31] In Germany, for example, the new campaign techniques were introduced by the Christian Democrats and copied by the Social Democrats.[32] In Britain, the Conservatives first began to employ mass media techniques during the 1950s, while the Labor Party did not begin to follow the Tory lead until at least a decade later.[33] The Conservative triumph in 1979 was in part a result of the large sums that the Conservatives spent on television, polling, and professional campaign consultants.[34] In 1983 they benefited greatly from the innovative advertising campaign mounted by Saatchi and Saatchi, one of the world's largest advertising agencies.[35] The history of campaign techniques in France parallels the British and German cases. Professional public relations, polling, and extensive media use was first introduced into French politics by General de Gaulle's party, the Union pour la Nouvelle République (UNR).[36]

In recent years American media consultants have been involved in a number of campaigns abroad. Significantly, the talents of these American experts are mainly employed by conservative forces. Thus Joseph Napolitan, head of Napolitan Associates, helped former president Ferdinand Marcos secure elec-

tion in the Philippines—before Marcos chose to terminate electoral democracy—and later worked extensively for President
Giscard's party in France.[37] Napolitan was also recently employed by Sir Seewoosagur Ramgoolam, a conservative who
sought, albeit unsuccessfully, to retain his post as Prime
Minister of Mauritius.[38]

Money, Technology, and Political Power

By the mid-1980s in the United States, parties and candidates
of every political stripe were using the new political techniques.
Nevertheless, the forces of the political right have continued to
be the chief devotees and principal beneficiaries of the new
campaign methods. Indeed, the ascendancy of the capital-
intensive technological format means that the balance of political power has shifted—perhaps decisively—in favor of the
right. First, because of their superior access to financial resources groups on the right will undoubtedly continue to be
able to make more extensive use of the electronic media, polls,
phone banks, and the other elements of the new technology. As
the new political technology continues to supplant the older
organizational format that generally favored the left, the political advantage will swing more and more toward the right.

At the same time, the new technology permits the right's
superior financial resources to be more effectively harnessed
and more fully exploited than was ever before possible. Always
an important campaign asset, money was seldom seen as the
critical factor in electoral competition.[39] Even today, superior
financial resources do not guarantee victory. In 1982, for example, several of the best financed candidates lost to less well-
heeled opponents. Nevertheless, on the aggregate, money is

now critically important. The introduction of the new technology was to money what the invention of the internal combustion engine was to oil—a development that substantially increased the utility and importance of this resource by permitting a fuller utilization of its inherent potential. Prior to the advent of the new political technology, money alone did not give political contenders the capacity to mount a potent campaign. No mechanism existed that could simply and directly translate financial resources into political effectiveness. With the new political technology, however, candidates can easily directly harness their financial resources to contact large number of voters, elicit electoral opinion, encourage supporters to go to the polls, and generally perform the tasks necessary to a successful campaign. Thus, in essence, the chief consequence of the new technology has been to make the traditional financial advantage of the right a much more significant political factor.

Money, more than some attitudinal shift to the right on the part of the electorate, was the key to the dramatic round of Republican electoral successes that began in 1978 and 1980. In 1978 the Republicans netted fourteen House seats and won control of the Senate by adding twelve more seats. The press attributed these successes to the increased conservatism of the mass electorate. Interestingly enough, however, there seems to have been little or no empirical relationship between Republican electoral success and changes in voters' ideological perspectives in 1978 and 1980.[40]

Republican success during these years was, however, associated with the GOP's financial lead over the Democrats. In 1978, according to FEC data, the Republicans spent an average of $283,000 in the twenty-one districts they took from the Democrats. The average expenditure across all congressional races in 1978 was only $106,000. In 1980 the Republicans outspent the Democrats in twenty-six of the thirty-seven districts that moved from Democratic to Republican hands. On average, the Republicans outspent the Democrats by $60,000—$325,000 to $265,000—in these thirty-seven districts. The average candidate expenditure across all districts in 1980 was some $200,000. Most significant is that the Republican gains of 1978 and 1980 were not erased during the depression-year election of 1982. In that year the Republicans were able to hold their losses to a mere twenty-four congressional seats and to retain control of the Senate despite the nearly 11 percent unemployment rate, which might have been expected to result in a Republican debacle. What is particularly interesting is that in 1982 the Democrats retook only eighteen of the total of fifty-eight congressional districts that the Republicans had captured in 1978 and 1980. Again, the Republican funding advantage figured prominently in the GOP's capacity to hold its gains. Republican candidates outspent their Democratic opponents in fifty-one of the fifty-eight races in question. The average Republican expenditure in these races was $340,000, nearly $75,000 more than the average Democratic expenditure of $266,000. A similar Republican advantage during the 1984 congressional elections contributed to the Republicans actually outpolling the Democrats on a national basis. District patterns favorable to the Democrats were the major factor that prevented the Republican majority of votes cast from becoming a majority of seats.

Redistribution of Political Power

These Republican successes must be seen as more than just short-term electoral phenomena. Rather they reflect a fundamental change in the underlying strength of political forces in the United States. The marriage of money and the new technology has given the forces of the political right a significant— perhaps a decisive—competitive edge, the full extent of which is perhaps best illustrated by the historic reversals that occurred in a number of congressional districts in 1978 and 1980. In both years the Republicans captured a sizable number of districts that had been Democratic strongholds for decades. In 1978 the Republicans captured a total of twenty-one congressional districts that had long been held by the Democrats. Several of these were longstanding Democratic bastions. The Arkansas Second District had not been won by a Republican since 1870. The Georgia Sixth had never been held by a Republican since its creation in 1844; the South Carolina Fourth not since 1874. In addition to these southern districts, the Republicans captured the California Thirty-fourth, held by the Democrats since its creation in 1962; the Iowa Second, held by the Democrats also since 1962; the New York First, Democratic since 1958; the Ohio Nineteenth, Democratic since 1934; Pennsylvania's Fourth and Fifteenth, held by the Democrats since 1946 and 1950 respectively; and Texas's Twenty-first and Twenty-second congressional districts, held by the Democrats in every election since their creation in 1934 and 1958. In addition, the Republicans were able to increase their level of voter support by 10 percent or more in another twenty-one districts that remained Democratic. Several of these had been held by the Democrats since the turn of the century.

In 1980 the Republicans captured thirty-seven previously Democratic districts. Five had been Democratic since the 1960s, four since the 1950s, five since the 1940s, two since the 1930s, and two since the nineteenth century. Two districts, the North Carolina Sixth and the Texas Eighth, had never been held by a Republican. In another twenty-eight districts that were won by the Democrats, the Republicans increased their voting margin by 10 percent or more. Three of these districts have been held by Democrats since the 1920s, three since the turn of the century, and four during the entire period of their existence.

In 1980, the Republicans, of course, also won control of the Senate, which they retained in 1982 and 1984. Several of the

newly elected senators were the first Republicans from their
states in decades: Jeremiah Denton, Alabama's first Republican
senator since 1868; Paula Hawkins, Florida's second Republican
since 1868; Mack Mattingly, Georgia's first since 1871; John
East, North Carolina's second since 1868; and Slade Gorton,
Washington's first since 1946.

In the course of American political history, major changes in
the relative strength of competing political forces have led to
partisan realignments—changes in the distribution of voter attachments to the party organizations that mobilized the electorate for political competition. The capacity of Republicans to
penetrate and hold significant positions in what had been traditional Democratic strongholds is indicative of an ongoing shift
in the relative power of competing political forces in the United
States.

This change in the balance of power has not yet produced a
realignment of electoral coalitions of the classic sort. Partisan
realignments historically reflected the fact that political parties
were the chief actors on the electoral stage and chief foci for
voters' attention. The present-day change in the underlying
strength of American political forces is a result precisely of the
displacement of political party organizations by new mechanisms of electoral mobilization. Few voters develop strong ties
to public relations firms. As a result, the contemporary reorientation of electoral forces has been what might be called an
apartisan realignment—a reorientation of electoral forces not
yet distinguished by the formation of strong new partisan loyalties. Of course, there remains the intriguing possibility that
disciplined national party institutions might ultimately emerge
from the new politics. To the extent that campaign funds come
to be controlled by parties rather than individual candidates,
the national parties might have the means of imposing a measure of discipline on legislators and other office holders. The
Republican National Committee is already the source of a good
deal of funding for Republican candidates, and the Democratic

National Committee is seeking to follow suit for its own partisan adherents. Indeed, legislative reforms are occasionally proposed that would require the channeling of a greater proportion of campaign funds through the parties. The result of such a development could well be a revival of partisan politics—though still a capital-intensive rather than the more labor-intensive politics once associated with organized parties.

Whatever the future possibilities, in terms of its implications and consequences the present apartisan realignment is not so different from the more fully partisan reorientations of the past. Since the seminal work of V. O. Key in the 1950s, analysts of political change in the United States have focused on realignments of voters as the "mainspring," to use Walter Dean Burnham's phrase, of American politics. Yet in an important sense realignments of voters have never been the mainsprings but have always been epiphenomenal, effects more than causes of shifts in the balance of political power in the United States. Partisan realignments of voters have been the tips of the iceberg. The iceberg itself has always been the emergence of powerful new economic interests or social forces that changed the balance of power among contending groups and interests. The voter realignment of the 1930s, for example, was a reflection and reinforcement rather than a cause of the emergence of powerful new economic and social interests that linked themselves to the Democratic party.[41] Major changes in the behavior and attitudes of voters reflect, register, and reinforce rather than cause such shifts in the underlying distribution of political resources and power.[42]

Today the shift in the underlying balance of political power favors the forces of the right. Obviously these forces will not win every election. Nevertheless, given the new capital-intensive, technological format of American electoral politics, the right is likely to be the dominant electoral force in the United States for the foreseeable future. Already this has had major policy consequences—the dismantling of many of the programs associated with the Great Society and partial erosion of some programs originating with the New Deal as well.[43] More can be expected if the right increases its hold on the state's structure.

Indeed, given the central role now played by the U.S. national government, this shift in the distribution of political power, once consolidated, could be the most significant in American history. As we have seen, the vaunted antistate bias of the right does not prevent conservatives from taking full advantage of their opportunities to control the levers of state power. In practice, if not in principle, American conservatives disagree with their liberal counterparts mainly about how—not whether—state power should be used. Ronald Reagan made this very clear from the first day of his administration. In his first inaugural address, as I noted earlier, Reagan declared, "Now so there will be no misunderstanding, it is not my intention to do away with government; it is, rather, to make it work."[44] It would, therefore, be ironic but not surprising if the political forces that claim to speak for tradition, stability, and, above all, limited government used their control of the state—a control acquired with the help of the new technology of opinion management—to seek the most far-reaching changes in American politics and society.

Chapter 6

Popular Opinion and Democratic Government

WHEN THEY DOMESTICATED opinion and forged institutional links between mass opinion and government during the nineteenth and twentieth centuries, western regimes not only created a firmer basis for national power, they also constrained the political impact of mass opinion. Western democratic processes—elections in particular—make governments formally dependent on mass opinion. It would, as a result, be foolish to argue that public opinion does not matter in the West. Clearly, rulers must take it into account when they formulate their plans. Groups that seek to influence policy or seize power are often, albeit not always, obligated to seek the support of mass opinion. Nevertheless, the creation of institutional links between government and opinion also delimited the role and influence of mass opinion in political life. This is particularly true in the case of the most important link between government and mass opinion in the West, democratic elections.

The Meaning of Elections

Elections are generally conceived to be the principal means through which ordinary citizens, as distinguished from members of the elite strata (who usually have other means at their disposal), can impose their views upon leaders' conduct. And certainly democratic elections permit citizens to routinely select and depose public officials, and thereby to influence the composition and behavior of the nation's ruling circle. But however effective the electoral sanction may be, it is hardly the only means through which even the most humble citizens can reward or punish public officials for their actions. Spontaneous or privately organized forms of political activity, or even the threat of their occurrence, can also induce those in power to pay attention to their subjects' opinions. The behavior of even the most rigid autocrats, for example, can be influenced by the possibility that their policies may provoke popular disobedience, clandestine movements, or riot and insurrection. To be sure, the likelihood that an autocrat will be removed from office may generally be less than the chance that an elected official will suffer defeat at the polls. At the same time, however, the potential cost of removal via popular insurrection can be significantly greater than the penalties associated with electoral defeat. Though American congressional representatives are occasionally retired to the private practice of law by their constituents, thus far at least few have lost their heads. Elections do not create a possibility of popular influence where none existed before. Rather, they substitute an institutional mechanism for the informal sanctions that might otherwise be available to a mass public. Elections transform citizens' capacity to influence their rulers' behavior from a matter of purely private activities and resources to a result of mass participation in a routine public function. This transformation has several critical consequences.

First, elections formalize and thus fundamentally alter the character of popular influence over governments' actions. As I noted earlier, while citizens' opinions could influence public officials long before the advent of elections, in the absence of formal mechanisms for its expression and enforcement, the influence of popular opinion tended to be inversely related to rulers' power. Rulers are likely to be most concerned with their subjects' wishes when their military and administrative capacity to compel obedience or forcibly maintain their positions is weakest and least concerned with citizens' views when their own power is most secure. Popular influence stemming from rulers' fear of disobedience—riot or insurrection, for example—is likely to be greatest when the state's military and internal security forces are weakest or least reliable. The advent of the democratic election, however, meant that even when rulers had the capacity to compel obedience, popular influence was no longer necessarily reduced. Citizens' capacity to influence their rulers' conduct had become at least partially independent of rulers' military and administrative power. The effectiveness of the electoral sanction, unlike that of the threat of riot and insurrection, does not necessarily vary with the state's power. Even the most powerful elected official can be voted out of office. With the advent of the democratic election, popular influence and rulers' power were no longer necessarily inversely related but could instead potentially coexist.

At the same time that they institutionalize the influence of public opinion, however, elections have a second consequence: they delimit popular influence. Elections introduce a means of mass influence that is itself subject to formal governmental control and manipulation. In every nation the electoral rules and procedures that translate individual opinions and choices into collective decisions and determine the impact of those decisions upon the government's composition are used by those in power to regulate electoral outcomes and their likely consequences. Electoral rules can obviously be employed to diminish or even to preclude the possibility of electoral influence. Examples of authoritarian elections without choice are numerous. But even where competition and choice are routine possibilities, election law can play an important role in preserving an established distribution of power. The democracies characteristically do not attempt to prevent mass influence via the ballot box. Instead, electoral law in the democratic context is typically used to organize the expression of mass opinion in such a way that its force is channeled to the advantage of the regime. Rather than prevent mass electoral influence, democracies attempt typically to "influence mass influence," so that the electorate's decisions themselves will accord with and thus reinforce the power and wishes of those who rule.

Third, whatever the precise character of the legal constraints on popular influence through voting, elections inherently limit mass intervention into governmental and political processes. To begin with, elections limit the frequency of citizen participation in politics. In the United States elections occur at fixed points in time and grant elected officials the freedom and authority to govern, without fear of citizen intervention, for a defined term. So long as participation is confined to periodic voting, officials have an opportunity to overlook public sentiment about the conduct of public affairs much of the time.

Moreover, elections limit the scope of mass political participation. Elections permit citizens to take part only in the selection of leaders. The mass public does not directly participate in subsequent policy making. Though there may be links between citizens' choices among candidates for office and choices about the government's actions, elections do not usually function as referenda on issues or policies. Indeed, as we shall see, elections in the United States tend for the most part to focus mass attention exclusively on the question of who shall govern and to divert it away from questions of how and what the government shall do.

Last, elections limit the intensity of mass political activity by converting it from a means of asserting demands to a collective statement of permission. In the absence of formal avenues for popular involvement, political participation serves almost exclusively as a device for the expression of strongly held beliefs and preferences. So long as political involvement is difficult, usually only those individuals with intense or extreme opinions will be sufficiently motivated to seek to become involved. Elections, however, facilitate participation sufficiently that large numbers of citizens take part despite their relative indifference or apathy about most public questions. Just as polls can dilute the weight of those with intense views, elections usually submerge those participants with strongly held views in a generally apathetic mass electorate.

Thus, while elections are usually seen as synonymous with mass political influence, their consequences are not so simple. Elections institutionalize popular influence but can at the same time constrain and delimit the effects of mass intervention into political life. It is undoubtedly true that popular influence through democratic electoral institutions is significantly greater than, say, the influence available to citizens ruled by a dictatorship sufficiently powerful to prevent dissent and disorder. But this comparison, often implicit when the importance of democratic elections is discussed, is not necessarily the most apt. In what at least historically has been the more usual case, governments often have not been powerful enough to stamp out clandestine oppositions or prevent political violence and disorder. And under such circumstances, the influence that the masses have been able to exert through these modes of political expression, or even their threat, has been substantial. The alternative to democratic elections is not clearly and simply the absence of popular influence but can instead be unregulated and unconstrained mass intervention into governmental processes. It is indeed often precisely because spontaneous forms of mass political activity can have too great an impact upon governments' actions that elections are introduced. Distinguished political commentator Walter Lippmann once observed that "new numbers were enfranchised because they had power, and giving them the vote was the least disturbing way of letting them exercise their power."[1] The vote can provide the "least disturbing way" of allowing the masses to exercise power because elections formally delimit mass influence that rulers are unable to forcibly contain. If the masses had no power without them, elections would never have been introduced.

Popular Influence and Rulers' Power

When the state's administrative and military forces are too weak or their loyalty too uncertain to enforce rulers' injunctions or suppress popular unrest, then those in power are likely to become more concerned with their subjects' needs and opinions. For example, European monarchs were generally most solicitous of their subjects' views when they lacked the military power and administrative means to collect needed taxes.[2] Thus the origins of representative government in Britain are closely linked with the crown's financial difficulties in the thirteenth and fourteenth centuries. Because it did not have the ability to forcibly acquire badly needed new revenues, the crown was compelled to summon knights and burgesses to obtain local consent for additional tax levies.[3] In exchange for this consent, the king often found himself obliged to grant a variety of concessions to local wishes. Or, to take a contemporary example, the Polish regime's inability to forcibly prevent riots in the fifties, sixties, and seventies—riots that led to the fall of two governments—made it at least temporarily quite sensitive to popular opinion. In 1976 price increases planned for meat, butter, vegetables, and other staples were quickly rescinded when workers in Warsaw staged a series of demonstrations and others set fire to Communist party headquarters in the city of Radom. Ultimately, fear of popular unrest led the government to establish a national Gallup-type poll on questions of public policy. Apparently the government concluded that its ability to satisfy popular opinion, and thus to avoid unrest, could be enhanced if it had a better notion of the content of popular preferences.[4] In the 1980s the government of the People's Republic of China also discovered the value of the scientific study of public opinion. China's Institute of Psychology endorsed the use of such polls as "tools in the science of management."[5] Thus the scientific public opinion poll serves as the twentieth-century technocratic equivalent of the representative assembly of provincial notables—helping the government to avoid trouble by providing it with some conception of what its subjects will tolerate.

So long as influence is informal, based simply on rulers' fear of riots or inability to forcibly levy taxes, its continuity is uncertain. An increase in the state's power or a diminution of subjects' capacity to resist its application almost inevitably reduces rulers' incentive to respond to their subjects' opinions. For example, in Brandenburg-Prussia the capacity of the nobility to obtain concessions from the crown in exchange for fiscal support was effectively undermined during the seventeenth century. Beginning with the reign of Frederick William, the Great Elector, in 1640, the creation of a state bureaucracy capable of administering tax collection and a peacetime standing army, capable of enforcing payment, opened the way to centralized absolutist rule.[6] A similar illustration of this phenomenon is the failure of the French Estates-General after 1600 to maintain the type of influence over the crown through control of taxation that developed in Britain. The growth of French rulers' military power, beginning in the fifteenth century, greatly diminished the possibility of taxpayer resistance. As this possibility decreased, so did the king's interest in bargaining with his subjects for their support.[7] In this context, it is hardly surprising that the contemporary Polish government's interest in public opinion surveys and independent trade unions ended when it mustered the capacity to forcibly halt popular disruption.

State Power and the Public Welfare

Some empirical indications of the consequences of elections can be obtained by comparing the relationship between social welfare expenditures and the size of internal security forces in nations that have institutionalized democratic electoral practices versus nations that have not. Social welfare expenditures, of course, cannot be said to measure popular influence per se. They do, however, offer one set of indicators of a government's attention to its citizens' needs. Similarly, the size of a state's internal security forces is certainly not a precise measure of governmental "power." Ideally, we would be able to take account of a variety of different aspects of governments' administrative, military, and policy capacities. Ideally we would also be able to consider variations in the loyalty and efficiency of internal security forces as well as cross-national variations in citizens' willingness and capacity to resist the application of force. The virtues of firearms regulation notwithstanding, a well-armed citizenry has, upon more than one occasion, served to discourage tyrannical behavior by those in power.[8] In addition, some governments with the military and policy capacity to suppress dissent lack the political ability or will to fully take advantage of the force at their disposal. Nevertheless, the size of a state's internal security apparatus offers one rough indicator of the government's potential ability to compel popular obedience.

My argument suggests that in the absence of formal electoral sanctions, a government's attention to its citizens' interests is likely to vary inversely with its capacity to compel popular obedience. By contrast, where formal electoral sanctions are available to citizens, we would expect to find little or no relationship between the state's coercive capacity and its attention to public welfare. To test these possibilities, all seventy-one nations for which the requisite social welfare and internal security data were available were divided into three groups on the basis of the classification of their electoral processes found in the *World Handbook of Political and Social Indicators.* [9] The first group consists of those nations whose electoral procedures the *World Handbook* termed "rigged." In these nations elections do not involve competition or permit the possibility of opposition to those in power. The second group consists of those nations whose electoral practices the *World Handbook* deemed to be marked by "substantial irregularity." That is, although a semblance of competition might be tolerated, electoral outcomes unfavorable to those in power are not likely to be permitted. The third category consists of those nations whose electoral practices the *World Handbook* labeled "competitive." In this group, which includes the western democracies, electoral competition and the electoral defeat of those in power is a routine possibility.

Taking each of these three groups of nations separately, I have correlated national expenditures for health and education with a measure of the effective size of each state's internal security apparatus. [10] To account for differences in national wealth, welfare expenditures are expressed as percentages of each nation's gross national product. Table 6–1 reports the results of these correlations. The pattern that emerges from this analysis indicates rather striking differences between the first two groups of nations, on the one hand, and the third group, on the other.

In the first two groups, nations whose electoral practices were deemed to be "rigged" or marked by substantial irregularities, social welfare expenditures generally tend to be inversely related to the size of the state's internal security apparatus. This association is clearly consistent with the argument that in the absence of formal electoral sanctions, governments' attention to citizens' needs is likely to diminish as their capacity to suppress potential dissent or resistance increases.

By contrast, in the third group of nations, those with competitive electoral practices, social welfare expenditures are not inversely associated with the size of the state's internal security forces. Expenditures for education in the thirty-one nations comprising this group show no relationship whatsoever with

TABLE 6–1

The Relationship Between National Social Welfare Expenditures and National Internal Security Forces in Dictatorships and Democracies[a]

	Expenditures for Education	Expenditures for Health
Size of internal security forces in nations whose electoral processes are rigged	−0.12 ($N = 21$)	0.01 ($N = 21$)
Size of internal security forces in nations whose electoral processes exhibit substantial irregularities	−0.15 ($N = 26$)	−0.10 ($N = 24$)
Size of internal security forces in nations with competitive elections	.00 ($N = 31$)	0.10 ($N = 30$)

[a]This interpretation is based on the Pearson correlation coefficients.
NOTE: Reprinted, by permission of the publisher, from Benjamin Ginsberg, *The Consequences of Consent* (New York: Random House, 1982), 71.

the size of internal security apparatus; health expenditures exhibit a positive association. In these nations, welfare expenditures do not appear to diminish as states' coercive capabilities increase. Governments' attention to citizens' needs does not appear to be inversely related to governments' power.

As is always the case, these results cannot be deemed conclusive. They depend, for example, on a rather indirect measure of popular influence, a measure of governments' power that is at best partial, and are based on data drawn from a relatively small number of nations. In addition, it is important to remember that the expenditure differences between electorally competitive nations and the other two groups do not necessarily represent differences in total welfare expenditures. Welfare expenditures in many nations in the rigged group are greater than or equal to expenditures in electorally competitive nations. The differences among the three groups of nations have to do with the *correlates,* not the *amounts,* of welfare expenditures. I shall return to this point later.

Even with these caveats, however, what emerges from this analysis is some empirical support for the argument that democratic elections tend to eliminate or erode the inverse relationship between popular influence and governmental power. By providing citizens with a formal capacity to select and depose leaders, elections permit popular influence and the state's power to coexist. It is for this reason that the advent of the democratic election potentially marks an enormous turning point in the relationship between the citizen and the state. For, given a formal electoral means of influencing their rulers' actions, a means independent of rulers' military and administrative power, citizens potentially stand to benefit from rulers' power rather than from their weakness. It is the advent of the democratic election that opens the possibility of citizens using rulers' power for their own benefit rather than simply benefiting from rulers' inability to muster sufficient power to compel citizens to obey their commands. It is indeed largely because of this characteristic of democratic electoral processes that the enormous expansion of the state's power in the twentieth century has not seemed to foreclose entirely the possibility of popular influence over governmental conduct.

Regulation of Mass Political Influence

The substitution of elections for informal modes of mass political action makes popular influence independent of the state's power. Yet, however important it may be, this change should not be mistaken for an increase in the extent of mass political influence. The correlates and extent of popular influence are two entirely different matters. That popular influence ceases to vary with changes in the state's power might only mean that it has become unvaryingly insignificant.

By eroding the inverse relationship between popular influence and the state's power, elections may sometimes give citizens a greater capacity to influence their rulers than they would otherwise have had. But at the same time, the introduction of elections can give the state an opportunity that it would not otherwise have had to formally delimit the extent of mass political influence. Elections are means of popular control of the state that are themselves controlled by the state. The substitution of elections for spontaneous modes of mass political action allows governments an opportunity if not necessarily to reduce, at least to regulate the likely consequences of popular intervention into policy-making processes. Whether citizens or their rulers have the most to gain from this substitution no doubt varies from case to case. And of course, once established, electoral processes may not be as easily amenable to control as rulers might have intended. But from the perspective of those in power, the alternative to elections can be unregulated and unlimited mass influence over their actions. Even democratic elections, by contrast, can permit governments to formally control the political consequences of mass opinion.

Though each has many variants, three general forms of control have played especially important roles in the electoral history of the western democracies. First, governments often attempt to regulate the composition of electorates in order to diminish the electoral weight of groups and ideas they deem to be undesirable. Second, governments almost invariably seek to manipulate the translation of voters' opinions and choices into electoral outcomes both through the organization of electorates and through organization of electorates' decisions. Third, virtually all ruling groups attempt at least to partially insulate policy-making processes from mass opinion by regulating the relationship between electoral decisions and the composition or organization of the government.

Electoral Composition

Perhaps the oldest and most obvious device used to control electoral outcomes and their likely consequences is manipulation of the electorate's composition. At the time of the initial introduction of elections in western Europe, for example, suffrage was generally limited, through property or other restrictions, to groups that could be trusted to vote in a manner acceptable to those in power. To cite just one illustration, property qualifications in France prior to 1848 limited the electorate to 240,000 of some 7 million men over the age of twenty-one.[11] During the same era, other nations manipulated the electorate's composition by assigning unequal electoral weights to different classes of voters. The 1831 Belgian Constitution, for example, assigned individuals anywhere from one to three votes depending on their property holdings, education, and position.[12] The well-known 1848 Prussian Constitution divided voters into three classes on the basis of property, tax payments, and official or professional position. Though the size of each class was unequal—in some districts the uppermost class contained only a handful of persons—each class selected an equal number of electors, who in turn selected representatives to the lower house of the legislature.[13]

But even in the contest of an ostensibly universal and equal suffrage, the composition of an electorate may still be amenable to manipulation. Examples range from the discriminatory use of poll taxes and literacy tests to such practices as manipulation of the placement of polls and scheduling of voting hours to depress participation by one or another group. Probably the most important example of the regulation of an electorate's composition despite universal suffrage is the personal registration requirement associated with voting in the United States.

Levels of voter participation in twentieth-century American elections are quite low by comparison to those of the other western democracies.[14] Indeed, voter participation in off-year congressional elections in the United States has barely averaged 50 percent in recent years. During the nineteenth century, by contrast, U.S. voter turnout was extremely high. Records indicate that in some counties as many as 105 percent of those eligible voted in presidential elections.[15] Some proportion of this total obviously was artificial—a result of the widespread corruption that characterized American voting practices during that period. Nevertheless, it seems clear that a considerably larger proportion of those eligible actually went to the polls in nineteenth-century American elections than is the case at present.

The critical years during which voter turnout declined across the United States were between 1890 and 1910. These years coincide with the adoption of laws across much of the nation requiring eligible citizens to appear personally at a registrar's office to register to vote some time prior to the actual date of an election. Personal registration was one of several "Progressive" reforms of political practices initiated at the turn of the century. Its ostensible purpose was to discourage fraud and corruption. But to many Progressive reformers "corruption" was a code word, much as "crime" has been a code word in recent years. Progressives objected to the types of politics practiced in the large cities where political machines had organized immigrant and ethnic populations. Reformers not only objected to the corruption that surely was a facet of machine politics but also opposed the growing political power of these polyglot urban populations and their leaders. From the point of view of middle-class reformers, the electoral system was corrupt, in part because it facilitated participation and influence on the part of the wrong types of persons.[16] Like some other Progressive reforms, voting reform may also have been congenial to the interests of the business elites that became dominant in American politics during the late nineteenth century. Personal registration created a more conservative electorate more amenable to the types of policies favored by business groups.

At any rate, personal registration imposed a new burden on potential voters and altered the format of American elections. While registration statutes existed in a number of states before 1890, these early laws had little consequence. It had not been uncommon in most areas for voters simply to walk into a polling place on the day of the election and cast ballots with little or no official interference. Those early registration laws that were enforced were similar in effect to the present-day European requirements, where the burden of registration is placed on election officials rather than on voters. It is the task of these officials to compose lists of qualified voters; no action on the part of the voter is necessary before the day of the election.

Under the new systems of personal registration adopted after 1890, it became the duty of individual voters to secure their own eligibility. During a personal appearance before the registrar, individuals seeking to vote were (and are) required to furnish proof of identity, residence, and citizenship. While the inconvenience of registration varied from state to state, usually voters could register only during business hours on weekdays. This, of course, meant that to many voters registration might entail the loss of some portion of a day's pay. Second, voters were usually required to register a long time, in some states up to several months, before the next election. This requirement forced potential voters to make an investment of time and effort just when their interest in electoral politics was likely to have ebbed. Third, in many areas citizens had to reregister periodically to maintain their eligibility. Most personal registration laws required a periodic purge of the election rolls, ostensibly to keep them up to date. Although personal registration requirements helped to decrease the widespread electoral corruption that accompanied a completely open voting process, they also made it much more difficult for citizens to participate in the electoral process.[17]

As might be expected, registration requirements have their greatest impact on the most poorly socialized segments of the electorate. As table 6–2 suggests, such requirements particularly depress participation on the part of those with little education and low incomes.[18] The explanation for this biased impact of registration is twofold. First, the simple obstacle of registering on weekdays during business hours is most difficult for working-class persons to overcome. Second, and more important, registration requires a greater degree of political involvement and interest than does the act of voting itself. To vote a person need only be concerned with the particular election campaign at hand. Yet as was noted, registration in many states is required up to several months prior to the next election. This requirement forces individuals to make the decision to register on the basis of an abstract interest in the electoral process rather than a simple concern with a specific campaign. As a number of studies have suggested, even if they become interested in specific campaigns, lower-class, poorly educated persons are less likely than middle- and upper-class individuals to have such an

TABLE 6–2

Socioeconomic Differences Between Registered Voters and Individuals Who Were Not Registered in 1972 and 1976

	Attended College (%)	Employed (%)	with Income over $10,000 (%)
1972			
Registered	33.4 (N=1066)	57.1 (N=1068)	51.9 (N=1024)
Not registered	14.1 (N=277)	47.5 (N=276)	27.8 (N=263)

	Attended College (%)	Employed (%)	with Income over $12,000 (%)
1976			
Registered	36.3 (N=1737)	55.9 (N=1743)	25.2 (N=1621)
Not registered	17.4 (N=489)	48.1 (N=491)	14.8 (N=466)

NOTE: Reprinted, by permission of the publisher, from Benjamin Ginsberg, *The Consequences of Consent* (New York: Random House, 1982), 85.

abstract or general interest in the electoral process, which is largely a product of education. Those with relatively little education may become interested in political events once the stimuli of a particular campaign become salient, but by that time it is too late to register to vote.[19]

That they have a greater impact on the voting turnout of individuals from lower socioeconomic strata means that personal registration requirements not only diminish the size of the electorate but also have a systematic impact on the electorate's composition. Personal registration tends to create an electorate that is, in the aggregate, better educated, higher in income and social status, and composed of fewer blacks and other minorities than the citizenry as a whole. Moreover, those groups particularly affected by registration requirements differ from the remainder of the electorate, in the aggregate, in their opinions about important public issues.[20] In particular, support for a variety of redistributive social programs is somewhat greater among individuals who are not registered to vote than among registered voters.

The implications of the differences reported by table 6–3 are relatively clear. Full electoral mobilization in the United States would create an electorate more receptive to a variety of broad social welfare initiatives than the present, relatively constricted, and, as a result, more conservative electorate. Presumably this is why many conservatives do not view favorably the elimination of personal registration requirements.[21] There is, of course, a major drawback to personal registration or any other mode of electoral regulation that inhibits voting participation. Should they seek to participate, groups barred from voting may instead select some other and perhaps less desirable form of political activity. Manipulation of the electorate's composition may work to the advantage of those in power during periods of political quiescence but can backfire when and if groups excluded from voting have some sudden incentive to participate in political life. In this respect, the implications of personal registration do differ somewhat from those of outright disen-

TABLE 6–3

Support for Social Programs Among Individuals Registered and Not Registered to Vote in 1976

	Favor Government Aid to Blacks and Minorities (%)	Favor Government Job Guarantees (%)	Favor Continued Private Role in Health Insurance (%)	Favor Job Safety Regulation (%)
Registered to vote	19.5 (N = 1492)	18.3 (N = 1439)	53.2 (N = 1735)	70.5 (N = 1422)
Not registered to vote	25.5 (N = 353)	25.6 (N = 347)	43.3 (N = 485)	80.8 (N = 364)

NOTE: Reprinted, by permission of the publisher, from Benjamin Ginsberg, *The Consequences of Consent* (New York: Random House, 1982), 87.

franchisement. Given sufficient stimulus, excluded groups may register to vote. The voter registration drive has been an integral part of minority protest activity in contemporary American politics up to and including the 1984 presidential election. Indeed, a federally sponsored drive to register southern blacks as voters was an integral part of the U.S. government's response to the problem of black political protest activities in the 1960s. Nevertheless, to attempt to control an electorate by discouraging some of its members from voting can negate the socialization of political action that is a major purpose of elections. In the twentieth century the United States has been among the few nations sufficiently quiescent politically to permit its leaders the luxury of excluding "undesirable" elements from the electorate. For the most part, twentieth-century electorate control has depended on techniques compatible with full electoral mobilization.

Organization of Electorates and Decisions

With the major exception of American personal registration requirements, control of electorates through regulation of their composition has in this century given way to control through manipulation of the relationship between individual voters' opinions and choices and collective electoral decisions. Rather than regulate who will choose, governments in the twentieth century generally prefer to allow—in fact to encourage—everyone to choose and then simply to manipulate the likely outcomes.

The translation of individual choices into collective electoral decisions can be influenced in two ways. The first of these is manipulation of the criteria by which popular votes are translated into governmental representation. For example, the selection of a majority, plurality, or some form of proportional criterion for the translation of votes into legislative seats obviously can have important implications for electoral outcomes and their likely consequences. Second, the organization of electorates themselves offers considerable potential for the management of electoral outcomes. The number and arrangement of electoral districts, for example, can have important consequences for the relative importance of different groups and forces. In combination, the organization of electorates and of electoral decisions offers governments a virtually endless array of possible ways to manipulate elections. Of course, not all of these possibilities are open to any given government at any point in time. Electoral arrangements conceived to be clearly "stacked," or illegitimate, may induce some segments of an electorate to refuse either to participate or to recognize the validity of the result. Some form of proportional representation, for example, may be necessary in nations severely divided along religious or ethnic lines.[22] Nevertheless, a good deal of electoral engineering is possible even within the limits imposed by governments' desire to uphold the legitimacy of electoral processes.

An enormous literature has been devoted to the comparison of majority, plurality, and proportional electoral systems as well as to the mathematical intricacies of various established and proposed modes of proportional representation.[23] This discussion can, therefore, be brief. In general, majority and plurality systems create higher thresholds for legislative representation; that is, they require more votes for the acquisition of a legislative seat and more severely overrepresent the most successful party than do proportional systems. Under the terms of a majority system, for example, a party may in principle need to acquire more than 50 percent of the popular vote before winning any legislative representation. On the other hand, a party that receives, say, 35 percent of the vote in a three-party plurality race may win 100 percent of the legislative seats. As a result, in nineteenth-century European political history, majority and plurality systems initially served the interests of established conservative parties by reducing the representation of emerging working-class groups. However, as working-class parties gained in strength and threatened to win electoral majorities, conservative groups came to see proportional representation as a barrier against socialism. In Sweden, for example, conservative groups first fought the introduction of proportional representation but later made it a precondition for their acceptance of universal manhood suffrage.[24]

Among proportional systems, there is a very wide range of variation in thresholds and in the degree of overrepresentation offered the largest parties. The "d'Hondt" system, which was among the first introduced in Western Europe, lowers the threshold of representation and degree of overrepresentation very little by comparison with majority and plurality systems. On the other extreme, what is called the method of the "greatest remainder" facilitates the representation of small splinter groups and under some circumstances actually tends to underrepresent the largest party. Though not directly related to the question of thresholds, modes of balloting can also be important. List systems, for example, probably tend to be more conducive to party formation and organization than preferential systems.

The precise consequences of any given proportional system, however, depend on the composition of the electorate, the number of legislative seats decided in each district, the number of established parties, and the extent and geographic distribution of support for each party. As a result, the consequences of any given proportional system can be different in different areas at different times. Considerable fine-tuning may be necessary to achieve a desired outcome. A well-known example is the electoral system devised for the French elections of 1951. The parties of the government coalition faced the Communists on the left and the Gaullist Rassemblement du Peuple Francais (RPF) on the right. Unfortunately, the distribution of electoral support for the government coalition meant that any single electoral arrangement would work to the advantage of either the Communists or the RPF or both. Therefore, the government coalition devised an electoral system with three different forms. First, in the rural areas of France, where the government coalition was strongest, the d'Hondt system of proportional representation was used to overrepresent the government's support. Second, in Paris and its surroundings, where the government coalition was weakest, the largest remainder system of proportional representation was introduced to underrepresent the Communists and Gaullists. Third, outside the Paris region, a system called *apparentement*, which awards all the seats in a district to any coalition of parties winning a majority of popular votes, was introduced to further maximize the government coalition's rural support. The consequence of this complex electoral engineering was that the government coalition was able to translate barely 50 percent of the popular vote into more than 60 percent of the seats in the legislature.[25]

Manipulation of the criteria by which votes are translated into representation has played some role in American electoral history. For example, the elimination of proportional representation in the selection of New York City council delegates was specifically designed to prevent the election of Communist party representatives.[26] On the other hand, the introduction of proportional representation for the selection of delegates to the Democratic party's 1972 national convention was designed in part to maximize the voting strength of minority groups and, not entirely coincidentally, to improve the electoral chances of the candidates they were most likely to favor.[27]

Despite these and other exceptions, however, the typical electoral arrangement in the United States is the single-member district plurality election. As a result, American electoral engineering has generally consisted of the manipulation of electoral districts to increase the likelihood of one or another desired outcome. The principle of the gerrymander hardly needs elaboration. Different distributions of voters among districts produce different electoral outcomes; those in a position to control the arrangement of districts are also in a position to manipulate the results. For example, during the 1950s Brooklyn's twelfth congressional district twisted and turned, almost fully bisecting the borough from northwest to southeast. The explanation of the district's peculiar shape was simple. "There are very few Republicans in Brooklyn and distributed in ordinarily shaped districts they would never make a majority anywhere. But the Republican legislature strung GOP areas into a district winding through the borough, and the result was Republican victories until this year."[28]

The Supreme Court's reapportionment decisions during the 1960s hardly put an end to the practice of gerrymandering. In fact, the Court's decisions appear to have prompted a wave of "incumbent gerrymanders" involving the redrawing of congressional district lines in such a way as to increase the safety of many legislative seats.[29]

Whether the means employed is organization of electorates or of their decisions, governments have the capacity to manipulate electoral outcomes. This capacity, again, is not absolute. Electoral arrangements conceived to be illegitimate may prompt some segments of the electorate to seek other ways of participating in political life. Moreover, no electoral system that provides universal and equal suffrage can, by itself, long prevent an outcome favored by large popular majorities. Yet faced with opposition short of an overwhelming majority, governments' ability to manipulate the translation of individual choices into collective decisions can be an important factor in preserving the established distribution of power.

Insulation of Decision-making Processes

Virtually all governments attempt at least partially to insulate decision-making processes from public opinion. The most obvious forms of insulation are the confinement of popular election to only some governmental agencies, various modes of indirect election, and lengthy tenure in office. In the United States, of course, the framers of the Constitution intended that only members of the House of Representatives be subject to direct popular election. The president and senators were to be indirectly elected for rather long terms to allow them, as *The Federalist* put it, to avoid "an unqualified complaisance to every sudden breeze of passion; or to every transient impulse which the people may receive."[30]

Somewhat less obvious are the insulating effects of electoral arrangements that permit direct, and even frequent, popular election of public officials but tend to fragment or disaggregate the impact of elections on the government's composition. In the United States, for example, the constitutional provision of staggered terms of service in the Senate was designed to diminish the impact of shifts in electoral sentiment on the Senate as an institution. Since only one-third of its members were to be selected at any given time, the composition of the institution would be partially protected from changes in electoral preferences. This would avoid what *The Federalist* called "mutability in the public councils arising from a rapid succession of new members."[31]

The division of the nation into relatively small, geographically based constituencies for the purpose of selecting members of the House of Representatives was designed in part to have a similar effect. Representatives were to be chosen frequently. However, Madison and others felt that since each was to be selected by a discrete constituency, the government's vulnerability to shifts in the national mood or, in particular, to any mass popular movements that might arise would be diminished. In a sense, the House of Representatives was compartmentalized in the same way that a submarine is divided into watertight sections to confine the impact of any damage to the vessel. First, the geographic particularization of the national electorate would increase the salience of local issues by granting local opinion its own national representative. Second, the salience of local issues would mean that a representative's electoral fortunes would be more nearly tied to factors peculiar to his or her own district than to the public's response to national issues. Third, given a geographical principle of representation, the formation of national policy majorities was conceived to be less likely than the formation of local majorities that might or might not share common underlying dimensions. No matter how well represented individual constituencies might be, the aggregate influence of constituents on national policy questions would be fragmented. In Madison's terms, the influence of "faction" would thus become "less likely to pervade the whole body than some particular portion of it."[32]

Another example of an American electoral arrangement that tends to fragment the impact of mass elections on the government's composition is the Australian ballot.[33] Prior to the introduction of the official ballot in the 1890s, voters cast ballots composed by the political parties. Each party printed its own ballots, listed only its own candidates for each office, and employed party workers to distribute the ballots at the polls. This ballot format had two important consequences. First, the party ballot precluded secrecy in voting. Because each party's ballot was distinctive in size and color, it was not difficult for party workers to determine how individuals intended to vote. This, of course, facilitated the intimidation and bribery of voters. Second, the ballot format virtually prevented split-ticket voting. Because only one party's candidates appeared on any ballot, it was very difficult for a voter to cast anything other than a straight party vote, unless, of course, he happened to bring scissors and paste to the polls with him.

The official Australian ballot represented a significant change in electoral procedure. It was prepared and administered by the state rather than the parties. Each ballot was identical and included the names of all candidates for office. This reform, of course, increased the secrecy of voting and reduced the possibility for voter intimidation and bribery. Because all ballots were identical in appearance, even the voter who had been threatened or bribed might still vote as he wished, without the knowledge of party workers. But perhaps even more important, the Australian ballot reform made it possible for voters to make their choices on the basis of the individual rather than the collective merits of the candidates. Voters were no longer forced to choose a straight party ticket. It was, indeed, the introduction of the Australian ballot that gave rise to the phenomenon of split-ticket voting in American elections.[34]

It is this second consequence of the Australian ballot reform that tends to fragment the impact of American elections on the government's composition. Prior to the ballot reform, it was not uncommon for an entire incumbent administration to be swept from office and replaced by an entirely new set of officials. In the absence of a real possibility of split-ticket voting, any desire on the part of the electorate for change could be expressed only as a vote against all candidates of the party in power. Because of this, there always existed the possibility, particularly at state and local levels, that an insurgent slate committed to policy change could be swept into power. A single popular insurgent could carry an entire new administration into office with him. The party ballot thus increased the potential impact of elections on the government's composition. In the absence of ticket split-ting, popular voting was more likely to produce a new adminis-tration controlling enough public offices to be in a position to effect significant changes in public policy. Though this poten-tial may not always have been realized, the party ballot at least increased the chance that electoral decisions could lead to policy changes.

Because it permitted choice on the basis of candidates' indi-vidual appeals, the Australian ballot lessened the likelihood that the electorate would sweep an entirely new administration into power. The result of ticket splitting was that the control of government came to be increasingly divided between the par-ties. In the State of New York, for example, until very recently voters had the opportunity to individually elect seven executive officers: governor, lieutenant governor, secretary of state, attorney general, state treasurer, state comptroller, and state engineer-surveyor. Staggered terms meant that the electorate seldom was asked to fill more than five of these positions in any one electoral year. Nevertheless, prior to the introduction of the Australian ballot, all the officials elected during any single point in time were invariably affiliated with the same party. Shifts in partisan control affected all available offices simultaneously. In 1893, for example, all five executive positions at stake in the election shifted from Democratic to Republican hands. This state of affairs gradually began to change after the introduction of the Australian ballot in 1895. In 1902 a Democratic attorney general was elected alongside a Republican treasurer, secretary of state, and lieutenant governor. In 1907 a Republican governor was elected at the same time that all six of the other executive posts were won by Democrats. This pattern of divided executive control became commonplace during the next decade and is the norm in contemporary New York politics.

Taken together, regulation of the electorate's composition, of the translation of voters' choices into electoral decisions, and of the impact of those decisions on the government's composition allow those in power a measure of control over the consequences of mass participation in political life. These techniques do not necessarily diminish citizens' capacity to influence their rulers' conduct. In the democracies, at least, these techniques are generally used to manage electoral influence. They permit governments a measure of control over what citizens will decide that governments should do. Perhaps the most clear-cut illustration is personal registration in the United States. Registration requirements do not diminish the impact of electoral decisions. Rather they influence the types of decisions that the electorate is likely to make. Though these decisions may in turn affect the government's behavior, their shape and content have been subject to prior manipulation. Similarly, regulation of the translation of voters' choices into collective electoral decisions cannot clearly be said to limit electoral influence. This form of regulation instead acts to channel the force of electoral influence itself into directions favorable to those in power.

As I noted previously, governments are often not completely free to establish whatever electoral rules they might wish. Electoral procedures generally conceived to be illegitimate can threaten to induce citizens to seek alternative forms of political expression. Election law in the democracies, moreover, can seldom by itself prevent outcomes favored by overwhelming majorities. But within these limits, even rulers who must dutifully bow to the voice of the people can take a hand in determining what that voice will tell them.

The Limits of Electoral Intervention

Whatever the precise character of the legal constraints, however, the substitution of elections for spontaneous forms of political activity inherently delimits mass intervention into governmental and policy-making processes. Elections limit to occasional voting what might otherwise amount to direct mass intervention into or resistance to administrative and policy-making processes. There is no doubt that voting can have implications for a government's actions. Democratic elections may permit citizens to select officials who represent their own interests and viewpoints. A fear of electoral reprisal may at times induce those in power to take account of citizens' policy preferences. It might indeed appear peculiar to suggest that an institution that permits citizens to select representatives and to hold officials accountable limits mass political intervention.

Yet these very concepts of representation and accountability that are central to democratic electoral institutions exemplify precisely the limited scope of electoral intervention in the governmental process. These concepts denote an indirect relationship between popular opinion and participation on the one hand and governmental decision making on the other. Popular acceptance of the doctrines of electoral representation and accountability itself constitutes popular acceptance of constraints upon political participation. Indeed, it is chiefly in order to induce citizens to accept limited participation that even dictatorial governments are often so careful to link voting with representation.[35] There is more than a grain of truth to Rousseau's observation that the moment a people agrees to the substitution of representation for participation it surrenders its political freedom.[36]

First, elections limit the scope of mass political intervention to leadership selection. Voters do not directly participate in policy making. Only in occasional referenda at the state and local levels do Americans vote for policies. Of course, leadership selection can serve as an indirect form of policy selection. Voters may conceivably base their choices on candidates' stands on important national issues or attempt to reward and punish incumbents on the basis of their records on major questions of public policy. But even though the electorates' choice of leaders can have policy implications, this indirect relationship between popular voting and the government's behavior is usually tenuous and ambiguous.

It is often quite difficult for voters to identify whatever policy differences may exist among opposing candidates for office. Even at the national presidential level, where candidate positions might be expected to be most visible, the electorate appears to have considerable difficulty distinguishing the candidates' stands on major issues.[37]

In 1972, for example, a year when the candidates exhibited unusually sharp differences on many public issues, voters' perceptions of the differences between Nixon and McGovern did not always accord with the candidates' actual positions. According to University of Texas political scientist Benjamin I. Page, Nixon and McGovern differed considerably more on women's rights, taxes, and pollution and less on marijuana and busing than the public was aware.[38] In 1968, a year when the war in Vietnam was an issue of overwhelming importance to most voters, the electorate was confused and divided over where the major candidates stood. Fifty-seven percent saw no difference between Nixon and Humphrey on Vietnam policy; 26 percent believed that Nixon was more "hawkish"; 17 percent saw Humphrey as the more hawkish of the two candidates.[39]

Part of the explanation of voters' inability to perceive policy differences between the candidates may be that candidates generally take similar positions. Some theories of electoral competition, of course, suggest that the strategies of both candidates in a two-candidate race usually lead them to adopt roughly equivalent issue positions.[40]

Another and perhaps more obvious explanation is that whatever the number of candidates in a race, contenders for office normally have strong incentives to make their issue positions as vague, ambiguous, and uncontroversial as possible.[41] Much of the subject matter of political debate consists of what Princeton University scholar Donald E. Stokes has called "valence issues." That is, candidates often attempt to define their positions in such a way as to support courses of action that all voters very likely favor or, alternatively, to express their disapproval of matters clearly opposed by everyone.[42] In recent years, for example, all presidential aspirants have condemned inflation, unemployment, and poverty. Some candidates have espoused such notions as "peace with honor" or "law and order with justice." And every political hopeful has taken a firm stand against "corruption," just as, in earlier eras, candidates advocated "a chicken in every pot" or opposed the spread of "communist totalitarianism." Presumably few voters opposed the elimination of inflation, unemployment, or poverty. Only the most perverse members of the electorate, it might be assumed, would oppose a candidate for his or her firm stand against corruption. From the perspective of candidates for office, such positions are potentially attractive to all voters and at the same time are unlikely to alienate any potential source of support. Yet what is perfectly rational behavior on the part of candidates makes it virtually impossible for voters to use their ballots to affect the course of national policy. Where no alternatives are available, no choices can be made.

Second, elections limit the frequency of mass political intervention. Voters are involved in the political process only occasionally, leaving public officials free to govern without fear of popular intervention most of the time. In the United States, except under the most extraordinary circumstances, public officials have fixed and secure tenure in office for a set period of time. The purpose of a fixed term in office was very clearly stated by Alexander Hamilton in *The Federalist:*

The republican principle demands that the deliberate sense of the community should govern the conduct of those to whom they trust the management of their affairs; but it does not require an unqualified complaisance to every sudden breeze of passion; or to every transient impulse which the people may receive. . . . When occasions present themselves in which the interests of the people are at variance with their inclinations, it is the duty of the persons whom they have appointed to be the guardians of those interested to withstand the temporary delusion in order to give them time and opportunity for more cool and sedate reflection.[43]

A fixed term allows public officials the opportunity to withstand the vicissitudes of public opinion and thereby the opportunity to make unpopular decisions. During officials' tenure in office, *they* govern. The popularity of elected officials and public approval of their behavior ebb and flow between elections, but without directly affecting them.

It is, of course, true that the prospect of ultimate electoral recall may induce those in office to obey their constituents'

TABLE 6–4

The Relationship Between Intensity of Preference and Nonelectoral Participation

	Intensity		
	0	1–3	4–9
Participated in two or more nonelectoral forms of political action	15.5%[a] (N = 45)	16.5% (N = 200)	28.2% (N = 936)

[a]That is, 15.5 percent of the least intense group engaged in two or more nonelectoral forms of political action. Intensity is defined in terms of the number of strong agreements or strong disagreements indicated by respondents in the 1960 Institute for Social Research survey to nine attitudinal questions. Data from 1960 were used because "strongly agree" and "strongly disagree" were dropped as response categories in subsequent surveys.
NOTE: Reprinted, by permission of the publisher, from Benjamin Ginsberg, *The Consequences of Consent* (New York: Random House, 1982), 102.

wishes. But given low levels of public awareness of the actual records of public officials and given the variety of other resources available to incumbents, even the threat of electoral defeat may not be enough to prompt them to work for programs desired by their constituents. For example, recent studies have suggested that the legislative records of incumbent congressmen in the United States have only a slight effect on their subsequent electoral fortunes.[44] Not only do voters appear to be little more than vaguely aware of representatives' legislative records, but also congressmen themselves often engage in a number of activities designed to increase their electoral chances while obscuring their actual records in office. Yale political scientist David R. Mayhew's discussion of "advertising," "credit claiming," and "position taking" as congressional strategies is instructive in this context.[45]

Finally, by virtue of the fact that elections make participation democratic, they diminish the intensity of mass political intervention. Public facilitation of political activity can compensate for low levels of political interest, motivation, and knowledge. Given sufficient public facilitation, even individuals with little interest in the result will take part in political affairs. By the same token, public facilitation compensates for lack of intensity of preference. In the absence of public facilitation of political activity, "spontaneous" participants tend to exhibit clear and intense issue and policy preferences.

If we compare, in table 6–4, the attitudes of voters with those of individuals who engage in political activities other than or in addition to voting, we see first that individuals who participate in forms of political action that are not publicly facilitated tend to exhibit considerably more intense preferences on public issues than do those who only vote.

Second, those who engage in forms of political action that are not publicly facilitated tend to cluster at the extremes of opinion on many public issues. The question of American policy in Vietnam in 1972 is an example. As figure 6–1 indicates, larger percentages of those favoring the more extreme Vietnam policy alternatives engaged in nonelectoral forms of political action than was true among those at the center of the opinion scale.[46] In the absence of public facilitation, participation tends to be an expression of strongly held preferences. With public facilita-

FIGURE 6–1

Percentage of Respondents Engaging in Two or More Nonelectoral Forms of Political Action in 1972

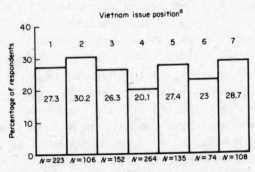

[a]Scale position 1 indicates a preference for "immediate withdrawl" of American troops from Vietnam. Position 7 indicates a preference for a "complete military victory."
NOTE: Reprinted, by permission of the publisher, from Benjamin Ginsberg, *The Consequences of Consent* (New York: Random House, 1982), 103.

tion, even those individuals who are relatively indifferent or unmotivated often participate. By virtue of the fact that they greatly expand mass political involvement, elections create more permissive constituencies and help governments to claim popular acquiescence without necessarily imposing any particular constraints upon their actions. Indeed, political leaders have often exhibited some awareness of this potential. Both Bismarck and Disraeli, for example, were convinced that suffrage expansion would create more conservative electorates.[47] In an electorate, as in the opinion poll just cited, those with strong preferences are usually submerged by the more apathetic majority. If balloting had occurred in 1776, for example, the American colonies would no doubt have remained part of the British Empire.

Voting and Mass Political Influence

Thus, while elections formalize and equalize, they can also delimit the potential for mass influence in political life. The character and effect of formal governmental control and manipulation of electoral processes varies from nation to nation and within any nation over time. As a number of observers have suggested, the potential for mass influence associated with nineteenth-century American electoral arrangements was, in several respects, greater than may be true in the twentieth century. The introduction of such mechanisms as personal registration and the Australian ballot enhanced the state's capacity at least to influence, if not to diminish, the impact of mass participation.[48] Yet whatever the precise character of prevailing electoral arrangements, by comparison with spontaneous or privately organized modes of political action, voting is inherently limited in scope, frequency, and intensity. The assumption often implicit in discussions of popular influence through elections is that democratic electoral processes create a possibility of mass influence where none would otherwise exist. But the potential for popular influence through elections must be assessed against the backdrop of electoral limits on mass political intervention.

Whether the influence citizens can exert through electoral means is greater or less than the possibilities associated with more informal modes of political action very likely depends on the state's military and administrative power. As noted earlier, it is undoubtedly true that the potential for popular influence through democratic electoral institutions is greater than the influence available to citizens ruled by a dictatorship sufficiently powerful to stifle dissent and suppress opposition. In this type of situation informal modes of political action would presumably be foreclosed or ineffective.

But because elections themselves formally delimit mass political action, where the state lacks the capacity to forcibly eliminate dissent and disobedience the potential for popular influence through informal means might well be greater than the possibilities stemming from voting. In this type of case, elections may formally delimit popular influence that the state could not otherwise forcibly contain.

Some empirical support for this view can be obtained if we reexamine the patterns of national welfare expenditures analyzed earlier. Welfare spending in electorally rigged and "irregular" nations appeared to vary inversely with the size of national internal security forces, while those in the electorally competitive nations did not. As I noted, however, despite these differences in the correlates of welfare spending, the actual proportions of GNP spent on welfare in the three groups of nations overlapped. As a number of other studies have also suggested, dictatorships and democracies do not necessarily differ in their average expenditures on social welfare programs.[49]

If we compare the three classes of nations while taking account of the propensity of welfare spending in the electorally rigged and irregular groups to vary with the size of national internal security establishments, a striking pattern begins to emerge. Table 6–5 indicates that, on the average, the proportion of GNP spent on health and education by the electorally competitive nations is greater than that spent by the authoritarian regimes with relatively large internal security forces. But at the same time, average social welfare expenditures by the democracies are generally smaller than those of the electorally rigged and irregular regimes whose internal security establishments rank in the smallest 20 percent.

Welfare spending certainly cannot be taken to be a fully satisfactory measure of popular influence. Nevertheless, to the extent that welfare spending offers at least some indication of governments' responsiveness to their citizens' needs, these findings provide a measure of empirical support for my argument. Welfare spending by the democracies is, on the average, greater than spending by the authoritarian regimes that rank relatively high in their capacity to forcibly suppress dissent and opposition. Yet those authoritarian governments with a more limited capacity to forcibly compel obedience appear to exhibit, on the basis of one indicator at least, a responsiveness to their citizens' needs that is greater than or equal to that of the electorally competitive nations. It would, of course, be inappropriate to conclude solely on the basis of this evidence that popular influence in electorally competitive nations is definitely less than that exhibited by the weaker authoritarian states. Yet the pattern of findings is quite consistent with the argument that elections can delimit mass influence in political life. When the state, for one or another reason, lacks the ability to compel obedience and suppress opposition, the potential for mass in-

TABLE 6–5

Average Social Welfare Expenditures in Dictatorships and Democracies

	Mean % of National GNP Spent on	
	Education	Health
Electorally rigged nations with relatively *large* internal military forces ($N = 18$)	3.5	2.2
Electorally irregular nations with relatively *large* internal military forces ($N = 21$)	3.1	1.7
Electorally competitive nations ($N = 27$)	3.8	2.1
Electorally rigged nations with relatively *small* internal military forces ($N = 5$)	3.7	3.2
Electorally irregular nations with relatively *small* internal military forces ($N = 5$)	4.5	2.2

NOTE: Reprinted, by permission of the publisher, from Benjamin Ginsberg, *The Consequences of Consent* (New York: Random House, 1982), 106.

fluence through informal mechanisms may be greater than that which would result from voting.

A concrete illustration of the limited potential of elections compared with more spontaneous modes of mass political action can be drawn from recent American history. The expansion of black voting opportunities during the 1960s is sometimes thought to have helped bring about important improvements in the lives of black Americans. It is true that the economic and material well-being of blacks in the United States improved somewhat during the 1960s. It is certainly the case that a variety of pieces of federal legislation, such as the Economic Opportunity Act of 1964 and the equal employment opportunity provisions of the 1964 Civil Rights Act, seemed to promise them

significant economic benefits. Nevertheless, such federal programs and whatever benefits they produced should probably be
seen primarily as responses to violent or disorderly modes of
political action on the part of blacks—sit-ins, demonstrations,
and riots—rather than as effects of black participation at the
polls.

Figure 6–2 reports, over time, black voter registration in the
southern states, the number of black elected officials in the
United States, the number of instances per year of black protest
activity, black family income, and the number of federal statutes enacted for the benefit of blacks between 1955 and 1977.[50]
During the 1960s black voter registration primarily in the South
increased dramatically; and at the same time the incidence of
more disruptive and violent forms of political action by blacks
also increased sharply. Coincident with these increases in both
formal and informal modes of political activity, blacks scored

FIGURE 6–2

Voting, Protest, and Mass Influence in Politics: The Case of Civil Rights

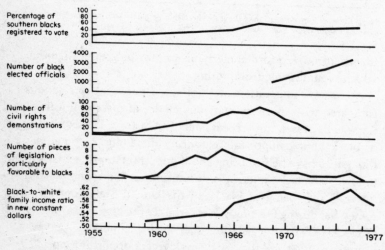

NOTE: Reprinted, by permission of the publisher, from Benjamin Ginsberg, *The Consequences of Consent* (New York: Random House, 1982), 103.

substantial economic gains and legislative successes. After the 1960s, however, black involvement in riots, demonstrations, and the like abated. Although blacks continued to vote in relatively large numbers and began to elect a fairly large number of public officials, their legislative success dwindled and their relative economic position began to deteriorate. As voting came to supplant more violent and disorderly modes of political action, federal policy began to shift in the direction of "benign neglect." Though the American government may have possessed the military and police capacity to suppress black protest during the 1960s, the costs would certainly have been enormous. And fortunately the government had neither the ability nor the will to fully employ the force ostensibly at its disposal. But the right to vote may, in effect, have helped to delimit what the state could not forcibly contain.

Neither the experience of American blacks over the past two decades nor the contrast between welfare expenditures in democracies and weak dictatorships means that citizens can exert no influence through democratic electoral processes. Surely they can. Moreover, it may well be that influence through informal modes of political action cannot be maintained for long. Eventually, perhaps, spontaneous and privately organized forms of action and opposition give way to a political quiescence that permits those in power to rule without interference. Yet spontaneous forms of political activity can, under some circumstances, be more effective modes of influence for ordinary citizens than voting. And as we saw in chapter 2, over time the availability of suffrage reduces the threat of just these sorts of action.

Chapter 7

A Window Closes

HOWEVER PROBLEMATIC it may be, it cannot be assumed that even the present level of subservience to mass opinion manifested by western regimes will endure. As I observed at the outset, the chief reason that western regimes became responsive to mass opinion during the eighteenth and nineteenth centuries was the fragility of state power at that time. Rulers sought to link themselves with public opinion because they lacked the means otherwise to curb disorder, collect taxes, and maintain adequate military power. Where ruling groups did possess the capacity to quell unrest, raise revenues, and bring their foreign and domestic foes to heel without having to rely on popular cooperation, they manifested no particular interest in the "will of the people." Thus, as we saw, in the nations of southern Europe—Italy, Spain, and Portugal—the bourgeoisie and gentry were able to come to terms with one another and fashion state instruments through which to coerce their working-class and peasant opponents, collect taxes, and so on. As a result, the rulers of these nations felt no compulsion to follow the liberal example of their less secure colleagues to the north. In a similar vein, ruling elites in those regions of the world that industrialized after the West were generally able to withstand political challenges without seeking popular cooperation by relying instead on the resources of the corporations, banking combines, or state agencies that have often had a dominant place in the economies of late industrializers.

In an important sense, the eighteenth and nineteenth centuries in the West represented a "window of opportunity" for mass opinion. During that particular time, in that particular place, and in very few others since, a conjunction of political and social circumstances compelled ruling strata to commit themselves to a measure of subservience to public opinion to shore up their power.

Does Government Still Depend Upon Opinion?

To the extent that they think about such matters at all, westerners tend to assume that this commitment on the part of eighteenth- and nineteenth-century rulers forever binds their successors, that is, that western regimes are permanently indentured to the service of public opinion. It is true that the institutional linkages—elections, representative bodies, and so on—between government and opinion developed during those centuries survived and indeed have flourished for nearly two hundred years. But while these linkages have been rather conspicuous successes, what has generally gone unnoticed is that the underlying conditions—the window of opportunity—that produced these institutions have, in many respects, closed behind them.

Unlike their predecessors, many contemporary western states do have sufficiently powerful administrative, military, and police agencies that they now could curb disorder, collect taxes, and keep their foes in check without necessarily depending on favorable public opinion. For example, contemporary western states have developed new forms of taxation that rely on sophisticated administrative machines like the value-added tax (VAT) that can generate enormous revenues in an unobtrusive manner.[1] Taxes like the VAT avoid the sort of direct confrontation between taxpayer and tax collector that is most likely to engender violent taxpayer resistance. At the same time, the VAT's mode of collection makes tax evasion extremely difficult. Similarly, contemporary western states have developed reasonably effective internal security mechanisms and procedures. In place of untrained and loosely organized amateur forces like nineteenth-century Britain's special constables, twentieth-century regimes generally have at their disposal rather well-disciplined police and riot control forces equipped with a variety of crowd control weapons and trained in effective means of curbing civil disorder.[2] The construction of such forces by the Polish government in recent years, for example, allowed it to deal remarkably effectively with enormous numbers of hostile demonstrators and, as a result, to stop worrying so much about the vagaries of public opinion. Finally, unlike their nineteenth-century predecessors, contemporary western governments can build and maintain powerful military forces without having to rely so heavily on popular support. Modern governments have combined technology and new modes of finance to construct enormous professional armies and so at least partially free themselves from a reliance on citizen-soldier armies of conscripts.[3] Thus, were it not for the persistence of their nineteenth-century democratic institutions, contemporary western governments might not be so dependent on the popular mood.

The growth of governmental powers and capabilities in the twentieth century has, in a fundamental sense, made these democratic institutions quasi-vestigial organs. The functions they were invented to perform are no longer as vital to the state as they were at one time. Does this mean that they will be removed or replaced? Not necessarily, certainly not all at once. But it is significant that interest in and support for judicial and bureaucratic as opposed to electoral and legislative solutions to domestic and foreign problems have grown in important segments of the western political class in recent years. Legislative power has declined relative to that of bureaucracies in most western nations in recent decades.[4] And, of course, the influence and coherence of political parties, the essential institutional foundations of a vital electoral politics, have also declined throughout the West in the twentieth century.[5] Political form does not necessarily follow political function, but to the extent that institutions of popular consultation cease to serve the interests of political elites, it is by no means preposterous to wonder just how much longer those elites will be willing to do much more than make a show of subservience to public opinion.

Government Over Opinion

Even if favorable popular attitudes are sometimes useful, the administrative capabilities and power of the modern state also extends into the realm of opinion. In the nineteenth century elites feared public opinion and sought to change its character but lacked the tools and capacity to do much to influence opinion in the short run. Indeed, rulers had little ability even to assess or analyze changing currents of popular thought. As Davison observed, "rulers looked upon public opinion with something akin to terror." Eighteenth- and nineteenth-century political elites often would have only the vaguest understanding of popular attitudes before "the government, the church hierarchy, and the aristocracy suddenly saw the roof blown off."[6] Before the twentieth century the two most important tools used by governments to manage opinion in the short term were secrecy and censorship. Rulers might occasionally attempt to sway popular feelings but the central thrust of official action was to block access to information about governmental plans and operations and to seek, through secrecy, to inhibit the development of potentially hostile opinion on as many matters as possible.

In the United States, secrecy became part of the official policy of the executive branch as early as 1792 when President Washington sought to prevent a congressional inquiry into a military expedition conducted by General Arthur St. Clair. Later, citing the importance of secrecy, Washington declined to provide the House with information concerning a proposed treaty with Great Britain. Subsequent administrations also asserted the need for secrecy in the activities of the executive branch and refused congressional requests for information. Attempts by private individuals to obtain information about governmental activities are often fruitless. Even the enactment of "freedom of information" legislation in recent years has by no means opened the process of government to full public scrutiny.[7]

All contemporary governments, of course, continue to employ some measure of censorship and secrecy to guard against real or imagined popular antagonism. But during the nineteenth and twentieth centuries national policies toward public opinion underwent an important change. Using polling, media, and public relations techniques, modern states have learned a good deal about the manipulation and management of mass opinion. Indeed, in the modern era the censor has been supplanted—or at least joined—by the public relations officer as the governmental functionary most responsible for dealing with public opinion.

In the United States, of course, efforts have been made by every administration since the nation's founding to influence public sentiment. But the management of opinion did not become a routine and formal official function until World War I. In some respects, this war was the point of transition from government-as-censor to government-as-manager of popular opinion in the United States. On one hand, the Wilson administration created a censorship board, enacted sedition and espionage legislation, and attempted to suppress groups that opposed the war, like the International Workers of the World (IWW) and the Socialist party. Eugene Debs, it might be recalled, was arrested and convicted of having violated the Espionage Law and was sentenced to ten years in prison, for delivering a speech that defended the IWW.[8]

At the same time, however, World War I was the first modern industrial war requiring a total mobilization of popular effort on the homefront for military production. The war effort required the government to convince the civilian population to bear the costs and make the sacrifices needed to achieve industrial and agricultural as well as battlefield success. The chief mechanism for eliciting the support of public opinion was the Committee on Public Information (CPI), chaired by journalist and publicist George Creel. The CPI organized a massive public relations and news management program aimed at promoting popular enthusiasm for the war effort. This program included the dissemination of favorable news; the publication of patriotic pamphlets, films, photos, cartoons, bulletins, and periodicals; and the organization of "war expositions" and speakers' tours. Special labor programs were aimed at maintaining the loyalty and productivity of the work force. Much of the CPI's staff was drawn from the major advertising agencies. According to Creel, the work of the committee "was distinctly in the nature of an advertising campaign . . . our object was to sell the war."[9]

The CPI's program was a temporary wartime effort. Within several months of the armistice, much of the government's opinion management apparatus was disbanded. The work of the CPI, however, was a harbinger of the permanent expansion of governmental opinion management that began with the New

Deal and has persisted to the present. The enlargement of the scope of governmental activity that began during the Roosevelt administration was accompanied by an explosion of official public relations efforts. Each new department, agency, bureau, office, or committee quickly established a public relations arm to persuade the citizenry to cooperate with its programs and support its objectives. The link between the expansion of governmental activity and the increased role of opinion management during the New Deal was put into very clear focus by Chester Bowles. Early in his long career of public service, Bowles served as Director of the Office of Price Administration (OPA). Under Bowles's leadership, the OPA developed an extensive public information program whose large budget eventually drew congressional criticism. Bowles's defense of the program is recalled in his memoirs:

At one point Congress threatened to cut our information budget. I testified that if they deprived us of the means of explaining our program to the people, our requirements for investigators and inspectors to enforce our regulations would be greatly increased. With a $5 million annual budget for information, I said I could keep the American people reasonably informed about our regulations and their own obligations and rights as citizens. But if Congress cut this $5 million, I would have no alternative but to make a public request for $15 million to hire law enforcement inspectors to prosecute the many people who, often through their own ignorance and lack of information, had acted illegally. If Congress preferred this, it was their prerogative. I myself preferred persuasion to police-state tactics.[10]

The Politics of the Market

The government's interest in "explaining programs to the people" has, of course, increased substantially since the New Deal. Many departments and agencies engage in opinion management efforts that dwarf the OPA's $5 million program. One recent estimate suggests that the annual salaries of federal public information and public relations personnel totaled almost $100 million. In 1976 the federal government spent over $30 million on television and motion picture products. In 1975 federal agencies paid almost $150 million to private agencies for advertising campaigns. In recent years the Defense Department's Defense Information School has graduated more than two thousand "public information specialists" each year. Every American citizen is exposed to some aspect of the federal government's information program—the news releases, films, public service spots, traveling exhibits, tours, open houses, commercial television programs and motion pictures produced with the cooperation of a federal agency, or one of the many other public relations efforts that have become such a routine part of the process of government in the twentieth century.[11]

At the same time, many of the forces in American society that traditionally defended the marketplace of ideas are succumbing to the temptation to make direct use of the powerful resources of the state to further their ideological interests and dispense with the market mechanisms that at least allow competition among upper classes, if not between elites and other strata. In recent decades both "liberal" and "conservative" elites have sought to use their access to governmental agencies to promote their ideas. Thus during the New Deal and postwar periods, liberal intellectuals were among the chief advocates of public broadcasting and government promotion of the arts and humanities. The agencies ultimately created for this purpose, such as the National Endowment for the Humanities (NEH), supported the development and dissemination of work whose themes were consistent with the views and values of liberal intellectuals. For example, during the 1970s the NEH funded a "street theater" troupe that visited corporate and government offices to perform skits on the oppression of women office workers. Similarly, the Corporation for Public Broadcasting has generally sponsored programs that supported the social and political values held by liberal intellectuals. For example, in recent years public television has aired programs critical of the arms race, documentaries painting a sympathetic picture of the Nicaraguan revolution, programs that questioned the safety of nuclear power, and so on. But has public television ever presented programming sympathetic to school prayer, favorable to the strengthening of American military defenses, or critical of government programs that give preferential treatment to minorities? In addition, various other governmental agencies and commissions whose ostensible mission was not chiefly ideological but that had been created and staffed to promote liberal policy goals, such as the Environmental Protection Agency, the Consumer Products Safety Commission, and the Civil Rights Commission, often sponsored and disseminated academic research whose questions—and answers—tended to support liberal views, as in the case of the U.S. Civil Rights Commission's journal, *Perspectives*. [12]

Conservatives, of course, bitterly attacked these ideological initiatives as dangerous governmental intrusions into the areas of thought and opinion and, with the Reagan victory in 1980, demanded a "defunding of the Left"—the elimination of governmental support for the burgeoning liberal cultural apparatus. However, as they solidified their own power, rather than dismantle this apparatus, conservatives began to take it over and use it to promote their own views. Thus federal agencies that had once sponsored and disseminated research by liberal scholars now perform the same service for conservatives. In some cases the shift has been quite dramatic. Take, for example, the case of the U.S. Civil Rights Commission's journal. Prior to the commission's capture by the Reaganites, the journal's contents consisted almost exclusively of articles and reports promoting and defending liberal causes. For example, issues of *Perspectives* featured articles on the problems of Native Americans, housing discrimination in Boston, the "salary gap" facing working women, the desirability of a black/Hispanic political coalition, and the difficulties encountered by gay police officers. Today the same journal, renamed *New Perspectives,* is a showcase for the views of the political and social right. Recent issues, for example, contained a critique of affirmative action by philosopher Sidney Hook, attacks on women's studies as a field of scholarship, and a hostile analysis of the proposed Civil Rights Acts of 1984 and 1985, which would have reversed the Supreme Court's "Grove City" decision (narrowing protections against discrimination on the basis of gender) by Jeremy Rabkin, a prominent conservative theoretician.

What is ironic about these developments is that the power that allows the state to infringe upon and—perhaps—dispense with opinion was in large part generated by the formal relationship with mass opinion that western regimes built during the eighteenth and nineteenth centuries. This relationship with opinion gave rulers access to a larger tax base, a broader base of political support, a more sizable pool of military manpower, and so on. Because of the formal linkage between government and opinion, citizens gladly acquiesced to the expansion of state power. Before the nineteenth century, people knew that the growth of state power always came at the expense of whatever influence they might have and ultimately at the expense of their liberties. But the advent of elections and representative bodies seemed to mean that even when rulers had powerful military and administrative machines, citizens' influence was no longer necessarily reduced. Citizens' capacity to influence their rulers' conduct seemed now to be independent of rulers' military and

administrative power. The effectiveness of the new formal linkages between government and opinion, unlike the traditional
threat of riot, revolution, or insurrection, did not seem necessarily to vary with the regime's power. With the advent of these
new institutions, popular influence and rulers' power seemed
no longer to be inversely related and, instead, seemed quite
compatible.

Because of this apparent possibility for coexistence between
popular influence and governmental power, elections, representative bodies, and the like appeared to transform the relationship between rulers and the ruled. For, given these formal
means of influencing their rulers' actions—means independent
of rulers' military and administrative power—citizens apparently stood to benefit from rulers' powers rather than from their
weakness. The construction of these democratic institutions
seemed to open the possibility of citizens using rulers' power
for their own benefit rather than simply benefiting from rulers'
inability to muster sufficient power to compel citizens to obey
their commands. It is largely because of this characteristic of
democratic institutions that the enormous expansion of the
state's power in the twentieth century did not seem entirely to
foreclose the possibility of popular influence over governmental
conduct. Citizens became overwhelmingly receptive to governmental intervention in economy and society because their rulers
seemed so responsive to opinion.

Freedom and Government

At one time westerners were concerned with freedom and fear-
ful of the state. But in the latter half of the twentieth century
they have become so enamored of government that they have,

for the most part, ceased even to perceive freedom and government as antipodes. Because, after all, they have responsive governments, citizens of the democracies believe that they can use the state's power without surrendering their liberties. Indeed, responsive government has actually come to be seen as a protector or guarantor of freedom. British political scientist Harold Laski, for example, once declared that "without democracy there cannot be liberty."[13] Philosopher H. B. Mayo, anticipating a point of view recently endorsed by the U.S. Supreme Court, avers that "democracy has a marked tendency to extend the freedoms from the political to other spheres."[14] Once freedom was understood as meaning the absence of a powerful government. Today some observers at least appear to believe that freedom is some sort of gift from government.

As I have argued elsewhere, governmental responsiveness in the form of democratic institutions emerged in free societies—societies in which citizens possessed the resources and capacities to resist state coercion.[15] Freedom was not a gift from the kindly and responsive state. Rather governments were compelled to be kindly and responsive where citizens were already free and had the capacity—often the armed capacity—to remain so. Over time, institutionalized responsiveness to opinion on the part of the state—the state's apparent subservience to opinion—induces citizens to succumb to the notion that they can have both the blessings of freedom and the benefits of government. Even most self-proclaimed conservatives have followed the well-worn path of Winston Smith and learned to love Big Brother. Partly as a result of this, in today's United States agencies of the state have considerable control over who may enter occupations, what may be eaten, what may be seen and heard over the airwaves, what forms of education are socially desirable, what types of philanthropy serves the public interest, what sorts of business practices are acceptable, what is and is not a religion as well as citizens' marital plans, vacation plans, child-rearing practices, and medical care. Is government still subservient to public opinion? Perhaps. Perhaps elections, referenda, parliaments, and the like mean that citizens will continue to control the state. But more and more the process of control is of the sort that de Tocqueville foresaw two centuries ago—interludes in which citizens proudly and cheerfully wave their own chains.

NOTES

Preface

1. Grateful acknowledgment is made to the following sources: The University of Texas Press (for Benjamin Ginsberg and Robert Weissberg, "Elections and the Mobilization of Popular Support," *American Journal of Political Science* 22 [February 1978], reprinted by permission, copyright 1978 by The University of Texas Press); M. E. Sharpe, Inc. (for Benjamin Ginsberg, "Money and Power: The New Political Economy of American Elections," in *The Political Economy: Readings in the Politics and Economics of American Public Economy*, edited by Tom Ferguson and Joel Rogers [Armonk, N.Y.: M. E. Sharpe, 1984], reprinted by permission of the publisher); and Random House, Inc. (for Benjamin Ginsberg, *The Consequences of Consent: Elections, Citizen Control, and Popular Acquiescence* [New York: Random House, 1982], reprinted by permission, copyright 1982 by Random House, Inc.).

Chapter 1

1. Benjamin Page and Robert Y. Shapiro, "Effects of Public Opinion on Policy," *American Political Science Review* 77 (March 1983): 175–190.
2. Harold Lasswell, *Democracy Through Public Opinion* (Menasha, Wisc.: Banta, 1941), 15.
3. Norman Luttbeg, ed., *Public Opinion and Public Policy* (Homewood, Ill.: Dorsey Press, 1974), 1.
4. Philip Selznick, *T.V.A. and the Grass Roots: A Study in the Sociology of Formal Organization* (Berkeley: University of California Press, 1949), 13.
5. James Bryce, *The American Commonwealth*, vol. 2 (New York: Macmillan, 1910), 259.
6. Nicholas Abercrombie and Bryan S. Turner, "The Dominant Ideology Thesis," *British Journal of Sociology* 29 (June 1978): 149–170.
7. Ibid., 159.
8. Ibid. See also Leon Trotsky, *The History of the Russian Revolution* (London: Sphere Books, 1965), esp. chaps. 1–6.
9. Eugen Weber, *Peasants Into Frenchmen* (Stanford, Calif.: Stanford University Press, 1976), chap. 5.
10. See, for example, Charles Tilly, "Reflections on the History of European

State-Making," in *The Formation of National States in Western Europe,* ed. Charles Tilly (Princeton, N.J.: Princeton University Press, 1975), 3–83.

11. Theda Skocpol, *States and Social Revolutions* (New York: Cambridge University Press, 1979).

12. E. E. Schattschneider, *The Semi-Sovereign People* (New York: Holt, Rinehart and Winston, 1960), 100.

13. Benjamin Ginsberg, *The Consequences of Consent* (New York: Random House, 1982).

14. Frances Fox Piven and Richard A. Cloward, *Poor People's Movements: Why They Succeed, How They Fail* (New York: Random House, 1979).

15. Rudolph Braun, "Taxation, Sociopolitical Structure and State-building: Great Britain and Brandenburg-Prussia," in Tilly, *Formation of National States,* 243–327.

16. Edwin R. A. Seligman, *The Income Tax* (New York: Macmillan, 1911), part 1.

17. Seymour Martin Lipset, "Radicalism or Reformism: The Sources of Working-class Politics," *American Political Science Review* 77 (March 1983): 1–18.

18. Martin Shefter, "Political Parties, Political Mobilization, and Political Demobilization," in *The Political Economy,* ed. Thomas Ferguson and Joel Rogers (Armonk, N.Y.: M. E. Sharpe, 1984), 140–148.

19. Lipset, "Radicalism or Reformism."

20. Stein Rokkan, "Norway: Numerical Democracy and Corporate Pluralism," in *Political Oppositions in Western Democracies,* ed. Robert A. Dahl (New Haven: Yale University Press, 1966), 70–115.

21. Eric J. Hobsbawn, *Primitive Rebels* (New York: Norton, 1965).

22. Karl Polanyi, *The Great Transformation* (Boston: Beacon, 1957).

23. Louis Chevalier, *Laboring Classes and Dangerous Classes in Paris During the First Half of the 19th Century* (Princeton, N.J.: Princeton University Press, 1981).

24. E. P. Thompson, *The Making of the English Working Class* (New York: Random House, 1966).

25. John Cannon, *Parliamentary Reform 1640–1832* (Cambridge, England: Cambridge University Press, 1973), 216.

26. Samuel Finer, "State and Nation-Building in Europe: The Role of the Military," in Tilly, *Formation of National States,* 84–163.

27. Ibid.

28. Max Farrand, ed., *The Records of the Federal Convention of 1787,* vol. 1 (New Haven: Yale University Press, 1966).

29. F. C. Mather, *Public Order in the Age of the Chartists* (Manchester: Manchester University Press, 1959).

30. Allan Silver, "The Demand for Order in Civil Society," in *The Police,* ed. David Bordua (New York: Wiley, 1967), 1–24.

31. Seligman, *Income Tax,* 36.

32. Finer, "State and Nation-Building in Europe."

33. Ginsberg, *Consequences of Consent,* chap. 7.

34. Shefter, "Political Parties."

35. Data were drawn from Arthur S. Banks, *Cross-Polity Time Series Data* (Cambridge, Mass.: MIT Press, 1971).

36. Walter Dean Burnham, "The Changing Shape of the American Political Universe," *American Political Science Review* 59 (March 1965): 7–28.

37. Samuel Huntington, "The United States," in *The Crisis of Democracy,* ed.

Michel J. Crozier, Samuel Huntington, and Joji Watanuki (New York: New York University Press, 1975), chap. 3.

Chapter 2

1. Harold Silver, *The Concept of Popular Education* (London: MacGibbon and Kee, 1965). See also Cyril Norwood, *The English Tradition of Education* (London: John Murray, 1929), and David V. Glass, "Education," in *Law and Opinion in England in the 20th Century,* ed. Morris Ginsberg (London: Stevens and Sons, 1959), 319–346.

2. Glass, "Education," 325.

3. Robert Ulich, *The Education of Nations* (Cambridge, Mass.: Harvard University Press, 1967), 110.

4. Silver, *Concept of Popular Education,* 208.

5. Ibid., 103.

6. Thomas Alexander, *The Prussian Elementary Schools* (New York: Macmillan, 1918).

7. Richard W. Gilder, "The Kindergarten: An Uplifting Social Influence in the Home and the District," *Journal of Proceedings and Addresses of the National Education Association* (1903): 390. For more general discussions of the role of mass education in the United States, see Michael B. Katz, *The Irony of Early School Reform* (Cambridge, Mass.: Harvard University Press, 1968), and Marvin Lazerson, *Origins of the Urban School* (Cambridge, Mass.: Harvard University Press, 1971).

8. Alexander, *Prussian Elementary Schools.*

9. P. W. Musgrave, *The Sociology of Education* (London: Methuen, 1965).

10. For a discussion of the actual extent of "middle-class delinquency," see Don C. Gibbons, *Delinquent Behavior* (Englewood Cliffs, N.J.: Prentice-Hall, 1970). See also Richard A. Cloward and Lloyd E. Ohlin, *Delinquency and Opportunity* (New York: The Free Press, 1960).

11. See Charles Honart, "Mobilizing Citizen Support: Elections as Legitimizing Agents." Bachelor's honors thesis, Department of Government, Cornell University, 1976.

12. See, for example, Joan Huber and William H. Form, *Income and Ideology* (New York: The Free Press, 1973).

13. Joel H. Wiener, *The War of the Unstamped* (Ithaca, N.Y.: Cornell University Press, 1969). Also Tom Burns, "The Organization of Public Opinion," in *Mass Communication and Society,* ed. James Curran (Beverly Hills, Calif.: Sage, 1979).

14. Charles Tilly, "Reflections on the History of European State-Making," in *The Formation of National States in Western Europe,* ed. Charles Tilly (Princeton, N.J.: Princeton University Press, 1975), 3–83.

15. "President Reagan's Inaugural Address," *New York Times,* 21 January 1981, p. B1.

16. Ibid.

17. Benjamin Ginsberg, *The Consequences of Consent* (New York: Random House, 1982), 239.

18. For a fascinating discussion, see Jack Citrin, "Do People Want Something for Nothing: Public Opinion on Taxes and Government Spending," *Na-*

tional Tax Journal 32 (June 1979, Supplement): 112–129. See also Paul Peretz, "There Was No Tax Revolt," paper presented at the Annual Meeting of the American Political Science Association, Washington, D.C., August 29–September 1, 1980.

19.   Poll conducted for the *New York Times.* Data copyright Benjamin Ginsberg, 1983. Some results of the survey were reported in Adam Clymer, "The Nation's Mood," *New York Times Sunday Magazine,* 11 December 1983, p. 47.

20.   Ibid.

21.   Ginsberg, *Consequences of Consent.*

22.   Sidney Verba and Norman Nie, *Participation in America* (New York: Harper & Row, 1972).

23.   For cost estimates see Richard Smolka, *The Costs of Administering American Elections* (New York: National Municipal League, 1973).

24.   Civic education is discussed by Charles Merriam, *The Making of Citizens* (Chicago: University of Chicago Press, 1931). See also Fred Greenstein, *Children and Politics* (New Haven, Conn.: Yale University Press, 1969); Robert D. Hess and Judith Torney, *The Development of Political Attitudes in Children* (Chicago: Aldine, 1967); and Robert Weissberg, *Political Learning, Political Choice and Democratic Citizenship* (Englewood Cliffs, N.J.: Prentice-Hall, 1974).

25.   University of the State of New York, State Education Department, Bureau of Elementary Curriculum Development, *Social Studies—Grade 1, A Teaching System* (Albany, N.Y., 1971), 32.

26.   Dean Jaros, *Socialization to Politics* (New York: Praeger, 1973).

27.   Lester Milbraith and M. L. Goel, *Political Participation* (Chicago: Rand McNally, 1977), 98.

28.   George Rude, *Paris and London in the 18th Century* (New York: Viking Press, 1970), 163.

29.   Charles L. Taylor and Michael C. Hudson, *World Handbook of Political and Social Indicators,* 2nd ed. (New Haven, Conn.: Yale University Press, 1972).

30.   A similar implication emerges from Adam Prezworski, "Institutionalization of Voting Patterns," *American Political Science Review* 69 (March 1975): 49–67.

31.   The effects of changes in economic conditions on voting behavior is discussed in Gerald Kramer, "Short-Term Fluctuations in U.S. Voting Behavior, 1896–1964," *American Political Science Review* 65 (March 1971): 131–143; see also Edward R. Tufte, *Political Control of the Economy* (Princeton, N.J.: Princeton University Press, 1978).

32.   Daniel Mazmanian, *Third Parties in Presidential Elections* (Washington, D.C.: The Brookings Institution, 1974). See also M. S. Stedman and S. W. Stedman, *Discontent at the Polls* (New York: Columbia University Press, 1950).

Chapter 3

1.   Robert Nisbett, "Public Opinion versus Popular Opinion," *The Public Interest* (Fall 1975): 166–192.

2.   See Walter C. Langer, *The Mind of Adolph Hitler* (New York: Basic Books, 1972); and Ivone Kirkpatrick, *Mussolini, A Study in Power* (New York: Hawthorn, 1964).

3.   For example, Harwood Childs, one of the most prominent of the early

academic analysts of public opinion, argued that "[the polls] bring public opinion into the open and thereby make governmental bodies more responsive to
that opinion." Harwood Childs, *Public Opinion* (Princeton, N.J.: D. Van Nostrand, 1965), 84. Similarly, George Gallup once averred that the quality of
representative government could be substantially improved if representatives
had "an accurate measure of the wishes, aspirations and needs of different
groups within the general public." George Gallup, *The Pulse of Democracy* (New
York: Simon and Schuster, 1940), 266.

4.   Measurement of human attitudes and behavior can often be "intrusive,"
changing rather than simply recording the phenomena in question. The standard discussion of the problem is Eugene Webb et al., *Unobtrusive Measures:
Nonreactive Research in the Social Sciences* (Chicago: Rand McNally, 1966). Though
the problem of intrusive measurement may be most acute in the social sciences,
it is hardly unknown in the biological and physical sciences. The problem of
"uncertainty" in the field of quantum mechanics, to take an obvious example,
derives from the fact that measurement of an electron's motion affects the path
the electron will take. The path of an electron is actually, as Lev Landau puts
it, "a product of its interaction" with a measuring instrument. L. D. Landau and
E. M. Lifshitz, *Quantum Mechanics,* trans. J. B. Sykes and J. S. Bell (Reading,
Mass.: Addison Wesley, 1958), 3.

5.   Chester F. Barnard, "Public Opinion in a Democracy" (Herbert L. Baker
Foundation, Princeton University, Princeton, N.J., 1939, pamphlet), p. 13.

6.   No doubt, federal regulatory legislation like the "truth in polling" bill
recently proposed to the U.S. House of Representatives as a means of curbing
polling fraud and bias would, if enacted, function as a federal endorsement or
guarantee of polling accuracy and thus further strengthen the polls' dominance
over other sources of information about public opinion. For a discussion of
truth in polling legislation see Michael Wheeler, *Lies, Damn Lies and Statistics* (New
York: Liveright, 1976), chap. 12.

7.   Robert Weissberg, *Public Opinion and Popular Government* (Englewood Cliffs,
N.J.: Prentice-Hall, 1976), 12–16.

8.   Robert E. Lane and David O. Sears, *Public Opinion* (Englewood Cliffs, N.J.:
Prentice-Hall, 1964), 105. See also Hadley Cantril, "The Intensity of an Attitude," *Journal of Abnormal and Social Psychology* 41 (1946): 129–135.

9.   Aage R. Clausen, Philip E. Converse, and Warren E. Miller, "Electoral
Myth and Reality: The 1964 Election," *American Political Science Review* 59 (June
1965): 321–332.

10.   For example, at the height of the Vietnam war in 1972, despite the fact
that public attitudes on American involvement were quite polarized, over 11
percent of those whose opinions were expressed only through the polls still
indicated that they "didn't know" whether the United States had been right to
become involved in Vietnam. Among individuals who engaged in some form
of political activity during that period, by contrast, only 5 percent remained
undecided about the question of American involvement. During the same year,
one in which the United States was beset by a number of serious crises, just
60 percent of those individuals whose opinions were expressed only through
the polls could identify two or more national problems. Seven percent of these
individuals could name none. Among those, on the other hand, who reported
engaging in some form of political activity, almost 90 percent could name two
or more national problems and only 2 percent were unable to name any. Source

of data: Center for Political Studies, Institute for Social Research, University of Michigan, 1972. Data were made available through the Inter-University Consortium for Political and Social Research.

11.   Walter Wilcox, "The Congressional Poll and Non-Poll," in *Political Opinion and Electoral Behavior,* ed. Edward C. Dreyer and Walter A. Rosenbaum (Belmont, Calif.: Wadsworth, 1966), 394.

12.   Richard M. Scammon and Ben Wattenberg, *The Real Majority* (New York: Coward-McCann, 1970).

13.   Wheeler, *Lies, Damn Lies and Statistics,* chap. 8.

14.   Ibid., chap. 7. See also Louis Harris, *The Anguish of Change* (New York: Norton, 1973), chap. 3.

15.   The percentage of Americans who believed that entry into the Vietnam war had been a mistake did not surpass the proportion who did not regret U.S. involvement until late in 1967. See John E. Meuller, "Trends in Popular Support for the Wars in Korea and Viet Nam," *American Political Science Review* 65 (1971): 363–364.

16.   Allan Silver, "The Demand for Order in Civil Society," in *The Police,* ed. David Bordua (New York: Wiley, 1967), 17–18.

17.   Bogdan Osolnik, "Socialist Public Opinion," *Socialist Thought and Practice* 20 (October 1955): 120.

18.   Walter D. Conner and Zvi Y. Gitelman, *Public Opinion in European Socialist Systems* (New York: Praeger, 1977), 77.

19.   Geoffrey Smith, "Can Marxism Stand Prosperity?" *Forbes*, 1 July, 1977, 41–46.

20.   Arthur L. Smith, Jr., "Life in Wartime Germany: Colonel Ohlendorff's Opinion Service," *Public Opinion Quarterly* 36 (Spring 1972): 1–7.

21.   Bernard C. Hennessey, *Public Opinion* (North Scituate, Mass.: Duxbury Press, 1975), 60.

22.   James L. McCamy, *Government Publicity* (Chicago: University of Chicago Press, 1939), chap. 5. See also Henry A. Wallace and James L. McCamy, "Straw Polls and Public Administration," *Public Opinion Quarterly* 4 (June 1940): 221–223.

23.   Jeffrey L. Pressman and Aaron Wildavsky, *Implementation,* 2nd ed. (Berkeley: University of California Press, 1979), 31.

24.   Wheeler, *Lies, Damn Lies and Statistics,* 133. Also Herbert I. Schiller, *The Mind Managers* (Boston: Beacon, 1973), 108–110.

25.   Hadley Cantril, *The Human Dimension* (New Brunswick, N.J.: Rutgers University Press, 1967), chap. 1.

26.   Ibid., chap. 15–18.

27.   Conner and Gitelman, *Public Opinion,* chap. 4.

28.   *Report of the National Advisory Commission on Civil Disorders* (New York: Bantam, 1968), esp. chap. 17. For an analysis, see Robert M. Fogelson, *Violence as Protest* (New York: Doubleday, 1971), esp. chap. 7.

29.   Richard M. Scammon and Ben J. Wattenberg, *The Real Majority* (New York: Coward-McCann, 1970), 49. The polls might also point to discrepancies between the views of those claiming to speak for "old people" and their constituents. Recently, for example, Representative Claude Pepper of Florida, the Democratic Chair of the House Select Committee on Aging, accused the Republican National Committee of attempting to "pervert and prostitute" a forthcoming White House Conference on Aging by conducting a poll of the political views of approximately nine hundred of the delegates. Representative Pepper,

who, of course, frequently claims to speak for the views and interests of older Americans, had planned to use the occasion of the conference to attack the Reagan administration's possible plans for cutbacks in the social security program. Presumably Pepper feared that the Republican poll might be designed to suggest that he did not fully reflect the views of those for whom he claimed to speak. See Warren Weaver, Jr., "G.O.P. Draws Fire for Polling Delegates for Forum on Aging," *New York Times,* 23 October 1981, p. B6.

30. Harris, *Anguish of Change,* chap. 9.

31. Charles W. Roll, Jr. and Albert H. Cantril, *Polls* (New York: Basic Books, 1972), 153.

32. Gerald W. McFarland, *Mugwumps, Morals and Politics 1884–1920* (Amherst: University of Massachusetts Press, 1975), 92.

33. Harold Gosnell, *Machine Politics: Chicago Model* (Chicago: University of Chicago Press, 1968 rev. ed.), 70.

34. Maurice Duverger, *Political Parties* (New York: Wiley, 1954), 426.

35. Gosnell, *Machine Politics,* 82.

36. See J. K. Javits, "How I Used a Poll in Campaigning for Congress," *Public Opinion Quarterly* 11 (Summer 1947): 220–226.

37. Richard Jensen, "American Election Analysis," in *Politics and the Social Sciences,* ed. Seymour Martin Lipset (New York: Oxford University Press, 1969), 229.

38. Ibid., 229–230.

39. For a discussion of newspaper polls see Claude Robinson, *Straw Votes* (New York: Columbia University Press, 1932), chap. 4.

40. Jensen, "American Election Analysis," 238.

41. See Wheeler, *Lies, Damn Lies and Statistics,* esp. chap. 3.

42. For example, see Rich Jaroslovsky, "New-Right Cashier," *Wall Street Journal,* 6 October 1978, p. 1. Appropriately enough, according to a recent *New York Times* report, President Reagan and his advisors have relied more steadily and extensively on polling for their political information than any previous national administration. B. Drummond Ayres, Jr., "G.O.P. Keeps Tabs on Nation's Mood," *New York Times,* 16 November 1981, p. A20.

43. See Schiller, *Mind Managers,* 108–110; also Cantril, *Human Dimensions,* chaps. 14–19.

44. Calculated from Dorothy Kattleman, ed., *Facts on File Five-Year Index, 1966–1970* (New York: Facts on File, 1971).

45. Calculated from George H. Gallup, *The Gallup Poll, Public Opinion 1935–1971,* vol. 3 (New York: Random House, 1972).

46. Calculated from Kattleman, *Facts on File,* and Gallup, *Gallup Poll.*

47. W. Phillips Davison, "Public Opinion Research as Communication," *Public Opinion Quarterly* 36 (Fall 1972): 314.

48. Wheeler, *Lies, Damn Lies and Statistics,* 4.

49. David Truman, "Public Opinion Research as a Tool of Public Administration," *Public Administration Review* 5 (Winter 1945): 62–72.

50. Ibid., 66.

51. George Gallup was among the most prominent of those who believed that polling would eventually lead to "government by opinion"—a state of affairs that James Bryce had once foreseen as the final evolutionary state of American democracy. Gallup, *Pulse of Democracy,* chap. 9. See also James Bryce, *The American Commonwealth,* vol. 2 (London: Macmillan, 1888), 220.

Chapter 4

1. Eugen Weber, *Peasants into Frenchmen* (Stanford, Calif.: Stanford University Press, 1976).

2. Ibid., esp. chap. 2.

3. Ibid., esp. chap. 1.

4. Louis Chevalier, *Laboring Classes and Dangerous Classes in Paris During the First Half of the 19th Century* (Princeton, N.J.: Princeton University Press, 1981).

5. Weber, *Peasants*, part 3.

6. See Ellwood P. Cubberley, *Changing Conceptions of Education*, excerpted in Sol Cohen, *Education in the United States: A Documentary History*, vol. 4 (New York: Random House, 1974), section 17.

7. Richard Hoggart, *The Uses of Literacy* (Oxford, England: Oxford University Press, 1970).

8. Weber, *Peasants*, part 3. See also P. W. Musgrave, *The Sociology of Education* (London: Methuen, 1965).

9. See Armand Mattelart, *Multinational Corporations and the Control of Culture* (Sussex, England: Harvester Press, 1979); also Jeremy Tunstall, *The Media are American* (New York: Columbia University Press, 1977); and Cees J. Hamelink, *Cultural Autonomy in Global Communications* (New York: Longman, 1983).

10. Joel Wiener, *War of the Unstamped* (Ithaca, N.Y.: Cornell University Press, 1969).

11. See C. Herman Pritchett, *The American Constitution* (New York: McGraw-Hill, 1968).

12. The best political discussion of this change is Martin Shapiro, "The Supreme Court from Warren to Burger," in *The New American Political System*, ed. Anthony King (Washington, D.C.: American Enterprise Institute, 1979), 179–212.

13. See *New York Times*, 16 October 1984, p. 1.

14. "Wallyball: A Sport is Born," *Newsweek*, 8 July 1985, 63.

15. Malcolm W. Browne, "Dinosaur Experts Resist Meteor Extinction Idea," *New York Times*, 29 October 1985, p. C1.

16. See Gillian Peele, *Revival and Reaction: The Right in Contemporary America* (Oxford: Clarendon Press, 1985); also Connie Paige, *The Right to Lifers* (New York: Summit, 1983).

17. An interesting albeit very critical account of the nuclear freeze movement is Adam Garfinkle, *The Politics of the Nuclear Freeze* (Philadelphia: Foreign Policy Research Institute, 1984). See also Fox Butterfield, "Anatomy of the Nuclear Protest," *New York Times Magazine*, 11 July 1982, pp. 14–39.

18. See Union of Concerned Scientists, *The Fallacy of Star Wars* (New York: Vintage, 1984).

19. Richard Ned Lebow, "Strategic Stupidity: The Quest for Ballistic Missile Defense," *Journal of International Affairs* 39 (Summer 1985): 57–80.

20. See the recent exchange between Nimroody and Hartung on the one hand and Nozette on the other. Rosy Nimroody and William Hartung, "Putting Industry Even Further Behind," and Stewart Nozette, "A Giant Step Forward in Technology," *New York Times*, 8 December 1985, p. C2.

21. Benjamin Ginsberg and Martin Shefter, "A Critical Realignment?" in *The Elections of 1984*, ed. Michael Nelson (Washington, D.C.: The Brookings Institute, 1985), 1–26.

22. For example, see Andrew S. McFarland, *Common Cause* (Chatham, N.J.: Chatham House, 1984); also Jeffrey M. Berry, *Lobbying for the People* (Princeton, N.J.: Princeton University Press, 1977).

23. Martin Shefter, "Political Parties, Political Mobilization and Political Demobilization," in *The Political Economy,* ed. Thomas Ferguson and Joel Rogers (Armonk, N.Y.: M. E. Sharpe, 1984), 140–148.

24. For a brilliant and novel analysis of the causes of the political weakness of the American working class, see Martin Shefter, "Trade Unions and Political Machines," in *Working Class Formation,* ed. Ira Katznelson and Aristide Zolberg (Princeton, N.J.: Princeton University Press, 1986).

25. The disappearance of civil rights as a news story is evident, for example, in the absence of its mention even in analyses of press coverage of American politics. Interestingly, in a book that properly calls attention to the lack of media coverage of subpresidential political campaigns, two prominent media analysts do not even take notice of the absence of media coverage of the race issue. See Michael J. Robinson and Margaret A. Sheehan, *Over the Wire and On TV* (New York: Russell Sage, 1983). Obviously the 1984 Jackson presidential campaign put race back into the news, but this was a temporary phenomenon.

26. David Garrow, *Protest at Selma* (New Haven, Conn.: Yale University Press, 1978).

27. For a discussion of the relationship between the media and an upper-middle-class protest movement, see Todd Gitlin, *The Whole World Is Watching* (Berkeley: University of California Press, 1980).

28. The relationship between media coverage and the interests of "desirable" audience segments is discussed in Tom Burns, "The Organization of Public Opinion," in *Mass Communication and Society,* ed. James Curran (Beverly Hills, Calif.: Sage, 1979), 44–230. See also David Altheide, *Creating Reality* (Beverly Hills, Calif.: Sage, 1976).

29. See Gary Paul Gates, *Air Time* (New York: Harper & Row, 1978); also Edward Jay Epstein, *News From Nowhere* (New York: Random House, 1973).

30. For the conservative view, see Edith Efron, *The News Twisters* (Los Angeles: Nash Publishing, 1971). An interesting sequel is Edith Efron, *How CBS Tried to Kill a Book* (Los Angeles: Nash, 1972).

Chapter 5

1. This is one of Madison's major points in E. M. Earle, ed., *The Federalist* No. 51 (New York: Modern Library, n.d.), 335–340. A similar perspective is the basis of Samuel Huntington's superb analysis of congressional power, "Congressional Responses to the Twentieth Century," in *The Congress and America's Future,* ed. David Truman (Englewood Cliffs, N.J.: Prentice-Hall, 1965), 5–31.

2. James Bryce, *The American Commonwealth,* vol. 2 (New York: Macmillan, 1910), 259.

3. This is one of the major points of what has come to be called the "issue voting" literature. See, for example, Benjamin Page, *Choices and Echoes in Presidential Elections* (Chicago: University of Chicago Press, 1978).

4. The relationship between these economic and political assumptions is discussed in Martin Shefter, "Party and Patronage: Germany, England, and Italy," *Politics and Society* 7, no. 4 (1977): 409.

5. Joseph Schumpeter, *Capitalism, Socialism and Democracy*, 3rd ed. (New York: Harper & Row, 1970), 263.

6. Thus, as Shefter observes, southern Italian peasants who migrated to northern Italian cities were recruited by Socialist and later Communist parties while their cousins who migrated to American cities became the mainstays of conservative patronage machines. See Shefter, "Party and Patronage," 407. In the same vein, conservative parties in all the western democracies have generally been able to recruit large numbers of working-class voters to stand alongside their middle-class countrymen. See, for example, Robert McKenzie and Allan Silver, *Angels in Marble* (Chicago: University of Chicago Press, 1968). In general, parties that rely on material rather than solidary incentives are likely to construct the most heterogeneous constituencies. The classic example is, of course, the nineteenth-century American patronage machine.

7. For example, the Basque peasantry, which had been a bastion of conservative Catholicism and reactionary Carlism at the turn of this century, generally supported the Loyalist cause during the Spanish Civil War and is, of course, a base of support for radical Socialism today. See Gerald Brenan, *The Spanish Labyrinth* (New York: Cambridge University Press, 1960), esp. chap. 9.

8. M. Ostrogorski, *Democracy and the Organization of Political Parties*, vol. 2 (New York: Macmillan, 1902), 211.

9. For an account of the "militarist style" of American campaigns during this period, see Richard Jensen, *The Winning of the Midwest* (Chicago: University of Chicago Press, 1971), chap. 6.

10. Maurice Duverger, *Political Parties* (New York: Wiley, 1954), 426.

11. Ibid., chap. 1.

12. The classic statement is the report of the American Political Science Association's Committee on Political Parties, "Toward a More Responsible Two-Party System," *American Political Science Review* 44 (September 1950, Supplement).

13. Larry J. Sabato, *The Rise of Political Consultants* (New York: Basic Books, 1981), 70.

14. Richard A. Joslyn, *Mass Media Elections* (New York: Random House, 1984).

15. Sabato, *Rise of Political Consultants*, 218.

16. James M. Perry, *The New Politics* (New York: Potter, 1968), chap. 6.

17. Crane's efforts are discussed in Sabato, *Rise of Political Consultants*, 250. Crane ultimately became disenchanted with his chief fund raiser, Richard Viguerie, when he learned that Viguerie's fees and expenses amounted to 64 cents of every dollar raised. Republican National Committee direct-mail efforts are discussed in Timothy Clark, "The RNC Prospers, the DNC Struggles as They Face the 1980 Election," *National Journal*, 27 October 1980, p. 1618.

18. For a discussion of the character of the various consulting firms, see William J. Lanouette, "The Selling of the Candidates, 1978," *National Journal*, 4 November 1978, pp. 1772–1777.

19. Joslyn, *Mass Media Elections*, 33.

20. Frank Lynn, "Political Consultants' Campaign Role Is Expanded," *New York Times*, 28 March 1982, p. 54.

21.   See Richard Jensen, "American Election Analysis," in *Politics and the Social Sciences,* ed. Seymour Martin Lipset (New York: Oxford University Press, 1969), 226–243.

22.   Ostrogorski, *Democracy,* 285.

23.   For estimates of nineteenth-century campaign costs, see Louise Overaker, *Money in Elections* (New York: Macmillan, 1932), 71–73. See also Herbert E. Alexander, *Financing Politics,* 2nd ed. (Washington, D.C.: Congressional Quarterly Press, 1980), 5.

24.   For a discussion of the costs of political polling, see Sabato, *Rise of Political Consultants,* 75–80.

25.   Lynn, "Political Consultants' Campaign Role."

26.   Clark, "RNC Prospers," p. 1619.

27.   See "Election Tab: A Billion Dollars, and Rising," *U.S. News and World Report,* 15 December 1980, 32–33.

28.   Adam Clymer, "PAC Gifts to Candidates Rose 45% in Latest Cycle," *New York Times,* 29 April 1983, p. A16.

29.   See John Felton and Charles W. Hucker, "Business Groups Gave GOP a Late Windfall," *Congressional Quarterly Weekly Report,* 11 November 1978, 3260–3262; also Glen Maxwell, "At the Wire, Corporate PACs Come Through for the GOP," *National Journal,* 3 February 1979, p. 174–177.

30.   See Rich Jaroslovsky, "New-Right Cashier," *Wall Street Journal,* 6 October 1978, p. 1.

31.   Epstein has called this phenomenon "contagion from the right." See Leon Epstein, *Political Parties in Western Democracies* (New York: Praeger, 1967), 257.

32.   Ibid.

33.   Ibid.

34.   Sabato, *Rise of Political Consultants,* 60.

35.   R. W. Apple, Jr., "Tory Campaign: Shrewd and Brutal," *New York Times,* 8 June 1983, p. A3.

36.   Epstein, *Political Parties,* 239.

37.   Sabato, *Rise of Political Consultants,* 58.

38.   See Joseph Lelyveld, "Isle Off Africa About to Undergo a Placid Upheaval," *New York Times,* 10 June 1982, p. A2.

39.   See, for example, Alexander Heard, *The Costs of Democracy* (Chapel Hill, N.C.: University of North Carolina Press, 1960), chap. 2; also Overaker, *Money in Elections,* chap. 4.

40.   See, for example, Arthur H. Miller and Martin Wattenberg, "Decision-making Dilemmas in the 1980 Election: Choosing the Lesser of Two Evils." Paper presented at the annual meeting of the American Political Science Association, New York City, September 3–6, 1981.

41.   See Thomas Ferguson, *Critical Realignment: The Fall of the House of Morgan and the Origins of the New Deal* (New York: Oxford University Press). Also Thomas Ferguson, "Elites and Elections," in Benjamin Ginsberg and Alan Stone, eds., *Do Elections Matter?* (New York: M. E. Sharpe, 1986).

42.   For a fuller analysis of the relationship between elections and the underlying distribution of power in society, see Benjamin Ginsberg, *The Consequences of Consent: Elections, Citizen Control, and Popular Acquiescence* (New York: Random House, 1982), chap. 4. See also Kenneth Prewitt and Alan Stone, *The Ruling Elites* (New York: Harper & Row, 1973), chap. 7.

43.   For an account of the Reagan administration's social policies, see Frances

Fox Piven and Richard A. Cloward, *The New Class War* (New York: Pantheon, 1983).

44. "President Reagan's Inaugural Address," *New York Times,* 21 January 1981, p. B1.

Chapter 6

1. Walter Lippmann, *The Essential Lippmann,* ed. Clinton Rossiter and James Lare (New York: Random House, 1965), 12.

2. For discussions, see Gabriel Ardant, "Financial Policy and Economic Infrastructure of Modern States and Nations," in *The Formation of National States in Western Europe,* ed. Charles Tilly (Princeton, N.J.: Princeton University Press, 1975), 196; and Rudolf Brown, "Taxation, Sociopolitical Structure, and State-Building: Great Britain and Brandenburg-Prussia," ibid., 253. See also Carl J. Friedrich, *Constitutional Government and Democracy* (Boston: Little, Brown, 1941), 259.

3. George L. Haskins, *The Growth of English Representative Government* (New York: A. S. Barnes, 1960), chap. 3. The title of this chapter, "Compulsory Self-Government," tells the whole story.

4. Geoffrey Smith, "Can Marxism Stand Prosperity?" *Forbes,* 1 July 1977, 41–46.

5. James P. Sterba, "Peking Backs Use of Opinion Polls," *New York Times,* 25 August 1980, p. A8.

6. Samuel E. Finer, "State and Nation-Building in Europe: The Role of the Military," in Tilly, *Formation of National States,* 134–144.

7. Ardant, "Financial Policy," 127. See also G. N. Clark, *The Seventeenth Century* (Oxford: Oxford University Press, 1929), chap. 6.

8. Note the discussion in E. M. Earle, ed., *The Federalist* No. 46 (New York: Modern Library, 1937), 46.

9. Charles L. Taylor and Michael C. Hudson, *World Handbook of Political and Social Indicators,* 2nd ed. (New Haven, Conn.: Yale University Press, 1972).

10. Obviously, a simple count of the number of troops available to a nation's rulers is not an adequate measure. Though the likely effectiveness of an internal security apparatus of any given size undoubtedly varies with a great many factors, at the very minimum, we should take account of cross-national variations in population and land area. Presumably an internal security apparatus large enough to quash any dissent that might emerge in a principality containing several hundred thousand inhabitants might not prove very formidable in a nation with tens of millions of citizens spread over a continent. At the same time, it is also important to take account of cross-national variations in vulnerability to violence and disruption. An internal military apparatus large enough to protect one nation's commerce and communications from disruption might not be adequate where communications, industry, and commerce were more complex or extensive. Modern industrial nations, in particular, depend on extensive industrial, transport, food, power, communications, and fuel networks that can be both difficult to patrol and quite sensitive to damage or disruption. It is partially for this reason, as we observed earlier, that modern industrial nations depend on relatively higher levels of popular acquiescence

than is required by their more traditional counterparts. Thus the indicator used in this analysis attempts to take account of cross-national differences in population, land area, and vulnerability. Internal security forces per population and land area can be expressed in terms of density of coverage, which is given by (I/capita) $(I/\text{square mile})$, where I is the number of relevant troops. I use size of gross national product as a surrogate for the various economic and technological characteristics likely to be associated with vulnerability. The indicator takes the form

$$\frac{(I/\text{pop.})\ (I/\text{sq. mi.})}{\text{GNP}}$$

which can be interpreted as the density of national internal security protection divided by the nation's vulnerability to disruption. Obviously, I have neither taken account of all possible sources of cross-national variation in the effectiveness of internal security forces nor constructed the only plausible indicator using the factors I do take into account. Because the data were collected during a period when they would likely have been affected by the Indo-China war, Laos, Cambodia, and Vietnam were excluded from analysis.

11.   Stein Rokkan, *Citizens, Elections, Parties* (New York: David McKay, 1970), 149.

12.   John Hawgood, *Modern Constitutions since 1787* (New York: D. Van Nostrand, 1939), 148.

13.   Charles Seymour and Donald P. Frary, *How the World Votes* (Springfield, Mass.: C. A. Nichols, 1918), 20–23.

14.   For comparisons of voter turnout in the United States and Western Europe, see Walter Dean Burnham, "The Changing Shape of the American Political Universe," *American Political Science Review* 59 (1965): 7–28. See also Kevin Phillips and Paul H. Blackman, *Electoral Reform and Voter Participation* (Washington, D.C.: American Enterprise Institute, 1975), chap. 3.

15.   Several counties in the State of New York, for example, appear to have had very enthusiastic electorates in the nineteenth century. Data are presented by Allan E. Mayefsky, "Personal Registration Laws and Voting Participation in New York State" (Honors Thesis, Cornell University, 1975). For discussions of nineteenth-century electoral corruption, see Joseph P. Harris, *Registration of Voters in the United States* (Washington, D.C.: Brookings Institution, 1929); and Philip E. Converse, "Change in the American Electorate," in *The Human Meaning of Social Change,* ed. Angus Campbell and Philip E. Converse (New York: Russell Sage Foundation, 1972), 263–335. See also Clinton R. Woodruff, "Election Methods and Reforms in Philadelphia," *The Annals* 27 (March 1901): 181–204.

16.   Two excellent discussions of the political character of Progressive reform are Walter Dean Burnham, *Critical Elections and the Mainsprings of American Electoral Politics* (New York: Norton, 197), chap. 4, and Samuel P. Hays, "Political Parties and the Community-Society Continuum," in *The American Party System,* ed. William N. Chambers and Walter Dean Burnham (New York: Oxford University Press, 1975), 152–181.

17.   See Converse, "Change in the American Electorate," p. 283; Walter Dean Burnham, "Theory and Voting Research," *American Political Science Review* 68 (September 1974), 1002–1023; and Converse, "Comment on Burnham's Theory and Voting Research," ibid., 1024–1027, for discussions of the historical, political, and methodological issues raised by the sharp changes in American voting patterns that occurred at the turn of the century. For a discussion of

contemporary nonvoting, see Arthur T. Hadley, *The Empty Polling Booth* (Englewood Cliffs, N.J.: Prentice-Hall, 1978).

18. The relationship between education and registration is discussed in Raymond E. Wolfinger and Steven J. Rosenstone, *Who Votes?* (New Haven, Conn.: Yale University Press, 1980), chaps. 2 and 4.

19. The relationship between social class and interest in politics is examined in Fred I. Greenstein, *Children and Politics* (New Haven, Conn.: Yale University Press, 1969), chap. 5, and Robert Weissberg, *Political Learning, Political Choice and Democratic Citizenship* (Englewood Cliffs, N.J.: Prentice-Hall, 1974), 100–103.

20. This interpretation differs from the one presented by Wolfinger and Rosenstone, who appear to conclude that registration requirements do not substantially affect the "demographic, partisan or ideological characteristics" of the electorate. However, they base their assessment on a comparison of the actual electorate to the electorate likely to result if every state adopted the registration laws in effect in the most permissive state in 1972. My assessment, by contrast, is based on a comparison of the actual electorate with the electorate that might result if all unregistered but otherwise eligible individuals were registered. In a sense, Wolfinger and Rosenstone compare the existing electorate to an alternative *likely* electorate. I compare the existing electorate to the *possible* electorate—possible if registration laws were eliminated altogether or if the burden of registration was assumed by the government, as it is in most European nations. See Wolfinger and Rosenstone, *Who Votes?* chap. 4.

21. See Phillips and Blackman, *Electoral Reform.* See also Wolfinger and Rosenstone, *Who Votes?* p. 81.

22. Rokkan, *Citizens, Elections, Parties,* 157.

23. A useful survey can be found in Wolfgang Birke, *European Elections by Direct Suffrage* (Leyden, Netherlands: A. W. Sythoff, 1961). For an analysis of the effects of alternative electoral systems, see Douglas Rae, *The Political Consequences of Electoral Laws* (New Haven, Conn.: Yale University Press, 1971). An excellent bibliography on electoral systems is presented in Rokkan, *Citizens, Elections, Parties.*

24. Rokkan, *Citizens, Elections, Parties,* 157–158.

25. Andrew Milnor, *Elections and Political Stability* (Boston: Little, Brown, 1969), chap. 3.

26. Frank Sorauf, *Party Politics in America* (Boston: Little, Brown, 1976), 241. See also Belle Zeller and Hugh A. Bone, "The Repeal of Proportional Representation in New York City—Ten Years in Retrospect," *American Political Science Review* 42 (1948): 1122–1148.

27. On Democratic party reforms, see Austin Ranney, *Curing the Mischiefs of Faction* (Berkeley: University of California Press, 1975). See also William J. Crotty, *Political Reform and the American Experiment* (New York: Crowell, 1977), chaps. 7 and 8; and Nelson Polsby and Aaron Wildavsky, *Presidential Elections* (New York: Scribners, 1980), esp. chaps. 6 and 7. A brief but excellent discussion critical of party reform can be found in Everett C. Ladd, Jr., "Party Reform since 1968—A Case Study in Intellectual Failure" (Paper presented at the Project '87 Conference on the American Constitutional System under Strong and Weak Parties, Williamsburg, Virginia, April 27–28, 1979). See also Everett C. Ladd, Jr., *Where Have All the Voters Gone? The Fracturing of America's Political Parties* (New York: Norton, 1978).

28. Anthony Lewis, *New York Times,* 27 November 1960, quoted in Sorauf,

Party Politics, 247. The term gerrymander was, of course, coined to describe a district allegedly drawn in the shape of a salamander by Massachusetts Governor Elbridge Gerry in 1812. Interestingly enough, Gerry was not responsible for this original gerrymander. Apparently he was opposed to what he considered an inequitable redistricting plan but signed the legislature's districting bill into law because he did not believe that a governor could properly oppose a state legislature on such matters. See Robert G. Dixon, *Democratic Representation* (New York: Oxford University Press, 1968), 459.

29.   David Mayhew, "Congressional Representation: Theory and Practice in Drawing the Districts," in *Reapportionment in the 1970s,* ed. Nelson Polsby (Berkeley: University of California Press, 1971), esp. 281–284.

30.   Earle, *The Federalist* No. 71, p. 464.

31.   Ibid., No. 62, p. 405.

32.   Ibid., No. 10, p. 62.

33.   For an analysis of the impact of the Australian ballot, see Jerrold G. Rusk, "The Effect of the Australian Ballot Reform on Split Ticket Voting: 1876–1908," *American Political Science Review* 64 (December 1970): 1220–1238. See also Converse, "Change in the American Electorate"; Burnham, "Theory and Voting Research"; and Converse, "Comment on Burnham's Theory."

34.   The Australian ballot reform should be seen as a "permissive" reform. It obviously did not cause split-ticket voting. Rather, the Australian ballot merely facilitated ticket splitting relative to voting a straight party ticket.

35.   On this point, see the excellent discussion by Nelson Polsby, "Legislatures," in *Handbook of Political Science,* vol. 5, ed. Fred Greenstein and Nelson Polsby (Reading, Mass.: Addison-Wesley, 1975), 257–303, esp. 266. See also William Gamson's discussion of representation as cooptation in *Power and Discontent* (Homewood, Ill.: Dorsey Press, 1968), chap. 6. Also very revealing is the statement by a Soviet legislator in Vikenty Narbutovich, "How I Became a Legislator," in *Legislative Politics, USA,* ed. Theodore J. Lowi and Randall B. Ripley (Boston: Little, Brown, 1973), 90–94.

36.   Jean Jacques Rousseau, *The Social Contract,* trans. and ed. by G.D.H. Cole (New York: E. P. Dutton, 1950), 94.

37.   The question of "issue voting" has received a good deal of attention in recent years. See Richard W. Boyd, "Popular Control of Public Policy," *American Political Science Review* 66 (1972): 429–449; Benjamin Page and Richard A. Brody, "Policy Voting and the Electoral Process," ibid., 979–995; Gerald M. Pomper, "From Confusion to Clarity: Issues and American Voters," ibid., 415–428; John L. Sullivan and Robert E. O'Conner, "Electoral Choice and Popular Control of Public Policy," ibid., 1256–1268; Arthur H. Miller et al., "A Majority Party in Disarray," ibid., vol. 70 (1976): 753–778; and David Repass, "Issue Salience and Party Choice," ibid., vol. 65 (1971): 389–400. See also V. O. Key, *The Responsible Electorate* (Cambridge, Mass.: Harvard University Press, 1966); and Robert Erikson and Norman R. Luttbeg, *American Public Opinion* (New York: Wiley, 1973). For an interesting discussion of the different forms that a relationship between electoral preferences and public policy might take, see Robert Weissberg, *Public Opinion and Popular Government* (Englewood Cliffs, N.J.: Prentice-Hall, 1976), chaps. 5 and 8.

38.   Benjamin I. Page, *Choices and Echoes in Presidential Elections* (Chicago: University of Chicago Press, 1978), 95.

39.   Ibid., 181.

40. See Anthony Downs, *An Economic Theory of Democracy* (New York: Harper & Row, 1957), esp. part 2.

41. Page, *Choices and Echoes,* chap. 6.

42. Donald E. Stokes, "Spatial Models of Party Competition," in *Elections and the Political Order,* ed. Angus Campbell et al. (New York: Wiley, 1966), 170.

43. Earle, *The Federalist* No. 71, p. 464.

44. On this point, see David R. Mayhew, *Congress: The Electoral Connection* (New Haven, Conn.: Yale University Press, 1974), chap. 1, esp. 28–49. See also Donald E. Stokes and Warren E. Miller, "Party Government and the Saliency of Congress," in Campbell et al., *Elections,* 199.

45. Mayhew, *Congress,* chap. 1.

46. For a similar line of argument, comparing the distribution of attitudes among voters with the attitudes of individuals who wrote letters to newspapers, see Aage R. Clausen, Philip E. Converse, and Warren E. Miller, "Electoral Myth and Reality: The 1964 Election," *American Political Science Review* 59 (June 1965): 321–332.

47. Rokkan, *Citizens, Elections, Parties,* 31.

48. The theme of electoral demobilization runs through Burnham's most provocative essays. See Burnham, "Changing Shape of the American Political Universe," and "Party Systems and the Political Process," in Chambers and Burnham, *American Party System,* 277–308; and Burnham, *Critical Elections,* especially chaps. 5, 6, and 7. For criticisms, see Converse, "Change in the American Electorate."

49. See Frederick L. Pryor, *Public Expenditures in Communist and Capitalist Nations* (Homewood, Ill.: Irwin, 1968). See also Harold L. Wilensky, *The Welfare State and Equality* (Berkeley: University of California Press, 1975), esp. chap. 2.

50. The black-to-white median family income ratio is reported by U.S. Department of Commerce, Bureau of the Census, "The Social and Economic Status of the Black Population" (Washington, D.C.: U.S. Government Printing Office, 1978), 31 and 1979 supplement. Data on the annual incidence of riots and demonstrations by blacks between 1955 and 1972 are compiled in the New York City Public Library's Schomburg Collection under the heading "The Civil Rights Movement (National Media)." Black voter registration figures from 1955 to 1968 are drawn from Converse, "Change in the American Electorate." Data for 1972 and 1976 are reported by U.S. Department of Commerce, Bureau of the Census, "Black Population," 145. The number of black elected officials in the United Staes is reported in ibid., 143. The graphic depiction of the number of major pieces of federal legislation designed to benefit blacks is based on a count of all newly enacted federal statutes pertaining to civil rights or economic opportunity cited by the *Congressional Quarterly Almanac* during each year between 1957 and 1976 (Washington, D.C.: Congressional Quarterly Service).

Chapter 7

1. The VAT is discussed in Henry J. Aaron, ed., *The Value-Added Tax* (Washington, D.C.: The Brookings Institution, 1981). See also Henry J. Aaron and Harvey Galper, *Assessing Tax Reform* (Washington, D.C.: The Brookings Institution, 1985).

2. On the developmental and historical importance of internal police see David Bayley, "The Police and Political Development in Europe," in *The Formation of National States in Western Europe,* ed. Charles Tilly (Princeton, N.J.: Princeton University Press, 1975), 328–379.

3. On the development of military forces see William H. MacNeill, *The Pursuit of Power* (Chicago: University of Chicago Press, 1982).

4. The most important statement of this position is Samuel Huntington, "Congressional Responses to the 20th Century," in *The Congress and America's Future,* ed. David Truman (Englewood Cliffs, N.J.: Prentice-Hall, 1965), chap. 1.

5. See Walter Dean Burnham, *The Current Crisis in American Politics* (New York: Oxford University Press, 1982). For a contrary view, see Xandra Kayden and Eddie Mahe, Jr., *The Party Goes On* (New York: Basic Books, 1985).

6. W. Phillips Davison, "Public Opinion Research as Communication," *Public Opinion Quarterly* 36 (Fall 1972): 313.

7. Adam C. Breckenridge, *The Executive Privilege* (Lincoln: University of Nebraska Press, 1974), chap. 3.

8. Marc Karson, *American Labor Unions and Politics* (Boston: Beacon, 1965), chap. 9.

9. George Creel, *How We Advertised America* (New York: Harper & Brothers, 1920); quoted in Frederick Irion, *Public Opinion and Propaganda* (New York: Crowell, 1952), 414.

10. Chester Bowles, *Promises to Keep* (New York: Harper & Row, 1971), 93.

11. See Charles Steinberg, *The Information Establishment* (New York: Hastings House, 1980); Robert Weissberg, *Public Opinion and Popular Government* (Englewood Cliffs, N.J.: Prentice-Hall, 1976), chap. 10; and J. William Fullbright, *The Pentagon Propaganda Machine* (New York: Vintage, 1971). See also David Wise, *The Politics of Lying* (New York: Vintage, 1973).

12. Published by the U.S. Commission on Civil Rights (Washington, D.C.).

13. Harold Laski, *Liberty in the Modern State* (London: Faber and Faber, 1930), 241.

14. H. B. Mayo, *An Introduction to Democratic Theory* (New York: Oxford University Press, 1960), 241. See also Justice Black's opinion for the Court in *Wesberry v. Sanders,* 376 U.S. 1 (1964).

15. Benjamin Ginsberg, *The Consequences of Consent* (New York: Random House, 1982), chap. 7.

INDEX

technology, 156, 159, 162, 164,
173; recent electoral losses,
175–76, 177–79
democratic theory, 4–6
demonstrations, 49, 53, 56, 57,
61, 62, 66, 67, 68, 112, 133,
218, 219, 222; *see also* protests;
riots
Denmark, 29
Denton, Jeremiah, 178
DeVries and Associates, 164
Dewey, Thomas, 167
d'Hondt system, 201, 202
dictatorships, 59, 209, 215, 216,
219; and polling, 69–70; *see also*
authoritarian regimes
"diffuse support," 36
dinosaur extinction debate, 110
direct mail, 162–63, 164, 167–68,
173
Disraeli, Benjamin, 14, 214
Dixon, Robert G., 247*n*28
Douglas, Stephen, 167
Downes, Anthony, 248*n*40
Dressner, Morris, and Tortorello,
165
Dreyer, Edward C., 238*n*11
Duverger, Maurice, 77, 156, 157,
158, 239*n*34, 242*n*10

Earle, E. M., 241*n*1, 244*n*8, 247
*n*30, 248*n*43
East, John, 178
Eastern European governments,
55; polling by, 69–70
economic downturns: and political activity, 55–57; and New
York City mayoral race of
1894, 76

Economic Opportunity Act
(1964), 217
education: civic, 50, 52–54; and
distribution of opinion, 100,
101–2; expenditures, and electoral practices, 190–91, 216;
and marketplace of ideas, 37,
92–93, 94, 139; mass, 8; and
perception, 94–95; reformers,
34, 35; social and political functions of, 33–36, 58; and voter
turnout, 197
Efron, Edith, 241*n*30
election campaign(s): cost of, 51,
167–69, 170–72, 175–76; of
1840, 157; fund raising, 163,
178–79; of 1978, 150, 175, 176,
177; of 1980, 150, 168, 169, 170,
171, 175–76, 177–78; of 1982,
150, 168, 169, 170–71, 176, 177;
of 1984, 168, 169, 170, 171–72,
178; *see also* elections; electoral;
presidential elections; voters;
voting
election(s): authoritarian, 184;
boards, 51; "competitive," 189,
190–91, 215–17; cost of, 51,
167–68, 169; direct popular,
23; and economic downturns,
55–57; "irregular," 189, 190,
215–17; majority system of,
200–201; money, political technology and, 149–80; and national authority, 23; nonpartisan local, 159, 160; plurality
system of, 200–201, 202; vs.
political disorder, 48–58; and
political influence of public
opinion, 182–86, 188–219, 229;
proportional system, 200,
201–2; regulation or manipula-